THEOLOGY, UNIVERSITY, HUMANITIES

THEOLOGY, UNIVERSITY, HUMANITIES

Initium Sapientiae Timor Domini

EDITED BY

Christopher Craig Brittain
& Francesca Aran Murphy

CASCADE *Books* · Eugene, Oregon

THEOLOGY, UNIVERSITY, HUMANITIES:
Initium Sapientiae Timor Domini

Cascade Books
An Imprint of Wipf and Stock Publishers
199 W. 8th Ave., Suite 3
Eugene, OR 97401

www.wipfandstock.com

ISBN 13: 978-1-60899-815-9

Cataloging-in-Publication data:

Theology, university, humanities : initium sapientiae timor domini / edited by
Christopher Craig Brittain and Francesca Aran Murphy.

viii + 244 p. ; 23 cm. — Includes bibliographical references and index.

ISBN 13: 978-1-60899-815-9

1. God (Christianity)—Study and teaching. 2. Knowledge, theory of (Religion). I.
Brittain, Christopher Craig. II. Murphy, Francesca Aran. III. Title.

BT108 T48 2011

Manufactured in the U.S.A.

Contents

Contributors

Christopher Craig Brittain is Lecturer in Practical Theology at the University of Aberdeen. His is interested in political theology, critical social theory and Christian Ethics. His publications include *Adorno and Theology* and *Religion at Ground Zero*.

Gavin D'Costa is Professor of Catholic Theology at the University of Bristol. His many books range from *Theology and Religious Pluralism: The Challenge of Other Religions* to *Theology in the Public Square*.

Laurence Paul Hemming is a Research Fellow in the Department of Organisation, Work and Technology in the Management School of Lancaster University. His numerous books include *Worship as a Revelation* and *Postmodernity's Transcending: Devaluing God* and *Heidegger's Atheism*. He is currently working on a book on *Heidegger and Marx: A Productive Dialogue*.

Christopher Insole is Senior Lecturer in Theology and Ethics, Durham University. He is interested in the conceptual and historical relationship between theology, metaphysics and ethics.

David Jasper is Professor of Literature and Theology at the University of Glasgow, and Changjiang Chair Professor at Renmin University of China. His most recent book is *The Sacred Body*. He was the founding Editor of the journal *Literature and Theology* and co-editor of *The Oxford Handbook of English Literature and Theology*. He has co-edited *Between Truth and Fiction: A Narrative Reader in Literature and Theology*.

P. Travis Kroeker is Professor of Religious Studies, McMaster University, Hamilton Ontario. His publications include, *Remembering the End: Dostoevsky as Prophet to Modernity*, *Christian Ethics and Political Economy in North America* and a series of articles on Pauline messianism and political theology.

David McIlroy is a practising barrister, Visiting Senior Lecturer in Law at SOAS and Associate Research Fellow at Spurgeon's College. His publications include *A Trinitarian Theology of Law*, *A Biblical View of Law and Justice*, a chapter in *God and Government*, edited by Nick Spencer and Jonathan Chaplin, as well as numerous articles on the theology of law.

Francesca Aran Murphy is Professor of Systematic Theology at the University of Notre Dame. Her books include *God is Not a Story* and a commentary on *I Samuel*.

Simon Oliver is Associate Professor of Philosophical Theology at the University of Nottingham, UK. His publications include *Philosophy, God and Motion* and *Creation's Ends: Teleology, Ethics and the Natural*.

Joachim Schaper is Professor in Hebrew, Old Testament and Early Jewish Studies at the University of Aberdeen.

John Webster is Professor of Systematic Theology at the University of Aberdeen, and has written widely on modern theology and dogmatics.

Introduction:
Theology, the Humanities, and the University

This Book

INITIUM SAPIENTIAE TIMOR DOMINI is a motto engraved over several stone portals in the University of Aberdeen, Scotland; the Professor of Systematic Theology has sometimes proposed, however, that *Initium Sapientiae Timor Cibi* might be engraved over the doorway to the dining room. The first motto states that the beginning of wisdom is the fear of the Lord. It was the title of a conference about theology and the humanities organized in Aberdeen by Philip Ziegler and myself, in the summer of 2009. This book presents the papers from that conference to a wider audience. I am very proud to be co-editor of this book. Each of the papers brought together here is a fine piece of intellectual craftsmanship, and the "building" completed by editing them into a book is an outstanding representation of the contribution made to the university by contemporary theologians.

The editors of books of conference papers sometimes write anxious introductions, turgidly attempting to persuade their readers that the disparate compilation they have toiled to assemble between hard-covers somehow presents an integrated vision. This book has no pretentions to intellectual unity, nor to giving a single response to questions about the relationship of theology to the humanities. Indeed, I suspect that many of its authors are replying to slightly different questions about the topic.

Each of them probably finds the topic problematic, and therefore interesting, for slightly different reasons. The book hangs together, not as a single answer to a single question about theology's status in the university, or its relationship with the humanities, but as a comprehensive snapshot of how Anglo-American theologians perceive that status and this relationship. Its achievement is to bring together a dozen first rate theological minds and let them think out loud about how theology stands in relation to our universities and to the humanities.

It does this at a time when theology is regarded by many as a pietistic sideshow that universities could well do without. The thought of execution concentrates the mind, and the external pressure of recognizing that a discipline that once had a firm and acknowledged status is now often denigrated by the builders of contemporary universities, has perhaps concentrated our contributors' thoughts. The topic may intrigue many readers for similar reasons, and they will not be disappointed by taking up this book. For they will discover a spectrum of polished and cheerful papers, ranging in their emphasis from the humanistic to the theological.

The Humanities and the Universities

For many today, the conjunction of theology, the humanities, and the university has no appeal. It makes sense to them to pair the problem or plight of the humanities and that of our universities. They'd rather leave it at that, without bringing theology into it. The humanities have taken important setbacks in recent years, and with them the meaning of "the university" as a place of academic study. The humanities are asked to demonstrate to university administrators and to students that one can "do something" with a degree in philosophy or literature in the same way that one can apply a degree in engineering or leisure management. And since what one learns by studying philosophy or any of the "humane arts" is less evidently "applicable" in the world of work than one in the applied sciences, it seems that the currency of the humanities—or what they can "buy"—has been devalued. Many in the humanities conceive of "adding" theology to the discussion as worsening rather than improving an already difficult case.

As they would tell the story, the humanities, that is, "useless" disciplines such as philosophy or literature, have lost ground to technical

subjects that can make a direct, vocational purchase. They think it sufficiently daunting to defend the worth of the "useless arts" without the
additional encumbrance of a discipline whose very name has become
synonymous with superfluity, as in "the question is *theological.*" At least
one aspect of this perspective is correct: the place of the humanities in the
universities has now to be *defended*, not assumed or presumed upon. It
is the assumption that vocationally "useful" subjects have a lesser, or no,
place in "the university" that has come to seem marginal and recondite,
whilst the belief that universities are primarily "about" study of the humanities for their own sake has moved into a position of defense. Once
one has to legitimate the educational worth of the humanities on the basis
of the transferable skills that they might implicitly impart, they seem to
have entered a state, not only of "defense" but of terminal "defensiveness,"
on grounds apparently outside themselves.

This is not the place to tell the tale of how the humanities came to
see themselves as torchbearers of useless knowledge, or even to explain
how the humane arts became guardians of the shrine of Knowledge for
Its Own Sake. It is a story of how the humanities became the Humanities,
and with the majuscule, became High Minded. The golden age of high
mindedness, on whose legacy the humanities lived until recently, was the
nineteenth century. Its heirs in the humanities frequently perceived their
disciplines as "useless," and prided themselves upon it: unlike vocational
subjects, like Engineering, a century ago, or Leisure Management or Den-
tistry today, the Humanities saw themselves as imparting an education
for no specified end. A degree in the Humanities would not make a student an engineer, a leisure manager or a dentist. Rather, as the founding
dogma of these wondrous Arts had it, it would make one more open and
critical, and thus more High Minded than the lowly, close-minded creature the student had been upon entrance through the university's doors.
The humanities perceived themselves, as, as it were, the "soul" of human
knowledge, as against its mechanical "body." The soul applied itself to the
"useless," mind-opening arts, which the body was trained in practical
skills by which the owner of both parts might earn a living. The humanities, that is, were conceived, not only as useless but, going one step further,
as aimless. These high-minded souls wore the air of the Kantian conception of beauty as the mind at rest, contemplating the aimless, undirected
play of the imagination. The humanities were about free play, the "useful"
disciplines intended merely to lead to a job of work. The university was

divided "territorially," with some parts or faculties doing the work of the body and others entertaining the aimless play of the soulful humanities. Universities were likewise divided up, over again, with some regarded by the high minded as mere mechanical training colleges, whereas the ones for the souls were taken to be pure ivory towers of infinite inquiry. Pursuing the "territorial" metaphor a little further, the demotion of the humanities would then be conceived as expulsion from their ivory turrets, with the body gaining the major territory and the technical university becoming exemplary, and the liberal arts college marginal to the popular conception of the function of higher education.

On that analysis, one could well doubt that in fact theology has been regarded as subsidiary or expendable as a result of being even more useless than the humanities themselves, and too redundant in applicability to support the "soulful" humanities in their battle with the applied sciences. Rather, it is unwelcome to those who still maintain this high-minded, idealistic conception of the humanities because theology is suspected by them of harboring a use, an aim, and a goal. It seems likely that theology looks useless to those who conceive of higher education as answering a call to a specifiable working vocation, and surreptitiously "useful" to those who think of universities as intended to impart the ability to ask questions, not to give answers, and is thus rejected on both hands. But this is perhaps excessively to clarify their thinking on the nature of the university. United in their rejection of theology, both sides are likewise united in their inability to *lead* the discussion of what a modern university is supposed to achieve. All too often, the discussion takes its direction from outside the university, from politicians and business leaders, for example. As John Webster puts it in his contribution to this volume, "Part of the travail of much contemporary higher education . . . is the flimsiness and ignobility of its understanding of what it is about, and, consequently, its helpless conformity to wider cultural expectations." Because no one of the different disciplines within the humanities can explain, on its own grounds, what a university is for, and because the most comprehensive discipline, theology, is regarded as one of these many disciplines with no wider brief, no one is able to give a leading answer. Webster says, "whether by intention or neglect, the demotion of theology to the status of being one—insecure—discipline alongside (and increasingly harried by) others inhibits theology from furnishing a comprehensive account of the nature and ends of intellectual activity *in toto,* and so of humane studies."[1]

It might in fact be the case that the humanities began to lose their quarrel with the "servile arts" when they took a high-minded role upon themselves, conceiving themselves as the playful and ultimately "useless" soul that is served by the body of the mechanical, working disciplines. For centuries after the foundation of the university, theology sheltered the humanities from the criticism of "uselessness" by its exemplary practice of the pursuit of knowledge that looks wholly useless from a worldly perspective, but which is at bottom profoundly needful. It may look useless to learn to articulate the Trinity without falling into Modalism or Arianism, but perhaps it is essential for salvation to be neither an advertent Arian nor a conscious Sabellian. In the first article of the *Summa Theologiae,* explaining why theology requires to be founded not only on philosophical reasoning but on the light of revelation, Thomas Aquinas stated that, if it had depended upon human reasoning alone, a tiny elite of reasoners would, after a long time, have only have achieved a largely false conception of the deity: "It was necessary for man's salvation that there should be a knowledge revealed by God besides philosophical science built up by human reason."[2] For centuries, theology examined intricate and recondite matters with the calm assurance that these problems have a supreme utility. And this assurance that the value of a discipline need not be immediately quantifiable cast its protective mantle over what was then known as the "Arts Faculty." Universities that believed that even *theology* discusses and imparts matters human beings need to know could readily acquiesce in the idea that studying literature, philosophy, and history is of some real if not obvious benefit to students. Then as now, theology had a practical goal, of training clerics. And if the apparently obscure doctrines their teachers thought future clerics must know, in order to serve their churches, were not at all far from serving the goals and ends of embodied human beings, then it made sense to think of an apprenticeship in the Quadrivium (of arithmetic, geometry, music, and astronomy) as serving goals as central as an apprenticeship in any trade. If theology was not *trivial,* then neither was the Trivium (of grammar, logic, and rhetoric). If "theological" questions about Christ, the Trinity, and the angels have

---

1. See below, 40.
2. Aquinas, *Summa Theologiae,* I, Q. 1, a. 1, reply.

an aim and purpose, then so too do the most obscure philosophical conundrums. But this is then to concede that, like theology, the humanities do indeed have aims and purposes, that they teach something more than open-mindedness and a critical spirit. The much-vaunted freedom from practical intent of the humanities, since the nineteenth century, was always something of a pretend uselessness, by comparison with the deep-seated, worldly uselessness of theology, and indefensible without its equally deep-seated supernatural aim. Theology can remind the humanities how to have a *practical aim* without being useful: that is, remind them how to distinguish between having an aim or purpose and offering quantifiability utility.

In short, adding "theology" to the question of the meaning of the humanities and the purpose of universities changes the story. For what this most apparently useless discipline has to add to the conversation is something practical. Nor, as some Modalists and Arians may be pleased to discover, is the practical purchase confined to reward in the next life. Addressing the problem of theology and politics in this volume, Christopher Insole remarks, "Now that the managers have taken over the university, and theologians are called upon to justify their existence in terms of their non-subject specific 'transferable skills', one of these skills at least is this: the ability to sniff out small gods. Theologians are well trained to find the gathering 'god concept' around which a particular discourse or practice is oriented" and one frequently discovers that "the gathering concept, rather like the Wizard of Oz, is largely unexamined at close quarters. When finally all the noise stops, and the concept appears, like the Wizard, it can often be exposed as an unimpressive and angry little squirt of a concept."[3] Theology can set the humanities *truly free*, and genuinely open them to infinite horizons, by evaluating them in the light of salvation, that is, the "reunion" of the incarnate, human person with the object of infinite, human desire, its architect and Creator. As Webster writes below, "A theology of the humanities is an account of the ways in which humane studies are an element in the moving of created intellect by God. Clarity about the relation of theology *to* the humanities is achieved only when we are able to provide a satisfactory theology *of* the humanities."[4] The founders of the European universities, for instance, Bishop Elphinstone who

3. See below, 191.
4. See below, 40.

obtained the charter for Aberdeen University from Pope Pius V, and perhaps even their nineteenth-century successors, like the men who commissioned the stone portal with the Latin tag, *Initium Sapientiae Timor Domini*, believed that learning to fear the Lord is a practical skill neither theology nor the humanities can do without.

The Relationship of Theology to the Humanities

Given that the story of the humanities, theology, and the modern university is of several centuries duration, the problem of the relationship between theology and the humanities is of much longer standing than the immediate, pressing issue of the survival of the humanities and of theology in centers of higher education prone to conceive themselves as technical training schools. It is in a sense a self-standing problem, which may outlast the teaching of the two disciplines in the same institutions, and which was already present before the universities took their current, utilitarian turn. It may be important, as Webster claims in this book, that theology does not conceive itself as one discipline amongst others. The distinctness of theology is important for the humanities themselves. The gloss of high-mindedness was knocked off the humanities conceived as the "soul" of human education long before "managerialism" set the tone in the universities: Nietzsche did that, by proposing to discern behind the high-minded mask the secret program of a quest for power. The further the humanities retreated into conceiving themselves as disembodied "soul-food," the more susceptible they became to the Nietzschean critique, that the soul is "really just" a will to power. What is actually being exercised behind the high-minded discourses of the various humanities, the reductionist argued, is not intellection, thought, or imagination, but something profoundly and entirely utilitarian, the will to obtain and retain power over others. The will uses reason and imagination as a "wax nose," turning this way and that, and producing a cloak of rhetoric that disguises what is actually entirely arbitrary, its own hold on power. Thus, for example, the law, and the study of law, would on this analysis reduce to the exercise of power by one group or individual over others; the discipline of law would come down to the framing, maintaining, and "justification" of laws for the single, arbitrary but entirely utilitarian purpose of exercising a willful domination over others. In one of the chapters about theology and law in this book, Travis Kroeker asks whether the discipline of law can avoid being reduced to voluntarism by grounding itself in liturgical practice. There seems to be little on earth less "practical" than liturgy. But if Kroeker is right to claim that "rights are related to rites," then liturgical rites serve the practical purpose and end of preventing legal theory from being grounded solely in the human will of lawmakers. And the student who responds to the question, "What are you going to *do* with a theology degree?" by saying, "Perform the liturgy," is stating that he intends to serve humanity by serving God. Getting the relationship between theology and the humanities right matters for the humanities.

It matters also for theology itself. For some of the contributors to this book, it is important that theology not see itself as one "humanities discipline" amongst others. But it is a long step from saying that theology is a distinct pursuit from the humanities to saying that, to the extent that it regards itself as one discipline amongst others, theology necessarily *founds* itself on the humanities. Some of our contributors take this step: Gavin D'Costa speaks of the "process of assimilation of theology to the various disciplines in the Humanities so that theology in turn it becomes deconstructive, feminist, structuralist, and so on." He advises us "to trace how this assimilation of theology to heathen gods and goddesses carries right through to the social sciences (in some brands of liberation theology that give hermeneutical priority to Marxism), and even the natural sciences (in some brands of eco-theology that configure God to gaia)."[5] But for others of our contributors, it would be a step too far to say that theology is not only distinguishable from the humanities, but that preserving that difference preserves it from idolatry. For some of our contributors, distinguishing theology from the humanities is not the end in view when one highlights its unique character. For Joachim Schaper, the crucial "need" "of our time" is to "reinstate theology as a subject that is able meaningfully to communicate with the humanities *and* the sciences." He argues that theology must recover its sense of its own historical character and its awareness of the historicity of its materials, thus "integrat[ing] Troeltsch . . . and tak[ing] the questions raised by historicism seriously by conceptualizing theology as a *Geisteswissenschaft* which is in dialogue with the whole of human knowledge."[6] Given the characteristic claims of

5. See below, 195.
6. See below, 90.

Christianity, and the nature of its Scriptures, it seems practically unavoidable that theology converge with history at crucial moments.

Diverse Conceptions of the Relationship of Theology to the Humanities

This book would not be comprehensive if it did not lay out diverse conceptions of the relationship between theology and the humanities. In principle, one could map out at least four conceptions of the relationship between the two. In the first place, the humanities could be subsumed into theology. This position was essayed by one of the benchmark works of contemporary theology, and one of the first to recognize that theology within the modern university is, as they say, "challenged." In 1990, in his *Theology and Social Theory*, John Milbank argued forcibly that theology cannot be grounded in the social sciences (as was commonly assumed at the time), precisely because the social sciences *are* theologies. Instead, as Milbank had it, the social sciences should be assimilated and absorbed into theology. Milbank's position is thus one to which our contributors pay attention, if not tribute. Christopher Brittain, for one, makes deft criticisms of the "assimilatory" maneuver, noting for instance that the refusal to seek any validatory norms outside the "narrative" of Christianity itself seems to leave that "narrative" with nothing to say for itself beyond sheer rhetorical force.[7] As overstated as it sounds today, Milbank's "assimilatory" notion of the relation of theology to social science (and by implication to the other humanities disciplines) was a crucial corrective to theology's complacent absorption into the social sciences in the 1970s and 1980s. It changed the game, paving the way for, and making thinkable, proposals more conducive to rational discussion.

A second conception of the relation of theology to the humanities sees the humanities as grounded in theology, but inassimilably different from theology. This conception is espoused in this book by Milbank's brilliant former student and current colleague at Nottingham University, Simon Oliver, and by the barrister and part-time theologian David McIlroy. Thus, on the one hand, according to McIlroy, "Legal theory has a legitimate, semi-autonomous discourse about *how* law functions, which is proper to it . . . [S]uch questions are not all directly theological." But on

7. See below, 150–72.

other hand, McIlroy stakes a claim for what Jacques Derrida called the "Mystical foundation to Authority," that is, a theological "foundation of law."[8] Travis Kroeker's contention that human "rights are related to rites, and ultimately to construals of the Right which have implications for religion, ethics and politics" is aligned to this perspective.[9] Responding to Pope's maxim that "the proper study of mankind is man," McIlroy observes that "a proper study of human beings must recognize that human beings are God's creatures."

A third possibility is that the difference between theology and the humanities is absolute: they have not the means to add or subtract a jot or a tittle from one another. For Lawrence Hemming, the abysm between the two is so steep that the positing of any kinship between them, or the use of a discipline like philosophy by Christians, leads ineluctably to the assimilation of theology into humanity—that is, it leads to idolatrous self-divinization, the Christian's eschewing his own baptism by attempting to "baptize" the humanities. On this view, the attempt to practice the humanities *as a Christian* is epitomized by Hegel's speculative equation of Christian dogmas with philosophical concepts. To practice "Christian philosophy" is according to Hemming to translate Christian doctrine into the self-development of human consciousness.

A fourth possibility states the direct contrary: rather than being mutually repellant when rightly understood, the humanities and theology have an equal amount to offer one another. The relationship between them is not foundational (neither the humanities founding theology, nor theology grounding the humanities), but, rather, the two mutually and equally nurture one another, both benefitting from drawing on the other's resources. For David Jasper, writing on "The New Theological Humanism," the advantage of such a position is that it avoids both "hypertheology" and "hyperhumanism," staking an Aristotelian mean between two extremes. He claims that conceiving theology as an "interdisciplinary exercise" "implies no conflation of its two elements. It is at once 'theological *humanism*' and '*theological* humanism' in creative, imaginative and energetic interchange." Taken in "isolation," theology "quickly becomes an obsession and a monomania," whilst "Overhumanization" promotes "the exclusive triumph of human power in the shaping of our reality which

8. See below, 145.

9. See below, 34.

brings about, sooner or later, an inevitable foreshortening and over-definition of aims in materialist, economic or absolutist myopias."[10]

Distrust of "hypertheology," or what Etienne Gilson simply called "theologism," is a point in common between the second and the fourth positions. Simon Oliver tackles the question of the relation of theology to the humanities by discussing modern philosophy's fascination with "potential" objects and potentiality at the expense of actual objects and actuality. Blaming William of Occam's "theologism" for originating this fault in modern philosophy in good Milbankian (and Gilsonian) fashion, Oliver notes that Milbank's French contemporary, Jean-Luc Marion, proposes a *purely* theological way out of the dilemmas generated by the Cartesian turn to the subject: though all *humanly constituted* objects are perforated with lacunae and absent meanings, the divinely constituted object, that is, revelation, is "saturated," filled to an excess, or superabundance of meaning and reality. Only revelation escapes constitution by the human "I," evading subjection to whatever human beings decide to denote as "being," and thus, paradoxically, only revelation is fully real and actual. And yet, for Aquinas, as Oliver says, the "I" is better known simply as a *creature*. He argues thus that by "reconfiguring" Marion's "scheme in terms of creation, all phenomena can be described as 'saturated' in Marion's sense in such a way that the whole of creation becomes, to some degree, revelatory and in excess of our attempts to grasp it or subject it to *a priori* conditions of knowledge—to possibilities rather than actualities."[11] Theology gives to the humanities an account of what it means to be a creature, and challenges each of the humanities, not only to be more humane but to be genuinely creaturely.

Theology and the Disciplines

David McIlroy remarks that "John Milbank's audacious book *Theology and Social Theory* challenged us to think of theology as social theory, criticizing secular social theories and exposing the ontologies of violence, the assumptions of original discord, which lie at their heart. One can perhaps imagine a parallel volume entitled *Theology and Historical Theory*, taking on historical materialism, the Whig view of history and other secular

---

10. See below, 65.

11. See below, 111.

historical meta-narratives and contrasting them with Christian under-standings of the purpose and unfolding of history."[12] The emergence of a genuine historical consciousness was as intellectually game changing, in the nineteenth century, as the rediscovery of the writings of Aristotle had been in the thirteenth. For this reason, it is good that this volume speaks to the issue, specifically with reference to biblical studies, but with wider relevance, in Joachim Schaper's chapter on "Historical Criticism." In an ideal world, this book would have contained not just one, however good, but two or three chapters about the relation of theology to history, and of history to theology. In the mid twentieth century, Christopher Dawson created a "Christian philosophy of history" that carries, in my opinion, no taint of Hegelianism. Its guiding metaphor is the "body of Christ," and it envisages the history of human cultures and religions in relation to this ecclesiology. The great Hungarian writer John Lukacs has produced an implicitly Christian philosophy of modernity and the postmodern, and he has written several works about the Second World War that rely on a specifically Christian anthropological and moral imagination. There are in addition many very fine historians who are also Christians, like Eamon Duffy. Taking the notion of "political religions" from Eric Voegelin, the historian Michael Burleigh has shown in several books the implicit reli-gious substructure of many modern political movements. The work of a Christian historian is one of imagination, imaging history in relation to the great Christian symbols of community. Biography would be one of its best vehicles. I think that the issue that Joachim Schaper raises will be central to future reflection on the place of theology in the universities. It needs wider consideration than we had the space to give it here.

Nonetheless, the book contains a thorough survey of the disciplines. Christopher Brittain speaks for *sociology*, discussing the contribution that the thought of Theodor Adorno can make to theology, especially his concept of the "social totality."[13] Like Jaspers, Brittain believes that the humanities can learn from, as well as teach, the humanities. He discusses how sociology can benefit from the use of mediating symbols. Symbols such as Adorno's image of the "social totality," which are neither wholly "sociological" nor doctrinally theological, but rather have their proper home "mid-way" between the disciplines, enable them to illuminate one

12. See below, 127.

13. See below, 169–70.

another. In other words, theology needs other disciplines in order to explain itself, and, for that to happen, these disciplines must be genuinely *different* from theology itself (they cannot just be theologies).

Politics is represented here by Christopher Insole. Analyzing the ideological caricatures of political liberalism that theologians have too often purveyed and that they still all too easily swallow, Insole argues that, despite this unfortunate history, "Theologians have a great deal to offer in separating out the complexity of normative strands in the various geological strata of liberalism, just because so many of these differences have their ultimate grounding in theological convictions and disputes. It is ironic that it is often the very same theologians who pride themselves both on being post-foundationalist, and properly attentive to *practices*, who . . . appeal to the 'foundations' of liberalism and neglect a range of concrete practices when thinking about politics."[14] In reality, one never has to do with "theology and the humanities" but with human theologians, in their concrete relationships with practitioners of the humane disciplines. As Insole argues, if one looks past the fog of the "isms," as a political practice, that is, in its actuality rather than its theoretical possibilities, liberalism has its roots in concrete ecclesial events, like the Conciliarist movement and, preceding it, the mediaeval separation of Church and State, which grounded the "modern" principle of the separation of powers, giving rise to a world that permits institutions to be independent without necessarily being isolated, or that harbors and shelters political diversity and freedom.

Philosophy is taken up by Lawrence Hemming and Simon Oliver, and not only as a topic. Both of them not only talk about philosophy in its relation to theology, but practice it, giving us dense and thought-provoking philosophical reflections. Whereas Hemming's piece seems to lead philosophy apart from theology, Oliver leads them together, suggesting that "theology reasserts the priority of the actual in all enquiry. Why? Because theology avoids the subject-object dualism by which conditions for possible knowledge are established in relation to knowing subjects. Instead, theology begins with creatures and the actuality of creation as it gives itself to be known in relation to an eternally actual creator."[15]

---

14. See below, 177.

15. See below, 96.

David McIlroy and Travis Kroeker both discuss aspects of the re-lation of theology to *law* and *legal theory*. The Christian Scriptures and central Christian doctrines like the atonement can and have been inter-preted from a "legal" perspective: the Christian God has at times looked primarily like a judge and law-maker. Rather than implicating himself in this procedure, McIlroy argues that "there are grave dangers of distorting the message of the Bible if we proceed from a particular understanding of law and punishment and use that as the grid through which we read the Bible. Doing so, in effect, sets up that particular theory of law and pun-ishment as the canon, the measure of what God's justice *must* look like. Instead, theological reasoning should proceed from the vision of God and of God's justice revealed in Scripture and use that to inform and reform theories of law and punishment."[16]

Travis Kroeker's contribution to thinking about the relation of law to theology is profoundly *literary,* or better, profoundly imaginative. He has taken to heart something like Jaspers' injunction that the humani-ties and theology need one another because "Perfection . . . can only be imagined . . . a deeply poetic act."[17] Both his and David Jaspers' chapters in their own ways draw on the relation of theology to *literature*. Kroeker does not merely claim or assert that "rights are related to rites" but makes us imagine the relationship by contrasting the "liturgy" of the courtroom scene in Dostoevsky's *Brothers Karamazov* with the "liturgy" of the mo-nastic cell of Father Zosima. Kroeker shows that "Dostoevsky's alterna-tive to the liturgy of retributive justice in the modern courtroom is the liturgy of restorative justice in monastic Christianity, which in *Brothers Karamazov* is taken out of the monastery and into the world by the novel's (anti)hero, Alyosha Karamazov. This establishes a very different context from Nietzsche's account for interpreting the meaning of punishment and torture."[18] As with Adorno's "social totality," mediating symbols such as the court of justice can ultimately only be attained by imagination.

16. See below, 134.

17. See below, 67.

18. See below, 34.

Theology and the Universities

These varied reflections on the relationships between theology and politics, sociology, philosophy, law, and literature describe how theology serves to give our universities aims and goals to which to aspire. They tell us about the functions that theology can play in modern universities. These essays make a comprehensive case for the necessary role of theology in all kinds of different universities. For one consequence of the diverse and comprehensive view of the relationship of theology and the humanities taken in this book is that no one conception of "the university" is envisaged. For Joachim Schaper, the model is Berlin's *Friedrich-Wilhelms-Universität*, which "established a theological faculty, yet denied it the dominant status it had been accorded in the mediaeval university system."[19]

In practice, there are many kinds of universities, and no one single model of "the university" exists. Many different sorts of university could recognize in diverse ways that the humane arts are expanded in themselves by engagement with theology. John Webster tells us that "A theology of the humanities recognizes the place of intelligence within the economy of God's life-giving and restorative love for rational creatures, and locates the ground of that economy in the eternal wisdom of God himself."[20] Although these premises could be espoused by theologians and practitioners of the humane arts in many diverse contexts, the question of grounding knowledge in the divine wisdom does seem to raise the question of "the Christian university." For some of our contributors, such is not an ideal to be aimed at: many of them, like John Webster, reject the notion that divine wisdom could best illuminate the human intelligence within the institutional context of a Christian university. For most, theology gives what it has to offer the humanities in local and ad hoc ways, in universities, not in an ideal, singular "University."

Holding the University to Ransom

Amongst the authors of this book, Gavin D'Costa stands out by boldly making a case for the Christian university. He claims that, "Only through

19. See below, 89.
20. See below, 40–41.

such a move can the 'secular', 'modern', and 'postmodern' institutions that shape our society be called into question in an institutionally embodied manner. The question of alternative knowledges affecting a wide range of disciplines is too important to be left to ad hoc individuals, notwithstanding their important contributions. Rather it requires structured and long-term institutional support and curriculum development if it is to be sustained."[21] As with Christopher Dawson, the notion of the transmission of grace and virtue through incorporation into a community is a key element in D'Costa's defense of the idea of Christian universities. Perhaps only theology can ransom "the university" from the universities' utilitarian enslavement.

One reason why proponents of the liberal arts and the humanities used to insist upon the "purposelessness" of these disciplines is that they conceived their subjects as radically free forms of enquiry. To have a set purpose seemed to them to entail being coerced and confined into achieving naught but that given purpose, and to be closed to the infinity of further possibilities. To the extent that theology was imagined as the representative closed discipline, it stood for coercive knowledge, knowledge that in some way does violence to the freedom of enquiry. To the extent that theology as thus conceived both represents and unifies the other disciplines, the disciplines taught in a university would not liberate their teachers and students, but would merely marshal and instrumentalize them. Willy-nilly, all of the disciplines, from theology to the least of the liberal arts would be tools in the service of a trade extrinsic to their best selves. It is such genuine and realistic anxieties, and such determination to preserve intellectual freedom, which lead some, like David Jasper here, to prefer love to truth.[22] Forcible integration of the university curriculum around an "objective" and predetermined goal existed down to the latter half of the twentieth century, in the Marxist universities of the Soviet Union, and of its involuntary satellites. Alasdair MacIntyre has contended that "theists" should recognize the Marxist university model as "more intellectually congenial" than the "liberal" model. For "the dialectical and historical materialist understanding of the nature of things" gave the universities of "the Soviet Union or Communist Eastern Europe between 1917 and 1991 . . . . a framework within which each of the

21. See below, 203.
22. See below, 64–74.

academic disciplines could find its due place. So physics, history, and economics were all taught in a way that made their mutual relevance clear, and Marxist philosophy was assigned the tasks both of spelling out this relevance in contemporary terms and of explaining how the philosophies of the past had failed, just because they were the ideologically distorted expressions of class societies."[23] It is possible that MacIntyre exaggerates the intellectual affinity between theism and Marxist historical materialism. There is a difference, which the Marxist conception of history elides, between goals and uses. The "use," the "purpose," and the goal of history are one and the same for it, and human beings are dragged into serving it. For Christian theists, on the other hand, the genuine purposes and goals of the human being, and thus the human mind, differ from the *uses* to which persons and minds can be put, in that genuine human goals can only be achieved non-coercively, that is, with the full and free cooperation of the human being. The theological model here is the free cooperation of the human being in his or her salvation. Restlessly to aim at resting in God is to be bent on the fullness of one's own natural desire. Love of God does no violence to the human soul, and this love freely serves a genuine goal. The human love for God is an exemplar of what human love for truth is like. It is with this model of knowledge, and not an instrumentalizing or coercive conception of human ends, that theology lays claims to its place in the university. One cannot love God, or literature, or history, or philosophy on the basis of compulsion.

Christopher Insole writes here both that the "opposite of good theology is not no theology, but bad theology" and that the "opposite of good liberalism is not no liberalism but bad liberalism." As for politics, so for philosophy, law, sociology, literature, and history: the university can either make good its debts to theology, or foreclose on those debts and make do with bad debts and bad theology, and it can either respect the humanities for their intrinsic worthy, or make do with bad, ham-strung "arts subjects" limping behind the applied sciences, not in universities, but in glorified technical colleges. It may be that in the not-so-distant future, the choice will be between such technical colleges and a singular, theologically grounded notion of "the university."

In short, theologians have the definite article, and we are not returning it until *universities* see sense.

---

23. MacIntyre, *God, Philosophy, Universities*, 16–17.

1

On the Difference Between Torture and Punishment: Theology, Liturgy, and Human Rights

P. TRAVIS KROEKER

IN HIS GIFFORD LECTURES, *The Lesser Evil: Political Ethics in An Age of Terror,*[1] Michael Ignatieff seeks to argue the case for emergency measures in the face of global terrorism and asks the question regarding what role human rights should play in deciding public policy during terrorist emergencies. While he holds that under such circumstances "neither rights nor necessity should trump" the other, he nevertheless argues that torture is a test case for the dilemma of liberal democracies' war on terror. It raises the question of the legitimate limits on the violation of human dignity rooted in the "necessities" of the security state. At what point, for example, does interrogation move from legitimate coercion and punishment to illegitimate torture? Ignatieff's extended defense of a "lesser evil" ethic advocates the development of democratic societies designed "to cope with tragic choice" required to ensure security in the face of terror and thus seeks a balance between "liberty" and "necessity."

Such ethical abstractions, however, are themselves of very limited value since precisely the line between (legitimate/warranted) punishment

1. Ignatieff, *Lesser Evil.*

and (illegitimate/unwarranted) torture is largely a conventional one. What is human dignity anyway? At the very least it is hard to define, predicated on complex judgments about the inner meaning of human life, the relations between body and soul, and between individual embodied souls in relation to the body politic. How are these judgments themselves to be related to views about visibility and invisibility of interrogation, the embodied and/or psychological character of such interrogations, and the larger meaning of the juridical subject who bears rights in relation to "state security," the institutionalized relations of power and knowledge in a given society, and so on?

Michel Foucault's famous study, *Discipline and Punish*,[2] is so valuable precisely because it puts the genealogy of such complex judgments on dramatic display. The graphic opening scene of Part I on "Torture," the gruesomely detailed eye-witness account of the horrible execution of the regicide (also called "parricide") Damiens in eighteenth-century Paris, is quite uncontroversially labeled torture by Foucault, as most non-psychopathic modern Westerners would automatically call it that—an unacceptably gratuitous violation of the bodily rights of a human being through the infliction of long-lasting and extended ordeals of intense pain. Most of us have difficulty reading the account, never mind imagining how anyone could stand to watch it as a public spectacle, as many apparently did on March 2, 1757. In contemporary Western societies we have become unaccustomed to *any* forms of corporal punishment. Witness the recent case of the removal of children from their parental homes in a small southern Ontario Mennonite community by Ontario social services authorities because their parents advocated the use of strapping with a belt as a normal, though socially invisible disciplinary practice. And yet anyone who observed the media images of traumatized children being forcibly extracted from their traumatized parents by police officers bearing weapons could not help but be struck by the ironies. How are we to make good judgments about such complex judgment scenes?

Oliver O'Donovan offers a fine generic definition of punishment that is designed to liberate us from the unhelpful abstractions of *theories* of punishment, when he calls it "a judgment enacted on the person, property, or liberty of the condemned party."[3] As such punishment is

2. Michel Foucault, *Discipline and Punish*.

3. O'Donovan, *Ways of Judgment*, 107. Further references to this will be given parenthetically in the text.

best understood as an expressive communication defending the order of society, an act of social definition that represents the truthful response to offense by a society (113). Hence it cannot but represent in symbolic terms a judgment on suffering that has been unjustly caused by communicating that suffering both to the offender and to the wider society. On O'Donovan's view, then, the problem with acts of torture is this: "They are performed in secret, without due process, without legal specifications as to duration or intensity; and in no way seek to tell the truth about the crimes they punish" (122). In this way are acts of torture subversive rather than expressive of social norms. It would seem that on O'Donovan's definition the execution of Damiens may not be considered an act of torture, insofar as it is public, governed by due judicial process that specifies each ordeal of pain as expressive of the enormity of the crime he committed against society—in this sense it is not "cruel or unusual" punishment. Indeed, it might even be possible to be moved by the extraordinary dignity displayed by Damiens in his consent and self-restrained subordination to his own punishment, especially in relation to his confessors and his executioners in the eyewitness account recounted by Foucault.

Finally, to take a more modern example of capital punishment, who can fail to be moved by the journey toward moral responsibility by the condemned murderer Matthew Poncelet in the film *Dead Man Walking*—a movement that is unimaginable without his impending execution and the loving, shriving presence of Sister Prejean, who, ironically, judges the death penalty itself to be immoral (and thus, it would seem, a form of torture). In the film it is only as the moment of death actually approaches that glimpses of the horrible crimes committed by the offender come to visible consciousness. The implication is that the offender can only acknowledge these deeds and confess them by confronting his own imminent punitive death. The judgment in conscience is clearly symbolized by the judicially authorized punishment and is existentially enacted in the complex expression of the sentence—though the film is nicely ambiguous about whether the violent punishment is indeed necessary, or whether simply the persistent caring rigor of Sister Prejean might suffice to facilitate the moral and indeed spiritual movement.

Is capital punishment torture? It seems Sister Prejean might think so, though she is no less horrified by the terrible murders committed by the offender. And what are we to make of the distinction between the execution of Damiens—with its drawn-out public infliction of grotesque ordeals of pain—and the hidden, rather clinical execution of Matthew Poncelet in *Dead Man Walking*, an execution designed to *appear* painless (not least by the medical administration of paralysis-inducing chemicals) and therefore more "humane." Both Oliver O'Donovan and Elaine Scarry make the connection between pain or suffering and mortality or death. O'Donovan argues that the basis of all retributive practice (and thus all punishment, which is always by definition also, among other things, retributive) is found here: "We are all mortal, and our life has a limited expectancy. That fact gives all crime and punishment its meaning" (122). The horizon of all punishment, then, is death itself. Every punishment is an assault on the offender's life, in return for assault on the victim's life. In Scarry's account of the structure of torture, she argues that "pain is the equivalent in felt-experience of what is unfeelable in death. Each only happens because of the body" (31)—and, of course, because of the human self-awareness of bodily mortality, the pain of death, the ultimate experience of "un-worlding."

On Scarry's account the speech enacted in torture, far from being the expression of true speech (a necessary condition in O'Donovan's definition of punishment), is precisely false. Both the speech of the torturer (rooted in the false motive of "information-gathering") and the speech of the tortured (the voice of pain, simply giving the answers sought by the torturer, without regard for truth) are therefore false. The effect of torture is thus to unmake the world in the shattering of language, in order to remake the world in the fictitious image of the torturer's power. Hence the covert disdain for the confession (often labeled "self-betrayal") of torture victims by their torturers. The interrelation of the infliction of pain and the interrogation in torture is designed precisely to create instability and disorientation in victims between the "real world" and "fiction," ultimately to prepare the way for the construction of a "second reality"—the power of the regime—as the only real or true one. All claims that challenge, threaten, or deny the truth of this reality must be eliminated. Such is the sovereignty of the absolutist or terrorist regime.

Here it may be instructive to return again to Foucault's *Discipline and Punish*. His thesis is that not only has the *context* of modern punishment shifted from public visibility to institutional hiddenness, but its *focus* has shifted attention away from the primacy of the body (and the infliction of pain upon it) to the primacy of the soul or subject and its reconstituting self-discipline. This entails an entirely different set of punitive and disciplinary practices, a new political technology that enforces a quite distinct—and ultimately more invasive and pervasive—sovereignty or regime of truth/power. Foucault's analysis suggests that the old public liturgy of bodily punishment displaying sovereign power—a liturgy both juridical and military, focusing on the punishment of evildoers as "enemies"—has gone underground in socio-political mechanisms that exercise more powerful ordering influence on the social body. These mechanisms are less personal, less immediate, and less visible, and yet very effectively deployed in the reformative rise of the "scientific-juridical complex" (19).

The power of this sovereignty is displayed less in a visible physical terror (that is reinforced in ceremonies of public torture as punishment) than in a pervasive disciplinary administrative regime, a "school" of inner interpretation or "apparatus of knowledge" (125) that governs conduct. It does this through a calculated economy using instruments of hierarchical observation, normalizing judgment, and examination in a "carceral" regime modeled after "panopticism"—the subjection of all citizens to a sovereign surveillance that establishes truth through a regime of control and inquisition that no longer needs to inflict pain upon the body in order to control its subjects, but in fact consolidates its power precisely through the promise to eliminate all such pain through comprehensive security. It would seem that Foucault would regard the discourse of universal human rights as yet another potential "knowledge apparatus" enforcing such a carceral sovereignty.

I do not wish to take up the details of Foucault's account of "normalization" and sovereign state control here. My concern has been to point up the ambiguities that exist between torture and punishment that render the making of moral judgments about them, including those rooted in human rights language, highly problematic. In order to begin to explore the thicket of possibilities theologically, I have found it helpful to turn to two nineteenth-century writers who have thought about the complex relationships between bodily punishment, the body politic, and the moral constitution of the agential practice of judging (sometimes called "conscience") from quite different theological and anti-theological perspectives—Friedrich Nietzsche and Fyodor Dostoevsky.

Nietzsche

Nietzsche, of course, is the great forerunner to Foucault in developing a "genealogy of morals" that unmasks the conventions of truth in our culture to be precisely that—the fictions of human language willfully imposed upon reality. Truth is always the imposition of perspectival conventions by the powerful, and punishment is the bodily-spiritual re-inforcement of these conventions in rituals that express sovereign human power. Nietzsche's compelling account of the role of crime and punishment in constituting moral conscience is provided in the second essay of his *Genealogy of Morals*.[4] Human beings have bred into themselves the conditions of "answerability [*Verantwortlichkeit*]," namely, a memory related to promises they have made, a "memory of the will" by which human beings become "calculable [*berechenbar*], regular [*regelmaessig*], necessary [*notwendig*]" (1). Such a responsible self is precisely a sovereign individual, one who has an independent will and has the right to make promises, to speak for him/herself in what has come to be called the "conscience [*gewissen*]" (2–3). According to Nietzsche the history of human responsibility is tied to the human animal's evolutionary development of the faculty of memory—promises made for calculable action in the future, a necessary feature of ordered human communities of speech. The beginning of the inner life of moral consciousness in which instinctual drives are countered and controlled, then, is dictated by social needs and is imprinted by rituals of punitive pain. The essence [*Wesen*] of human consciousness is memory grounded in pain—a "*mnemotechnics*" (3) of cruelty, the cruelest of which are religious.[5]

That is, in contrast to Kant's autonomous moral agent, Nietzsche's sovereign will is formed not by seeking universal moral ends given in the invisible structure of reality, but through the struggle to realize *my* aims and values in an agonistic world. The origins of memory are to be located in the history of human punishment in which the demands of social existence are imprinted upon the instincts in legal promises, judgments

---

4. Nietzsche, *On the Geneaology of Morals*. References to the "Second Essay" will be made by section number in parentheses in the body of the essay.

5. Nietzsche writes, "life operates *essentially*, that is in its basic functions, through injury, assault, exploitation, destruction and simply cannot be thought of at all without this character" (11); and again: "Thus the essence of life [*das Wesen des Lebens*] is *will to power* [*Wille zur Macht*]" (12).

and enactments (5ff.). Instincts are thus ordered with reference to legal obligations, moral laws of behavior, "soaked in blood and torture" (6). These are not simply retributive relations—punishment is also rooted in the pleasure of imposing suffering on another, a "genuine *festival*." Indeed, says Nietzsche "Without cruelty there is no festival: thus the longest and most ancient part of human history teaches—and in punishment there is much that is *festive!*" (6). Part of the enjoyment of violation in administering punishment is the experience of the free exercise of sovereign power, and this experience has been deeply sublimated in the cruel religious spectacles of divine punishment that undergird the moral conscience of the European West (7).

The two distinctive features of punishment according to Nietzsche are: a) its customary, dramatic character, which is relatively enduring, and b) the meaning, purpose or expectation associated with the performance of the dramatic act, which is fluid (13). The concept "punishment," therefore, cannot be reduced to one meaning but rather has a whole range of meanings related to particular performative acts: deterrence, preventing harm, recompense, isolation of a disturbance, inspiring fear, repayment, expulsion, festivity, mnemonesis, revenge, declaration of war, etc. Thus is punishment over-determined by various utilities, but Nietzsche insists that "bad conscience" did not grow on the soil of punishment. Rather the effect of punishment is a heightening of prudent memory that tames human desires and instincts (15).

Nietzsche's hypothesis about the origin of "bad conscience" is related to a kind of Hobbesian evolutionary account of the origin of the security state (16), as the most fateful evolutionary shift in the human animal from a creature of instinct to a creature of consciousness. This is the "internalization" of the human in the development of "soul" or psyche, and it is coincident with the birth of the religious consciousness. Only though the invention of divine spectators and "otherworldly eyes" could the external violence of active instinct be internalized in the inner agon of the divided, self-lacerating, suffering soul. That is, the taming process of political sovereignty is accompanied by a religious self-surveillance that internalizes the conflictual drama of pleasurable punishment, the "war of all against all." This inner war becomes the condition for social peace. In a self-regulating, self-punishing, self-torturing society, the more natural punishment of the body may be safely minimized as people are able to enjoy their own self-imposed punitive suffering:

> You will have guessed what has really happened here, beneath all
> this . . . this man of the bad conscience has seized upon the presup-
> position of religion so as to drive his self-torture to its most grue-
> some pitch of severity and rigor. Guilt before *God*: this thought
> becomes an instrument of torture to him. He apprehends in "God"
> the ultimate antithesis of his own ineluctable animal instincts: he
> reinterprets these animal instincts themselves as a form of guilt
> before God . . . he stretches himself upon the contradiction "God"
> and "Devil" . . . . In this psychical cruelty there resides a madness
> of the will which is absolutely unexampled [*nicht seines Gleichen
> hat*]: the *will* of man to find himself guilty and reprehensible to a
> degree that can never be atoned for [*Unsuehnbarkeit*] . . . his *will*
> to infect and poison the fundamental ground of things [*untersten
> Grund*] with the problem of punishment and guilt . . . what *bestial-
> ity of thought* [*Idee*] erupts as soon as he is prevented just a little
> from being a *beast in deed* [*Tat*]. (22)

We are familiar enough with this Nietzschean account of modern
human beings as the "heirs of the conscience-vivisection and self-torture
[*Selbsttierquaelerei*] of millenia," possessors of an "evil eye [*boesem Blick*]"
for natural inclinations, ultimately hostile to life. But what does it mean
for interpreting the relation between punishment and torture? Surely at a
minimum it requires a critique of the kind of conformist humanism that
underlies the bourgeois citizens of modern security states devoted to the
unnatural, nihilistic taming of the truly human—the desire for a perfect
carceral society of equal rights for all that "overcomes" (bodily) suffering by domesticating and destroying human beings by taking over their
consciences and taking away the freedom of their wills by imposing a civil
religious "evil eye" of moral surveillance. Ultimately, for Nietzsche, it will
require an agonistic effort to overcome the great juridical straitjacket that
characterizes the "sovereignty" (in theory and practice) of modern statist
humanism. Modern justice will itself have to be "overcome" through a
mercy that goes beyond the law (10).

Dostoevsky

There is of course another, quite different yet equally penetrating and critical nineteenth-century approach to interpreting conscience in relation
to crime, punishment and torture offered by Fyodor Dostoevsky, particularly in his great novels, such as *Demons* and *Crime and Punishment*.

His last and greatest novel, *The Brothers Karamazov*, is a novel about the political and religious meanings of justice and at the heart of this lies the discernment of conscience—an insight shared but differently resolved by the novel's two central ascetic figures, the Grand Inquisitor and the elder Zosima. Interestingly, it is precisely the punitive, indeed tortuous suffering of conscience that the Inquisitor seeks to relieve in his regime of external state power rooted in a Christian civil religion. Such a regime promises a secure and painless existence for all who submit to its authority. According to the elder, on the contrary, such relief is not a human prerogative, since conscience is not finally socially constituted or guided by the conventional norms and authorities of a community (*pace* both Nietzsche and the Grand Inquisitor). Conscience is a knowledge constituted also "before God," whose divine law measures human beings—a divine law that is not primarily understood in juridical or retributive terms, but rather the messianic law dramatically enacted in the restorative practices of "active love" (56).[6] The "security" of the Inquisitor can only result in ongoing psychic and bodily suffering, as the "second reality" it constructs is destructive of the human spirit and of human social life; indeed, on the Elder's view, it is destructive of justice itself. Richard Peace, however, misses the mark when he suggests that Zosima "points to the individual conscience as the only true instrument of punishment,"[7] since for the elder conscience is neither simply "individual" nor "instrumental"—punishment is not extrinsic to the relational, embodied life of human society. Nor is conscience the "mnemotechnical" internalization of contractual power relations rooted in rituals of pain. The pain and punishment of conscience is rooted in the memory or consciousness of divine love (not acts of human or divine violation), which exposes one's (willed) separation from its fullness. Pain is an important symptom of a deeper illness that is ignored or dulled at peril of death. As such, conscience cannot work mechanically or instrumentally. Indeed, to treat conscience that way "only chafes the heart" (64).

Yet clearly the punishment related to conscience is also related by the elder (and Dostoevsky) to ritual socio-political contexts, and I wish to reflect on these here, as I believe they may be helpful in developing a distinction between punishment related to restorative justice and

6. All parenthetical references in this section are to Dostoyevsky, *Brothers Karamazov*.

7. Peace, *Dostoievsky*, 276.

punishment related to forms of retributive justice that move inevitably toward torture. In some respects I have taken a cue from William Cavanaugh's argument in *Torture and Eucharist* that the failure of human rights language has been to construe torture primarily as an attack on individual bodies, and that "true resistance to torture depends on the reappearance of social bodies capable of countering the atomizing performance of the state."[8] He contrasts the liturgy of torture in the idolatrous state with the liturgy of the Eucharist in the Chilean church as the disciplined formation of two alternative social imaginations.

My argument is that the radicalism in Dostoevsky's contrast between retributive and restorative justice is artistically depicted in the two central ritual settings of justice in *Brothers Karamazov*—the monastic cell of elder Zosima and the modern secular courtroom. It is no accident that the meeting between father and brothers Karamazov to mediate their dispute in the elder's cell early in the novel is a classic Dostoevskyan scandal scene, widely enjoyed for its sacrilegious buffoonery. Less well understood is the profound liturgical expression of spiritual discernment and restorative social justice it represents in the novel as a whole. The by contrast very lengthy and serious justice scene in the final third of the novel (by far the longest scene in a very long novel) is played out in the liturgical setting of the modern Russian courtroom, regarding the crime of parricide that gives the novel its central literal and symbolic dramatic movement. This scene is taken seriously as Dostoevsky well knew because we psychically "buy" the liturgical structure of the secular courtroom, and we consider its rituals to be endowed with absolute political and religious authority. The courtroom, its liturgy, liturgical players and icons—above all enshrining the sovereign rule of law understood as structuring and protecting the rights of contractual individuals—is the symbolic heart of one of the largest colonizing missions in human history: the global export of modern Western civilization as the model of the highest, happiest, most prosperous and most just form of human life ever attained. Dostoevsky's scandalous claim is that this ritual of retributive justice travesties true justice.

8. Cavanaugh, *Torture and Eucharist*, 4.

The Elder's Cell

The monastic tradition is central to Eastern Orthodoxy and in *Brothers Karamazov* it is the vision of the Russian monk that articulates and embodies the prophetic challenge and alternative to the orthodoxy of secular modernity.[9] This is for Dostoevsky not only a religious vision but a political one, and the institution of monastic elders founded upon the vows of complete obedience and self-renunciation stands in contrast to the secular path of absolute autonomy and self-realization. The root assumption of the monastic path is that freedom may be attained only through a "whole life's obedience" (27) to the rule of Christ and the difficult practices of serving, forgiving love. As the elder Zosima puts it: "Obedience, fasting, and prayer are laughed at, yet they alone constitute the way to real and true freedom," namely liberation "from the tyranny of things and habits" (314). Only one freed from the isolation of self-love can truly love others and build up the human community through deeds of humble love. The justice of this human community, moreover, is not to be found in the mechanics of procedural justice or in "rights" (313)—it is situated in the "consciousness of one's own conscience" (64). The elder states: "Remember that you cannot be the judge of anyone. For there can be no judge of a criminal on earth until the judge knows that he, too, is a criminal, exactly the same as the one who stands before him, and that he is perhaps most guilty of all for the crime of the one standing before him. When he understands this, then he will be able to be a judge" (320–21). Precisely such a posture of discernment is displayed by the elder in the opening scenes of the novel, and it is a posture of spiritual and political authority that stands in stark contrast to the Grand Inquisitor's.

The gathering of the Karamazov family in the elder's cell has a false pretext. The conflict over inheritance money between the father Fyodor and the eldest son Dmitri has intensified, and is of course complicated by their erotic pursuit of the same woman. Apparently as a joke Fyodor suggests they gather in the elder's cell—not for direct mediation but to see whether "the dignity and personality of the elder might be somehow influential and conciliatory" (32). Also attending is the relative of Fyodor's first wife and early guardian of Dmitri's, Miusov, a free-thinking atheist who is engaged in a lawsuit with the monastery (which borders his

---

9. This position is given extensive treatment in Kroeker and Ward, *Remembering the End*.

estate) over property and logging and fishing rights. Alyosha, the young-
est Karamazov son, a monastic novice devoted to elder Zosima and the
hero of the novel, suspects the motives of these various "quarrellers and
litigants," but has reluctantly approached the elder with the request. The
elder reluctantly agrees, citing (with a smile) the words of Luke 12:14—
"Who has made me a judge over them?" (Jesus' response to a request that
he settle an inheritance dispute). The visit therefore has both a litigious,
juridical context and an explicitly religious context.

The meeting is set to follow immediately the late morning liturgy,
and of course the guests show up *after* the liturgy. None but Alyosha
truly orders his life under the authority of Christ or the disciplines of
the church and so the avoidance of the liturgical ritual that orders the elder's enactment of justice attests to the motives and predispositions of the
claimants. Of course attendance at the liturgy, like consultations with the
elder, are voluntary, not required. The foundation of the elder's authority
is neither civically mandated nor based upon coercive state power. Hence
the elder's words "Who has made me a judge?" echo his teachings on
criminal justice rooted in the knowledge that is "the crown of the monk's
path, and of every man's path on earth," namely, "that each of us is un-
doubtedly guilty on behalf of all and for all on earth, not only because
of the common guilt of the world, but personally, each one of us, for all
people and for each person on this earth" (164; cf. 289). Precisely such a
personal penitential posture based upon Eucharistic self-giving and the
discernment of humble love is displayed by the elder in the meeting.

This also means, however, that the elder displays no sense of worldly
honor and treats all his guests the same, whether important estate own-
ers or poor peasant women, which offends the liberal-minded, worldly Miusov who thinks he is being snubbed by the elder. The monks,
moreover, greet one another ritually with deep bows and mutual bless-
ings, which also offends Miusov and the secular guests who scorn this
as religious pretentiousness, in keeping with their scorn for the liturgy
of the evening office. In effect, then, the ritual and liturgical setting of
the practice of justice in the monastic cell is scorned by all of the guests
except Alyosha. Furthermore, the monastic cell itself is small, the furni-
ture, the narrator tells us, is crude and poor, and the room is dominated
by icons—a large Mother of God lighted by an icon lamp, and a motley
combination of expensive engraved prints of eighteenth-century Italian
art alongside cheap Russian lithographs of saints, martyrs, and hierarchs,

an egalitarian pluralism that offends Miusov's good taste. The liturgical and ritual setting, then, is lacking all conventional worldly markings of authority: wealth, power, high art, aesthetic formality. As Alyosha has feared, no reverence or even respect is paid either to the monastery or to the elder by family members. To the contrary, Fyodor's blasphemous buffoonery combined with Miusov's offended liberal vanity leads to a quintessentially Dostoevskyan scandal scene.

The elder Zosima, by contrast, is neither offended by the antics of his guests nor scornful of their impiety, and what follows cannot be easily summarized or represented, since it is really an extended informal conversation about theories of church and state and crime and punishment as well as deeply personal revelations that expose the roots of the familial conflict, punctuated by vignettes involving the elder's acts of discernment with others seeking his counsel. In all it is a rather chaotic and disordered scene, and yet Zosima manages to address the root causes of the familial conflict—pride, shame, false honor, habitual lying—offering both an interpretation and a prescribed cure: "Above all, do not lie to yourself" (44), he repeatedly tells Fyodor. Preserving the conscience from self-deception is the first step toward just discernment and fitting action in human beings. He also addresses Ivan's intellectual conflicts as the torments of an unresolved heart, a conflict of loves in the conscience that requires decision. Finally, in response to Fyodor's histrionic demand that, in relation to the son "against whom I am seeking justice from you . . . Judge and save us!" (71), and the ugly exchange between father and son that follows, degenerating into talk of duels and parricide, the elder does a strange thing. He kneels deeply before Dmitri, even touching the floor with his forehead, and then begs forgiveness of all his guests. It is a gesture no one understands, and it evokes different responses in all his guests: Dmitri flees with his face in his hands, while Miusov takes it as a display of religious madness. Later Zosima explains it to Alyosha as a prophetic gesture: "I bowed yesterday to his great future suffering," in response to what he detected in Dmitri's eyes and non-self-justifying confession.

It may be useful here to recall what the elder says about crime and punishment in that same conversation. A true judgment ordered by Christ's law of love, which sees clearly the cause of the crime and how the criminal might be transformed, cannot "essentially and morally be combined with any other judgment, even in a temporary compromise. Here it is not possible to strike any bargains" (65). Hence Zosima's judgment on the "false consciousness" of the "establishment" churches of Western Christendom, in which the church's authorizing image (the law of Christ) has in some manner been falsely externalized and replaced by another form of rule (the juridical state)—symbolized in the sovereignty of the Grand Inquisitor. Ivan's Inquisitor covertly opposes the true authority of Christ (the freedom of the loving heart) in order to establish an external judicial political order that nevertheless claims the name of Christ. This is the founding "lie" of his sovereignty. It is a noble lie, claims the Inquisitor, premised on a "truer" image of human nature and history; and it is also a "lie in the soul" that uses false images, speeches and signs about the divine in the service of social order. On the Inquisitor's view, of course, human beings are not created in the divine image—they are merely clever beasts who must be tamed. For the elder, such lying is disastrous, as we may see in his account of the psychological anatomy of the liar (44, 58). Lying to oneself leads to a loss of discernment of truth, both within the self and in the world. This leads in turn to contempt, fear, disrespect—of self and others—and the inability to love. Such a self becomes the slave of changing passions and abstract, self-glorifying fantasies that can reach "complete bestiality" in a social order dominated by violence and fear, and the need for a security state.

The Secular Courtroom

It is Dmitri of course who will be formally (and falsely) charged with the murder of his father Fyodor, and this represents a kind of poetic justice, since he is of all the brothers the passionate sensualist most controlled by his desires. This gets him into trouble not only with women but causes him to abuse physically three central fathers in the novel—Fyodor, Snegiryov, and Grigory the servant who treated him like a father. Yet Book 12 of *Brothers Karamazov*, which concerns the courtroom trial of Dmitri, is entitled "A Judicial Error," and concerns not only a conventional miscarriage of justice on technical grounds but provides Dostoevsky's display of the erroneous measure of justice embodied in the modern adversarial judicial process, which stands ritually and existentially over against the elder's understanding.

Let us note first of all some of the differences in this liturgical context of justice. The courtroom, in contrast to the elder's cell, is described by the narrator as "the best hall in town, vast, lofty, resonant" (659)—in keeping with its status as civic cathedral of public justice. At the center, in front of the presiding judges, is the table holding the objective "material evidence" of the crime committed, which will become the focus for the competing narratives interpreting the evidence. This particular trial has generated a great deal of public notoriety and journalistic attention both because of the nature of the crime, that of parricide in the context of complex erotic rivalries, and the fame of the defense lawyer Fetyukovitch. The gallery is filled with dignitaries and ladies whose faces exhibit "hysterical, greedy, almost morbid curiosity" (657) for an event that promises to deliver up sensational gossip and a gripping forensic contest between ambitious, articulate, and aggressive lawyers. The rivalries displayed passionately in the crime will be experienced vicariously by the spectators of the courtroom drama. The ritual legal performances will consciously exploit these rivalrous desires, though the lawyers will not be interested in them for any moral reasons. Their interests are focused on the contemporary legal and social significance of the case, to which their careers and public reputations are attached.

We should also note that there is nothing optional about attending the liturgy of the courtroom for its main participants. All are required to defer formally to its authority by standing for the judges, maintaining decorous silence, testifying under oath, wearing proper clothing, and allowing its designated ritual experts to follow a strictly formal procedure. In contrast to the elder's cell, for example, Dmitri's passionate and conscience-laden speechmaking is disallowed and immediately silenced, with threats. Above all this is to be a public contest between legal representatives about the objective data completely indifferent to, and in fact essentially abstracted from, any personal considerations. The thing most to be avoided in this liturgical ritual is spiritual discernment, which could only contaminate and render invalid the public and secular enactment of justice.

This does not mean that all kinds of appeals to "Christian values" will be disallowed, or that language of conscience is ruled out. But the ritual setting requires a quite different understanding of the meaning of such appeals and the ends to which they are dedicated. I do not have the time here to describe the liturgical performances in the courtroom. Suffice it to say that all of the legal liturgists share a commitment to Westernizing legal reforms. The detached, scientific exactitude of the secular progressivist judge stands in sharp contrast to the engaged spiritual disposition of the elder toward matters of justice. The role of medical, legal and psychological experts in the adversarial construals of the evidence by opposing lawyers, and indeed the technical evidentiary process itself, are displayed by Dostoevsky as devoted to retributive ends, but not discerning the real relations of the human beings involved, nor much concerned about the truth behind the evidence.

A frequent observer of criminal trials, Dostoevsky believed that the liturgical practices of modern adversarial justice often not only do not serve justice but that its rituals and rhetoric actively corrupt it, breeding cynicism and lack of discernment in its practitioners and in the public observing the spectacle. He argued that the mechanisms of adversarial justice, which cater to appearance, external evidence, and spectacle, should be replaced by the disciplined pursuit of truly restorative justice. In *Brothers Karamazov* such an alternative set of rituals is offered in the practical institution of elders and the monastic disciplines. I have only been able to give a brief glimpse into Dostoevsky's rich artistic display of the correlation between ritual and justice in *Brothers Karamazov*. The point is that rights are related to rites, and ultimately to construals of the Right which have implications for religion, ethics and politics. Rites orient practitioners liturgically—in the etymological sense of *leitourgia* (*leitos*, public; *ergos*, performance or work/service)—and entail disciplines of speech and action that affect the enactment of political justice. Dostoevsky's alternative to the liturgy of retributive justice in the modern courtroom is the liturgy of restorative justice in monastic Christianity, which in *Brothers Karamazov* is taken out of the monastery and into the world by the novel's (anti)hero, Alyosha Karamazov. This establishes a very different context from Nietzsche's account for interpreting the meaning of punishment and torture.

Conclusion

I began this essay with reference to Michael Ignatieff's rather abstract consideration of the difference between punishment and torture "in an age of terror" in terms of a "balance" between liberty or rights and necessity. While I have argued that such abstractions are of very limited help (and indeed may be used to legitimate increasingly global "empire necessities") in making judgments about the differences between punishment and torture, I wish in conclusion to turn to the thinker who has perhaps most burdened Western political ethics with necessity language—namely, Augustine. In contrast to ethical abstractions, however, Augustine gives us in *City of God* XIX, 6 his vivid image of the anxious wise judge who is called upon to exercise public political responsibility to make judgments with the full awareness that in a sinful world those judgments will be flawed. They will entail a measure of evil necessity, evident in such practices as judicial torture, rituals of pain designed to evoke confessions of truth.

Augustine's image is both moving and deeply disturbing. It is moving not least for its uncompromising honesty (some call it "realism") about the presence of evil in the world and the dutiful necessity to act politically despite the necessary limitations on our capacities—for example, we cannot see into the souls of those we judge, and so have to do the best we can with the appearances of things (including bodily pain and interrogation). It is also moving because Augustine will advert repeatedly to what he calls the rallying cry of the Christian church in the midst of such miserable necessities: "forgive us our sins," and "deliver me/us from my/our necessities," a penitential disposition of humility. Yet it is also disturbing in that it authorizes practices, such as various forms of corporal (and capital) punishment and judicial torture, that are not necessarily to be viewed as "necessary" but perhaps as strictly evil and thus avoided, even on Augustine's own account of messianic politics, which, though I do not have the space to argue it here, is finally not so different from Dostoevsky's.

While Augustine clearly envisions the ritual of judicial torture as a secular and civil, not ecclesial and religious, liturgy, his position is nevertheless problematic on several levels. The first is that it does not conform to Augustine's theological understanding of truth and lying—for him clearly not a bodily matter but a matter of the soul[10]—and this would pertain no less in the secular than in the ecclesial domain. In fact, Augustine's description of the "necessity" of judicial torture shows a clear awareness that innocents will often confess to crimes they have not committed under pain of torture: "And when [the accused] has been condemned and put to death, the judge still does not know whether he has slain a guilty man or an innocent one, even after torturing him to avoid ignorantly slaying the innocent. In this case, he has tortured an innocent man in order

10. For helpful discussions of Augustine's interpretation of truth and lying, see Rist, *Augustine*, 193–97; and Griffiths, *Lying*.

to discover the truth, and has killed him while still not knowing it."[11] The second is that judicial torture stands in egregious contradiction to the defining liturgical drama of his political theology, namely, the Eucharist—itself a sacrificial meal in which the church receives and offers itself in humble and penitential service to God and to the neighbor in an act of dispossessive self-giving. This is done in memory of another criminal torture and punishment, indeed under the sign of crucifixion, that both puts on cosmic display the sinful pretension of falsely sovereign human judgment and reveals the martyr form of the servant (not domination and coercive control) to be the sovereign and liberating form of God in a world of evil necessity. Clearly the torments of Augustine's judge derive from this more primary liturgical enactment. It is hard to see how appeals to "necessity" make any sense, then, with regard to the practice of judicial torture. Indeed, it is possible to see in Augustine's conscience-plagued figure the origins of the despised priest of Nietzsche's genealogy—one who is able to move adroitly between juridical inquisitorial torture (and why not use rituals of pain to evoke confessions also in an ecclesial setting where, even more, the eternal soul's salvation/condemnation, is at stake?) and the many possible pastoral uses of conscience-vivisection and tortuous self-surveillance to keep citizens and Christians in a state of moral conformity.[12]

It is my view that Augustine cannot have it both ways. He cannot participate in the Eucharistic liturgy and then advocate participation in the liturgy of judicial torture. If the former is true, the latter must be a lie—as the elder Zosima puts it, the messianic law of love may not "be combined with any other judgment, even in a temporary compromise." Furthermore, while I have not argued it here, I have assumed it is the

11. Augustine, *City of God*, 927. Augustine's reflections continue: "[The wise judge] does not consider it a wickedness [*nefas*] that innocent witnesses should be tortured in cases which are not their own, or that the accused are so often overcome by such great pain that they make false confessions and are punished in spite of their innocence. Nor does he think it wicked that, even if not condemned to die, they very often die under torture or as a result of torture . . . Witnesses may lie in giving testimony; the defendant himself may be obdurate under torture and refuse to confess; and so the accusers may not be able to prove the truth of their accusations, no matter how true those accusations may be, and the judge, in his ignorance, may condemn them." The key point, for Augustine, is that the wise judge's *intention* is not to do harm.

12. Here one finds the narrow opening for Connolly's Nietzschean-Foucauldian interpretation of Augustine's political theology, in *Augustinian Imperative*; see Dodaro's excellent critique of Connolly's too narrow reading, in "Augustine's Secular City," 231–59.

case that language of human dignity, rights, forgiveness, and the Right (I mean this as a synonym for the Good, not an ideological partisan political term) in the secular West is heavily indebted to religious practices and ideas. It is therefore important to draw analogically and comparatively upon these interrelations in thinking through the question of torture and punishment, and not simply in institutional or doctrinal terms. Above all it would be dangerous to impose a strict institutional dualism (e.g., the church represents "mercy," while the state represents "judgment"[13]) upon these questions in a manner that precludes a fully critical analogical consideration. Here Book XIX of *City of God* may itself provide a helpful structure. Augustine is convinced that the same existential relations of human love and justice hold true from the most intimate levels of self and household to the civic and international domains, from the most visible bodily level to the cosmic spiritual context concerning the origin and end of all things. No false boundaries will enable us to sort this out more simply. This does not mean that divine justice or judgment is transparent in the world, but it does mean that those ordered by the liturgical practices of penitence and self-offering may not presume to mediate divine judgment in anything but the servant form enacted therein. To the extent that judicial torture and indeed any retributive judicial practices are devoted to the possessive and dominating "order" of the security state that claims to mediate a non-penitential justice, such practices are rooted in evil necessity and contribute to the "lie" of a strictly human sovereignty. They are subject to the Nietzschean critique of a Christianity that seeks coercively to impose its humble and confessional truth through internal and external disciplinary mechanisms of sovereign control. On the other hand, as I hope this essay has also shown, Nietzsche's reading of conscience, crime, punishment, and torture, is not the only possible reading—either of the Christian tradition or of the rise of the "sovereign" moral self in the modern (and postmodern) West. Dostoevsky (and Augustine) points to another possibility that is utterly pertinent to these questions, that no less than Nietzsche and Foucault, problematizes taken-for-granted assumptions about the difference between punishment and torture, and yet interprets and addresses them in a very different way. The sources I have drawn upon in this essay enable us to go beyond the often unhelpful abstractions of conventional technical ethics in order to wrestle theologically with the

---

13. This is the approach of O'Donovan in *Desire of the Nations*, 259ff.

challenging lived complexities, including the religious ones, of our inher-
ited moral discourses and practices concerning torture and punishment.
The outcome of such a wrestling, just perhaps, may be a less confident
limping through that nevertheless mediates political blessing.

2

Regina Artium:
Theology and the Humanities[1]

JOHN WEBSTER

Every good endowment and every perfect gift is from above,
coming down from the Father of lights. (Jas 1:17)

I

Two topics should be distinguished: that of theology *and* the humanities, and that of a theology *of* the humanities. The first concerns the relation of theological studies to humane studies, and has evoked two sorts of inquiries. In the period before theology embedded itself in the university as a distinct academic discipline, treatments of this topic took the form of questions about the propaedeutic function of the liberal arts, the cycle of studies whose origins lay in the educational culture of antiquity: theology is contemplation of the revealed wisdom of God, the liberal arts are its (potentially unruly) *ancillae*, in the service of a Christian culture at whose center lay the exegesis of Scripture. As theology acquires some of

1. A version of this material was delivered as the Danforth Lecture at Hope College, Holland, Michigan, in March 2010.

the properties of an academic discipline, and especially after the growth of the modern research university from the mid-eighteenth century, the question shifts to become one about the relation of theology as one discipline to the humanities as another cluster of disciplines. This more recent way of asking the question, forms of which remain the conventional approach in the modern university, has rarely proved fruitful; the very terms in which the question is asked defeat in advance any theologically satisfactory answer. This, because whether by intention or neglect, the demotion of theology to the status of being one—insecure—discipline alongside (and increasingly harried by) others inhibits theology from furnishing a comprehensive account of the nature and ends of intellectual activity *in toto*, and so of humane studies.

This leads to the second topic, that of a theology *of* the humanities. A theology of the humanities is an account of the ways in which humane studies are an element in the moving of created intellect by God. Clarity about the relation of theology *to* the humanities is achieved only when we are able to provide a satisfactory theology *of* the humanities. In formal terms: didascalics—the question of what is to be studied and in what sequence—is a function of metaphysics. Theology supplies such a metaphysics of created intelligence, its origin, nature and ends, grounding the arts of human intelligence in the eternal self-communicative wisdom of God himself. The domain of the intellectual life, theology tells us, is not simply one of education and research, *Bildung* and *Wissenschaft*, and the various disciplinary and curricular forms by which they may be ordered. These are temporalities, whose end lies not wholly in themselves but in serving as instruments of God's illumination of us as he conducts us towards the light of truth after primitive disaster cast us in the shadows.

Why inquire into this second topic? Because all intellectual enquiry and educational practice, all research and teaching and learning, are informed by an underlying account of the intellectual life and its goals, even when our thinking about such matters is not made explicit. Part of the travail of much contemporary higher education (especially in British universities) is the flimsiness and ignobility of its understanding of what it is about, and, consequently, its helpless conformity to wider cultural expectations. Theological reflection can release us from these expectations; indeed, only theology can do so, by speaking of the arts of created intelligence in the light of God who knows all things and makes creatures to know. A theology of the humanities recognizes the place of intelligence within the economy of God's life-giving and restorative love for rational creatures, and locates the ground of that economy in the eternal wisdom of God himself. Theology, that is, sees that the movement of created intellect is not self-bestowed or self-derived, but a movement from above, a gift that comes down.

Theology can release us from the instinctive secularity in which we think of intellectual inquiry in the humanities or any other domain as a matter of free natural spontaneity. In practice, however, theology has often failed to effect the release. In large part this has been because theology has allowed itself to be outwitted or captivated by the very conventions whose malignity it ought to have exposed. Theology has commonly been content to take refuge in a lesser calling, to settle into the reduced role of being one discipline alongside others, and to permit its content to be supplied by natural religion rather than by the wisdom which comes down from the Father of lights. Theology's capacity to explicate and commend a way of thinking about the humanities depends upon its willingness to think out its own understanding of the economy of knowledge, trusting that its exegetical and dogmatic resources are adequate to the task. Most of all, theology is required to contribute to the flourishing of the universe of letters by pressing the claim—utterly counter-intuitive within the constraints of contemporary research cultures—that the motion of the mind is of God.

It has often proved illuminating to trace the issues by studying epochs in which theology's relation to the liberal arts (or philosophical faculty, as earlier nomenclature had it) became a matter of intense dispute, such as the twelfth and thirteenth centuries, or the later eighteenth and earlier nineteenth centuries.[2] The disputes might be studied through key episodes (the foundations of the universities of Paris, Göttingen or Berlin), or key texts (Bernard's Letter 190, Kant's *Conflict of the Faculties*, Schleiermacher's *Kurze Darstellung*). This may be useful in displaying the issues in sharp profile; but it too readily persuades us to consider them in agonistic terms, to think that conflict between the theology faculty and the faculty of arts is the natural state of affairs. To break free of this, we may ponder a text in which the harmony of theology and the arts is considered not merely possible but normal, and in which their occasional

---

2. On the earlier period, see, for example, Evans, *Old Arts and New Theology*; de Ridder-Symoens, *A History of the University in Europe*; Pedersen, *First Universities*, esp. 271–301; on later developments, see Howard, *Protestant Theology*.

conflict is explained in terms of the way in which intellectual activity is caught up in the as yet unfinished redemption of all things. The text is Bonaventure's *Reduction of the Arts to Theology*, written probably quite late in the life of the Seraphic Doctor (perhaps around 1270).[3] It is an exquisite text, an elegantly patterned, economical, and spiritually charged articulation of a Christian metaphysics of created intelligence in which all the arts are moved by divine wisdom. Such virtues are in themselves enough to commend the text to our attention. But there is more: both in his person and in his particular historical location, Bonaventure stands at a point in the development of theology as a university discipline at which speculative theology has not yet lost touch with positive divinity and retains a sense of theology's contemplative character and of its saturation by Holy Scripture. As an inheritor of the sometimes conflictual reappraisals of the relation of theology to the liberal arts in the twelfth century, Bonaventure offers a theological rationale for the arts which goes far beyond simply registering their utility to the student of Scripture, as had been done earlier in the tradition of Augustine by, for example, Rupert of Deutz or Hugh of St. Victor in the *Didascalicon*. Drawing on Neo-Platonic antecedents, Bonaventure proposes that the arts are intrinsic to the mind's ascent to God because they are themselves irradiated by the same divine wisdom in which theology instructs us; the mind's performance is itself a movement by and towards its creator. We shall have cause to question Bonaventure's slight treatment of the mind's estrangement from God. Yet, that aside, he may help derail some of the conventions through which we are kept from making progress—by his uncluttered sense that created intelligence is flooded by divine light, and by the simple fact that it never occurs to him to think that the arts of the mind may be secular.

I proceed by (1) a reading of Bonaventure's text, (2) some reflections on his understanding of the divine economy which undergirds the *Reduction*; (3) some more general comments on the theology of the intellect, the humanities, and institutions of humane learning.

II

The *Reduction* in its entirety is governed by the text from Jas 1:17 with which it opens: "Every good gift and every perfect gift is from above,

3. Bonaventure, *On the Reduction of the Arts to Theology*.

coming down from the Father of lights."[4] The citation of a biblical text might easily be passed over as casual or merely decorative; but—as in other writings of Bonaventure on the nature of creaturely knowledge[5]—it serves as the "authority" for what follows. The citation is not so much the identification of data or the statement of a norm as it is the evocation of the given epistemological and ontological order within which his reflection takes place and by which it is directed. Bonaventure is a positive divine, one for whom the mind's powers are encompassed and accompanied by a gift and light which are not of the mind's invention. Scripture is the presence of this *positum* of divinity, and, as Scripture is announced at the beginning of a passage of reflection, an entire conception of the nature of created intelligence breaks to the surface.

The James text speaks of a single source of light variously refracted. It identifies "the source [*origo*] of all illumination" but "at the same time it suggests that there are many lights which flow generously from that fontal source of light" (§1). It is this liberality of emanation which is for Bonaventure fundamental in understanding the nature and operations of the arts of the mind, for each of the arts is illuminated by a light which itself flows from the Father of lights. For Bonaventure, the term "arts" encompasses both intellectual skills and practices; the arts are the deliberate ways in which rational creatures make material and intellectual culture. Bonaventure offers a four-fold division. First, there is the "exterior light" or "light of mechanical art" (§1) which "sheds its light on the forms of artefacts," by which he means those arts directed towards the production of things "external to the human person and intended to supply the needs of the body" (§2), and so "servile and of a lower nature" (§2) in that they furnish only external consolation and comfort. (It is worth noting by way of parenthesis that a couple of deft sentences from Bonaventure are all it takes to expose the miserable shallowness of our present "knowledge economy" and its incapacity to envisage goods beyond bodily consolation and comfort). Bonaventure lists seven such arts—his list derives from Hugh's *Didascalicon*,[6] but is later expanded to cover the whole sphere of material and aesthetic culture as Bonaventure knows it: weaving, armor

4. Inexplicably, the English translation renders *descendens a Patre luminum* as "from the God of lights."

5. Such as the sermon *Christus unus omnium magister* or the fourth and eighth of the *Collationes de septem donis Spiritus Sancti*.

6. Hugh of Saint Victor, *Didascalicon*.

making, agriculture, hunting, navigation, medicine, the dramatic arts. Second, there is the "inferior light" or "light of sense perception" (§1), in which natural forms are illuminated "by the aid of corporal light" (§3); here Bonaventure offers a brief account of the operations of the five senses derived from Augustine's *On Genesis* in terms of "similarity and correspondence between the sense-organ and the object" (§3).[7] Third, there is the "light of philosophical knowledge," that is, the light "which enlightens the human person in the investigation of intelligible truths" (§4). This is called "interior" because "it inquires into inner and latent causes through principles and learning and natural truth, which are connatural to the human mind" (§4)—it asks what happens not just when we produce or sense, but also when we engage in intellection. Bonaventure provides a threefold division of this knowledge as rational, natural and moral philosophy, considering respectively the truth of speech, of things and of conduct. "Just as we find in the most high God efficient, formal or exemplary, and final causality, since 'God is the cause of being, the principle of intelligibility, and the order of human life', so we may find these in the illumination of philosophy, which enlightens the mind to discern the cause of being, in which case it is physics; or to know the principles of understanding, in which case it is logic; or to learn the order of living, in which case it is moral or practical philosophy" (§4). Alongside this, Bonaventure offers another anatomy of philosophical knowledge which almost corresponds to the seven liberal arts as studied in the philosophical faculty: rational philosophy divides into grammar, logic and rhetoric, natural philosophy considers physics, mathematics and metaphysics (music is absent and the other *quadrivium* subjects are assimilated to physics and mathematics).

Over and above these three lights there is a fourth, "which provides illumination with respect to saving truth"; this is "the light of sacred Scripture" (§5). For Bonaventure, what is illumined by this light is not simply one domain alongside the others. The light of Scripture is "superior," partly because of its object and purpose—"it leads to higher things by revealing truths which transcend reason" (§5)—and partly because of its mode of acquisition—*non per inventionem sed per inspirationem a Patre luminum*, not by invention but by inspiration. But it is also clear that the light of Scripture is superior because it is not simply one of the set of other illuminations of the arts of the mind, but that which affords

---

7. Augustine *Literal Meaning of Genesis* III.6–7.

comprehensive illumination of technical, intellectual and moral culture in its entirety. The illumination given by Scripture pervades and interpenetrates the whole of creaturely knowing; it is its surrounding atmosphere, not simply another set of materials to go to work on.

Holy Scripture is to be understood according to its one literal and three-fold spiritual senses. As Bonaventure's text proceeds, the latter three senses come to the fore as basic to the process of reduction. The allegorical sense is that "by which we are taught what to believe concerning the divinity and humanity" (§5), namely, the eternal generation and incarnation of the Word; the moral sense is that "by which we are taught how to live" (§5), that is, "the pattern of human life" (§5); and the anagogical sense is that "by which we are taught to cling to God" or, "the union of the soul with God" (§5).

At the beginning of the *Reduction*, then, Bonaventure presents the several arts of knowing, hierarchically ordered from technical to philosophical, as acts in which creatures illuminate the world only insofar as their acts are themselves illuminated. Only as acts of knowing are bathed in light can they be the means of seeing our way around the world or of giving ourselves a truthful picture of it. This is why the light of Holy Scripture is not commensurate with the other lights, but the light upon which their particular lights depend. "[A]s all these lights have their origin in a single light, so too all these branches of knowledge are ordered to the knowledge of sacred Scripture: they are contained in it; they are perfected by it; and they are ordered to the eternal illumination by means of it. Therefore all our knowledge should come to rest in the knowledge of sacred Scripture, and particularly in the anagogical understanding of Scripture through which any illumination is traced back to God from whom it took its origin" (§7). It is precisely this process of tracing all knowledge back to God [*refertur in Deum*]—scarcely imaginable by us in a culture in which the finality of all things in God has ceased to stir the mind—which is the heart of the project of *reductio*.

Bonaventure announces that project in the simplest terms: "Let us see . . . how the other illuminations of knowledge are to be traced back [*reduce*] to the light of sacred Scripture" (§8). We may pause a moment over the term "reduction" itself.[8] To offer a "reduction" on the various arts of human knowledge is to secure their unity on the basis of a principle

---

8. On the wider metaphysical and cosmological setting of *reductio*, see Bérubé, *De la philosophie*, 265–72. More generally, see Allard, "La technique de la 'reductio,'" 395–416.

which is at once metaphysical, cosmological and theological or spiritual, namely that all created realities, including created acts and arts of knowing, are caught up in the process of coming from and returning to God the supreme good. This circular history, the economy of emanation from and return to the point of origin, is what creaturely being is, and it is what is known when creatures know themselves and other created realities. Created being and knowing are not a mere random assemblage of disparate entities and operations; they are at their deepest level one thing, by virtue of their origin and term in God. A "reduction" of the history of creation isolates for thought and contemplation the single rhythm that underlies all its disparate manifestations. Creatures have their being as they are conducted back to God; their form *is* this movement of return, a movement made explicit in theology or Holy Scripture. Reduction of the arts to theology is, therefore, a matter of plotting the arts as undertakings within the comprehensive movement of created being. The reduction brings to consciousness this unified process. It answers the questions: "What do we know when we know?" and "What do we do when we know?" by referring them to a prior question: "In what movement do creatures participate?" Answering this question in terms of a scriptural economy of the coming forth of creation from God and its return to him, reduction thinks of creaturely being and knowing as more than phenomenal, more than surface motion. It is worth pointing out that this is not "reductive" in the bad sense—not, that is, a repudiation of the "surface" of created being and activity, a refusal of exteriority or the triumph of pure intelligibility over the merely visible.[9] Rather, reduction discloses what such surfaces are: created beings and acts, phenomenal beings and acts with depth, and so, in their very visibility, *signs*.

Most of Bonaventure's text is given over to undertaking such a reduction in the three realms illuminated by the first three lights—the realms of mechanical art, sense perception and philosophical knowledge. It would be laborious to trace all three in detail, and for our present purposes we may restrict ourselves to one example, namely, the reduction of rational philosophy to theology (§§15–18).

As each element in his reduction proceeds, Bonaventure gives an analysis of the elements of a particular art, that is, of some act which we might call "intelligent making." The aim of the reading is to make us aware

---

9. For worries along this line, see Allard, "La technique de la 'reductio,'" 403.

of the deeper motion of this particular art, and so to show how the operation of human intelligence signifies the active presence of divine wisdom. This is accomplished by applying the techniques of spiritual exegesis, thereby disclosing the allegorical, moral and anagogical layers of meaning within the art under discussion. By so doing, reduction shows that this art participates in, and in its own operations manifests, the wider history of God's dealings with creatures, the most salient features of which are the incarnation of the eternal Word, the moral life and the union of the soul with God. How, then, may "divine wisdom" be "found in the illumination of rational philosophy" (§15)? Rational philosophy concerns itself with speech, the topic dividing into inquiries into the person of the speaker, the delivery of speech and its purpose. In considering the speaker, the reduction unearths the allegorical weight of that with which rational philosophy is concerned. Speech signifies a "mental concept" (§16); the process of signifying is to be understood as communication of what has been interiorily conceived through the assumption of external form. The "inner concept is the word of the mind and its offspring which is known to the person conceiving it. But in order that this concept becomes known to the hearer, it assumes the form of the voice; and by means of this clothing, the intelligible word becomes sensible and is heard externally. It is received into the ear of the listener and yet does not depart from the mind of the person uttering it" (§16). And, the reduction continues, "It is something like this that we see in the eternal Word. God conceived the Word by an eternal act of generation . . . but that the Word might be known by human beings who are endowed with sense, the Word assumed the form of flesh, and 'the Word was made flesh and dwelt among us,' while remaining 'in the bosom of the Father.'" (§16, translation altered).

Again, in considering the delivery of speech, we may discern "the pattern [*ordo*] of human life" (§17). Speech fulfils its nature when it displays "fittingness [*congruitas*], truth [*veritas*] and style [*ornatus*]" (§17). And "[c]orresponding to these qualities, all acts of ours should be characterised by measure, beauty and order so that they may be measured by reason of modesty in external works, rendered beautiful by purity of affection, and ordered and adorned by uprightness of intention" (§17). Thus, the *moral* sense of rational philosophy. Finally, in relation to its purpose, speech aims "to express, to instruct and to persuade" (§18)—ends which can only be achieved by correspondence to the soul. Speech "never expresses except by means of a likeness; it never teaches except by means of a convincing light; it never persuades except by power; and it is evident that these effects are accomplished by means of an inherent likeness, light and power intrinsically united to the soul" (§18). Hence, rational philosophy harbors an anagogical meaning: "As nothing can be known perfectly by means of speech except by reason of a power, a light, and a likeness united to the soul, so, too, for the soul to be instructed in the knowledge of God by interior conversation with the divine, there is required a union with the one who is 'the brightness of the divine glory and the image of the divine substance, upholding all things by the word of divine power'" (§18).

It would, doubtless, be easy to dismiss this and the rest of Bonaventure's reduction as fanciful, no more than a set of quaint analogies between the various arts and the truths of Christian dogma, morals and ascetics. But that response may well indicate our instinctive preference for the literal and the secular—for surfaces beneath which nothing lies—which reading Bonaventure ought to unsettle, because for him human culture is *layered*. Put differently, for Bonaventure there is no literal or natural meaning and activity which is not illuminated by and ordered towards the wisdom of God. The arts, therefore, are an economy of production, communication and speculation constituted by that wisdom, and their very performance is suffused by and drawn towards the light of God. "It is evident," he concludes,

> how the manifold wisdom of God, which is clearly revealed in sacred Scripture, lies hidden in all knowledge and in all nature. It is clear also how all divisions of knowledge are servants of theology, and it is for this reason that theology makes use of illustrations and terms pertaining to every branch of knowledge. It is likewise clear how wide the illuminative way may be, and how the divine reality itself lies hidden within everything which is perceived or known. And this is the fruit of all the sciences, that in all, faith may be strengthened, God may be honoured, character may be formed, and consolation may be derived from union of the spouse with the beloved, a union which takes place through charity: a charity in which the whole purpose of sacred Scripture, and thus of every illumination descending from above, comes to rest—a charity without which all knowledge is vain because no one comes to the Son except through the Holy Spirit who teaches us all the truth, who is blessed forever. (§26)

With this in place, we may take a step back and look at some underlying principles of the *Reduction*. First, Bonaventure's text is informed throughout by exegesis and doctrine. We have already noted the role played by the opening quotation from the Letter of James in giving explicit direction to the argument. No less important is the dogmatics, even though in this severely economical text dogmatic principles are largely implicit (they could be reconstructed from elsewhere in Bonaventure's writings: the sermons, the collations on the gifts of the Spirit and on the hexameron, the *Sentences* commentary). The project of reduction presupposes a theology of God and creatures, and of the order of their relations enacted in the economy of creation and salvation through which their union is perfected. For Bonaventure, the sheer liberality of the triune Creator is rooted in his infinite blessedness in himself, such that he gives life not out of need for self-completion, but out of love. This liberality takes form in the divine Word, who, by virtue of his eternal generation shares the fullness of the divine essence and *sapientia* and so is the origin, principle and cause of all created wisdom; and God's liberality is shed abroad among creatures by the Spirit. The creatures of such a God have their being in his infinite resourcefulness, and their temporal course in all its activities is the realization of union with God. Contemporary readers of mediaeval texts, eager to discover in them a metaphysics of participation prior to the fateful separations of the fourteenth century, are sometimes prone to treat their exegetical and dogmatic content in too cursory a way and to turn them into exercises in metaphysics. Bonaventure certainly offers a metaphysics of the arts of intelligence; yet it is a metaphysics in which the Trinity, Christ the teacher, and the Spirit who gives all good things are not illustrative but primitive.

Second, the theological metaphysics of the arts of intelligence which Bonaventure sets out concerns the graced character of created being and its operations, by virtue of which creatureliness is a *sign*. To be a creature is to be "anticipated . . . by divine grace," *praeventus . . . divina gratia*.[10] In terms of the arts of the mind, this means that intellectual acts are not in themselves illuminative but illuminated, flooded by the light of God, who alone is the *origo omnis illuminationis*, the *fons lucis* (§1). In the collation *De dono intellectus*, Bonaventure argues that the mind enlightens only as it is enlightened. "Every act of the intelligence comes from that fount

---

10. Bonaventure, *Itinerarium*, prologue iv.

of intelligence;"[11] the mind's activity requires "a brightening through a divine influence,"[12] or "the assistance of a superior and higher light."[13] To change the image somewhat: creaturely intelligence takes place in the ordered double movement of divine giving and creaturely return. "If," Bonaventure says in *De dono scientiae*, "the Lord is a great teacher and grantor of gifts . . . it is proper that we run back to that fount to pursue illumination."[14] Notice that what Bonaventure is describing is not simply some sort of spiritual preparation for intellectual work, but rather the intellect in act: the work of the mind *is* the act of running back to God as *doctor*, *grantor* and *fons*. This is why intelligence and prayer cannot be pried apart, the latter made into pious preliminaries to aid the mind in directing itself along the right course. "No one can illumine the hearts of men except him who knows the consciences of men;" and so, "in the beginning, let us beg God."[15] That act—*in principio rogemus Deum*—is the basic act of intelligence.

All this shows that the distinction of uncreated and created being and intelligence is entirely natural to Bonaventure, and is not effaced by what he has to say in the *Reduction* about how divine wisdom lies hidden within the arts of human intelligence and about how such arts may serve in the return of creatures to God. Bonaventure, of course, makes much use of the notion of exemplarity in his theological metaphysics of creation. Created realities are external expression of the divine Word, the internal divine self-expression who contains within himself all the divine ideas which are the exemplars of creatures. Leaving aside the question of whether this is too closely wedded to an emanationist understanding of the act of creation, we may nevertheless note how decisive exemplarity is for the project of reduction. Objects of knowledge, knowing subjects and their acts of knowing all stand in relation to anterior eternal ideas by which they are informed, and are most fully understood within that relation, which is essential, not accidental. A reduction of the arts of the mind is a raising to consciousness of the relation which these arts bear to their

---

11. Bonaventure, *Collationes*, VIII.6.

12. Ibid., VIII.15.

13. Ibid., VIII.20.

14. Ibid., IV.1

15. Ibid., VIII.1; see also IV.1; *Itinerarium*, prologue i, I.

exemplars in God's own wisdom and knowledge, and of the path along which they move to their end in God.

The arts, we might say, *signify*.[16] They are not pure acts of will or of instrumental reason, because in their very intentionality and productiveness they are illuminated by and directed towards divine light. We find this reduction oddly forced (can sense perception really be an analogy of eternal generation and incarnation? we ask), lacking Bonaventure's conviction that the surface does not exhaust the reality of any creaturely act. The phenomenal surface is significative, disclosing its origin and term. What seem random associations are indications of the ontological depth of creatures and their acts, which bear a reference to the *fons* at a level beyond that of consciousness or intention. All sorts of cultural activities—making shelter and food, commerce, drama, arts of speech and speculation—are disclosive once they are "read" within the comprehensive context of creatureliness as a movement of divine love. In performing such acts, creatures do more (but not *less*) than what presents on the surface; as they do these things, they are moved by and move towards God.

Theology's primary task in the reduction of the arts is to draw attention to this movement, because theology is the knowledge of the ways of God and creatures, which is proffered in Holy Scripture. Bonaventure does not think of theology as one discipline or art alongside others, partly because he is writing at a time when the conception of theology as a discrete field of inquiry is still coalescing, more profoundly because he does not consider theology to be a special science treating a special set of transcendent objects alongside or over against disenchanted "natural" objects. Theology is a comprehensive account of all things in the light of God. There is no conflict of the faculties between the arts and theology, because theology is not a "faculty" but a culture, a mode of thought, prayer, and holiness which permeates all acts of intelligence.[17] Further, the reduction is a refusal of the secularity of the arts, for there is no secular realm, no entity or act or art that has its being and motion in itself and is knowable apart from God. There is no pure nature and no pure reason; but there is nature, and reason, and so there are the human arts.

16. On the work of human intelligence as sign, see Milbank, "Conflict of the Faculties," 39–57; Davies, *Creativity of God*; Williams, *Grace and Necessity.*

17. By contrast, in distancing his account of Bonaventure from Gilson's, C. Cullen tends to separate theology and philosophy more sharply: Cullen, *Bonaventure.*

III

Bonaventure invites us along what have become unfamiliar paths in thinking about the relation of theology and the humanities. On the one hand, a reduction of the arts to theology suggests that theology need not cast itself as a homeless discipline, hovering on the edge of the academy and wondering how to secure a place for itself; from its exegetical and dogmatic stores, theology is capable of providing a sort of "first philosophy" of the life of the mind, a description of the condition and operations of created intelligence. On the other hand, a reduction of the arts to theology declines to consider the intellectual arts as wholly profane phenomena, which must either be repudiated as necessarily hostile to theology or affirmed in their independence as the triumphant revenge of the philosophical faculty. Within the terms of Bonaventure's theocentric humanism, there need be no final contest between the arts and theology, because "reduction" affirms and orders both, setting them within a vision of created being and its illumination by God. "The university of things is the stairway to ascend to God."[18]

Before moving to some wider issues, a doctrinal question looms over the project of reduction. What is the place of reconciliation in Bonaventure's economy of human intelligence? What would become of the reduction of the arts if, alongside the image from James of the breadth of divine illumination we set the Pauline notion that what distinguishes the gentiles from the church is "the futility of their minds; they are darkened in their understanding, alienated from the life of God because of the ignorance that is in them, due to their hardness of heart" (Eph 4:17ff.)? Is Bonaventure's reduction seriously shaken by the realities of the futility, darkness, alienation, ignorance and callousness of fallen intelligence? Does the distinction between the church and the nations extend into the liberal arts?

The *Reduction* itself is quite generously optimistic, even perhaps a little naïve, about the way in which created intelligence participates in the gathering of all things back to God. The economy of the arts that Bonaventure sketches is not redemptive, and there is little reference to sin. It should immediately be recognized that elsewhere Bonaventure does address the effects of the fall on the realm of the arts. In the collations of the gifts of the Spirit, Bonaventure writes that "the first brightness, that

18. Bonaventure, *Itinerarium* I.2.

of philosophical knowledge, is great according to the opinion of worldly men; but it is easily eclipsed unless a man himself beware the head and tail of the dragon. If anything is interposed between himself and the Sun of justice, he will suffer the eclipse of stupidity."[19] The forms of the mind's fallenness against which Bonaventure warns his readers are the classical sins of the Augustinian tradition: pride,[20] presumption,[21] ingratitude,[22] disorderly, and concupiscent appetites which capture the intellect,[23] arresting the movement of knowledge and so failing to press ahead to its proper term. "Philosophical knowledge is the way to the other sciences but he who wants to stand still there falls into darkness."[24]

There is more here than protest against the pretentions of Averroism: we are touching deep currents of Bonaventure's thought. Yet it is curious that they do not find their way into the *Reduction*, with its emphasis on the breadth of the illuminative way. It is a great accomplishment of the *Reduction* to counter the secularity of the arts of intelligence by setting them within the realm of God's resplendent glory. The corollary weakness is inattention to the fact that the glory which illumines all things is not only that of the Father of lights, of Christ the teacher, and of the Holy Spirit, but also the glory of the *mediator*. The one by whom the mind is moved to return to God is the one who in the sphere of knowledge has overwhelmed and invalidated a regime of vanity, untruth and self-absorption, and is now renewing the spirit of the mind (Eph 4:23). Christ is not only *doctor* and *magister* of the mind, nor only the mover and governor of intellectual motion, but also its *priest*, overcoming ignorance and alienation (Eph 4:18).

To begin to see how the movement of reconciliation extends into the arts of the intelligence, we may briefly recall Augustine's later reflections on the liberal arts in the *De doctrina christiana* and the *Confessions*, well beyond Augustine's post-conversion commitment to the value of philosophical retreat and cultivation of the arts which produced the *Soliloquies*, *De academicis*, *De beata vita*, and *De ordine*.[25] Brooding over the period

19. Bonaventure, *Collationes* IV.12.

20. Ibid.

21. Ibid., VIII.1.

22. Ibid., VIII.2.

23. Ibid., VIII.3–5, 7.

24. Ibid., IV.12.

25. I prescind from engaging the long-standing debate over Augustine's place in the

in his late twenties when he wrote a now-lost work *On the Beautiful and the Fitting*, Augustine asks himself in the *Confessions*: "What did it profit me that I could read and understand for myself all the books I could get in the so-called 'liberal arts,' when I was actually a worthless slave of wicked lust? I took delight in them, not knowing the real source of what it was in them that was true and certain. For I had my back toward the light, and my face toward the things towards which the light falls, so that my face, which looked towards the illuminated things, was not itself illuminated."[26] For Bonaventure the arts of intelligence are intrinsically illuminated by the Father of lights: the necessity of the conversion and sanctification of those arts and their agents does not break the surface of the *Reduction*. Augustine does not share this serenity, experience having made him quite bitterly aware of the potential for wickedness in the practice of the liberal arts and the rhetorical culture of which they formed part—of the pervasiveness of disordered intellectual appetite, of the terminating of the arts in the knower, of ingratitude. "Whatever was written in any of the fields of rhetoric or logic, geometry, music or arithmetic, I could understand without any great difficulty and without the instruction of another man . . . yet for such gifts I made no thank offering to thee. Therefore my abilities served not my profit but rather my loss, since I went about trying to bring so large a part of my substance into my power."[27] For Augustine it is not enough to think of the arts as divinely irradiated means of journeying to God, because fallen creatures incorporate the arts into a different and wicked movement of vanity and carnal absorption. In part this is because Augustine does not detach the arts from the way in which the educational arrangements in which they are embedded are a social embodiment and instrument of corruption. His curt summary of his nine years as a teacher

---

transition from classical to Christian culture, generated by Marrou in *Saint Augustin*. In the first edition of his work, Marrou portrayed Augustine as the central figure in the passage from classical intellectual culture (with the liberal arts at its centre) to the culture of mediaeval Christianity. Marrou himself began to call his own argument into question some years later in the second edition of his book, as did others, notably Hadot in *Arts libéraux et philosophie*, who argued that Augustine did not simply appropriate a settled and systematic classical educational ideal because there was no such ideal for him to take over (for example, from Varro) until at least Cassiodorus in the sixth century. More recent interventions in the debate include Harrison, *Augustine*; Pollmann and Vessey, *Augustine and the Disciplines*; Paffenroth and Hughes, *Augustine and Liberal Education*.

26. Augustine *Confessions* IV.15.30.

27. Ibid.

of rhetoric runs: "I was deceived and deceived others, in varied lustful projects."[28]

Where Bonaventure has a quite tranquil sense of the way in which the arts of intelligence are caught up in the mind's ascent to God, Augustine is a good deal more guarded, as is indicated by his particular use of the image of despoiling the Egyptians in the *De doctrina christiana*:

> Like the treasures of the ancient Egyptians, who possessed not only idols and heavy burdens, which the people of Israel hated and shunned, but also vessels and ornaments of silver and gold . . . which on leaving Egypt the people of Israel, in order to make better use of them, surreptitiously claimed for themselves . . . similarly all the branches of pagan learning contain not only false and superstitious fantasies and burdensome studies that involve unnecessary effort, which each one of us must loathe and avoid as under Christ's guidance we abandon the company of pagans, but also studies for liberated minds which are more appropriate to the service of truth . . . these treasures . . . must be removed by Christians, as they separate themselves from the wretched company of pagans, and applied to their true function, that of preaching the gospel.[29]

This points us in a different direction from Bonaventure's calmly ordered universe of the human arts. Augustine's appeal to the image of the exodus is at once more social, more conflictual, and more discriminatory. The Christian picks over the arts to see what can be salvaged, what must be cast aside by the people of God in the flight from captivity.

Augustine's ambiguity concerning the place of the arts in the Christian and scriptural way of life, his sensitivity to the friction between the divinely-instituted culture of the church and the vanity of pagan inventions, comes across in Letter CI, written to an inquirer who had asked for the revised text of Augustine's *De musica*. Augustine speaks at length of the spurious liberty of the liberal arts:

> For to men who, though they are unjust and impious, imagine that they are well educated in the liberal arts, what else ought we to say than what we read in those writings which truly merit the name of liberal,—"if the Son shall make you free, ye shall be free indeed." For it is through Him that men come to know, even in those stud-

---

28. Ibid., IV.1.1.

29. Augustine *On Christian Doctrine* II.40.60.

ies which are termed liberal by those who have not been called to this true liberty, anything in them which deserves the name. For they have nothing which is consonant with liberty, except that which in them is consonant with truth; for which reason the Son Himself hath said: "The truth shall make you free." The freedom which is our privilege has therefore nothing in common with the innumerable and impious fables with which the verses of silly poets are full, nor with the fulsome and highly-polished falsehoods of their orators, nor, in fine, with the rambling subtleties of philosophers themselves, who either did not know anything of God, or when they knew God, did not glorify Him as God, neither were thankful, but became vain in their imaginations, and their foolish heart was darkened; so that, professing themselves to be wise, they became fools, and changed the glory of the incorruptible God into an image made like to corruptible man, and to birds and four-footed beasts, and to creeping things, or who, though not wholly or at all devoted to the worship of images, nevertheless worshipped and served the creature more than the Creator. Far be it, therefore, from us to admit that the epithet liberal is justly bestowed on the lying vanities and hallucinations, or empty trifles and conceited errors of those men—unhappy men, who knew not the grace of God in Christ Jesus our Lord, by which alone we are "delivered from the body of this death," and who did not even perceive the measure of truth which was in the things which they knew.[30]

Yet even here there is a vestige of Augustine's earlier esteem for the liberal arts as means whereby, prompted by divine wisdom, we may ascend to truth:

Forasmuch, however, as the powers belonging to numbers in all kinds of movements are most easily studied as they are presented in sounds, and this study furnishes a way of rising to the higher secrets of truth, by paths gradually ascending, so to speak, in which Wisdom pleasantly reveals herself, and in every step of providence meets those who love her, I desired, when I began to have leisure for study, and my mind was not engaged by greater and more important cares, to exercise myself by writing those books which you have requested me to send.[31]

The restlessness which sets Augustine apart from Bonaventure is partly explicable as the reaction of one who, educated to assume a place

30. Augustine *Letter* CI.2
31. Augustine *Letter* CI.3.

among the governing elite, found himself precipitated by conversion and ecclesiastical vocation into a new Christian culture which was apostolic and scriptural, rather than rhetorical, in character. "Men uninstructed in any branch of a liberal education, without any of the refinement of heathen learning, unskilled in grammar, not armed with dialectic, not adorned with rhetoric, but plain fishermen, and very few in number,— these were the men whom Christ sent with the nets of faith to the sea of this world, and thus took out of every race so many fishes, and even the philosophers themselves, wonderful as they are rare."[32] A society with such a foundation, one whose authoritative text lacked literary sophistication and was, indeed, vulgar, could have at best a circumspect attitude to the arts in which Augustine had earlier immersed himself and from which he had expected much. Moreover, the exercise of his pastoral office required Augustine to direct himself not only to a cultural elite but to the uneducated, reinforcing the incommensurability of the Christian society and high culture.

Yet none of this need call into question the project of reduction, even if it chastens complacent versions of it. For Bonaventure, theology describes what, according to Holy Scripture, the world is: the temporal passage of created being back to its creator. This history is irreducible to other terms, and so there can be no profane understanding of the arts of the mind, because creatureliness is basic. For Augustine, too, the arts of the mind are not secular, but of divine institution; but they are caught up in wickedness, and discriminating use of them—most of all in the interpretation of the Bible—depends on their being broken away from captivity to vice.[33] The setting for the arts is therefore not simply that of emanation and return but rather the paschal mystery, figured in baptism and repeated in sanctification. "In the symbol of the cross every Christian act is inscribed."[34]

IV

Finally, some more general extensions of what has been found in Bonaventure. First: a theology of the humanities derives from a more general

---

32. Augustine *City of God* XXII.5.
33. See Augustine *On Christian Doctrine* II.39.58.
34. Ibid., II.40.62.

theology of the intellectual arts—that is, from a theological portrayal of what happens when the reconciled creaturely intellect is at work. That portrayal does not just pick out certain practices, habits or virtues of rational creatures; it speaks of intellectual activity in terms of its origin and end in God. The chief concern of a theology of created intellect is with the hidden inner movement which is the setting for all that the rational creatures of God undertake, including their intellectual dealings with the world in the humanities. What we have found in Bonaventure is a description of the work of the intellect as an element in the economy of God's illuminating presence and gift, an activity in the domain in which all things come down from the Father of lights. To study the humanities is to participate in this movement, to inhabit this domain.

Why is it that we so often find it such an awkward business to articulate the life of study in these terms? Partly, of course, it is because teachers and learners are usually preoccupied with tasks more immediately to hand, and do not often pause to consider the depth of the undertaking in which we are enlisted. But there is a more malign aspect to this failure to set our intellectual activity in relation to God. We have been schooled, both by long-standing cultural convention and by the perversity of fallen nature, into settled antipathy to the theological idea that the movement of the mind derives from God. By instinct, we do not consider that God supplies the mind's motion, preferring to associate rational acts with absolute spontaneity or originality. Talk of divine motion—of God's providential and redemptive acts in which he sustains, governs, purifies and directs the intellectual life—seems to us to threaten rational autonomy and responsibility. In the sphere of the intellect, we customarily tell ourselves, we must be our own prime mover, our own first cause. As with moral freedom, so with the life of reason: to speak of God is to take something away from ourselves.

Such oppositions ought not be admitted. There is every good reason for us to renounce the vicious habit which imagines that divine illumination and human intellectual activity are competitive forces, and that the work of the mind must be attributed *either* to God *or* to ourselves. God does not move the mind as an archer propels an arrow, for what God moves is precisely the proper power of the intellect in its dependent but real spontaneity; God moves *from within*, not simply as a causal force from without. Yet in order to grasp this, we have to detach ourselves from the assumption that the *natural* life of creatures is *secular* life, only natural if cordoned off from God's presence and action. Further, we have to retrieve some pieces of theological doctrine which were second nature to Bonaventure but which have drifted to the margins: teaching that createdness is humanly basic, encompassing everything that we do, and teaching about God's presence in the Spirit, sustaining all things in their created integrity.

It is worth adding that this account of the life of the intellect has considerable critical potential. One of the services which it may perform is to offer resistance to the instrumentalizing of the life of study, as it is found in, for example, an understanding of education in which the chief end of intellectual training is the development of the practical skills required for the acquisition of wealth. Study of the humanities is not this; it is, rather, one of the ways in which ignoble appetite is chastened, in which the reconciled children of Adam may find occasions for sanctification by coming to see the human cultural world as suffused by God's illuminating and redemptive judgment.

Second, how does this theology of the intellect shape the practice of studying the humanities? Theology is not competent to make direct recommendations about how the humanities are to conduct their business: it may not, for example, enable us in any straightforward way to decide between empirical or interpretative social science, or between formalism and historicism in literary studies. Rather, theology approaches such matters indirectly, posing questions about the origin and end of humane studies, asking about the movement to which these arts belong. As it contemplates the ways in which all things are taken up into the history of redemption, theology tries to indicate where we are, who we are, in what we are engaged, when we study; and it tries also to depict the intellectual virtues which are fitting in the presence of God the creator and reconciler. Theology says, in effect: humane studies are creaturely arts, ways in which we inhabit in a reflective way the domain in which God has placed us. And so, for example, though it would be intolerable for theology to prescribe methods of historical study, theology may legitimately articulate an understanding of created and redeemed time, on the basis of which the historian may make determinations about the nature and goals of historical inquiry, and about the methods most suitable to those goals.

Yet theology may only *try* to articulate the nature of the humanities. The queen of the arts is gentle and modest, not a high-handed dominatrix. To be sure, theology is an exercise of apostolic intelligence from which we may legitimately expect instruction about what it means to be and think as a creature: there is no reason for theology to be embarrassed about voicing its understanding of the humanities. But—like all the sciences—theology participates in our fallen condition; as ectypal, not archetypal, knowledge, as science *in via*, not *in patria*, it knows only in part, and can lay no claim to comprehension of the wisdom of God, because its learning is not finished. And yet, again, what theology has been given to know, it knows, and what it knows it seeks to commend.

Third, what are the entailments of this theology of the intellect for the ways in which institutions of higher education are to be understood? It is of course the case that a metaphysics of the arts of the mind is not a sufficient condition for the realization of intellectual life; but it is a necessary condition. Academic institutions are places of thought, including thought about themselves. Members of such institutions who persist in raising issues about the nature of intellectual activity often encounter resistance in the form of amusement, boredom or bureaucratic exhaustion. The prudent Christian response is dogged cheerfulness in asking the really important question: What is the place of higher studies, including study of the humanities, in the redemption of created intelligence after the fall?

By way of an answer, the Christian offers—as we have seen both Bonaventure and Augustine to do, albeit in rather different ways—an account of the life of the mind which talks about human intellectual arts by talking about the creative, revelatory and redemptive works of God. Like any other human activity, the intellectual arts need ordering according to their natures if they are to flourish and be perfected. Such ordering, including the disposition of intellectual fields and of their several modes of inquiry, is not a matter of management but of wisdom, and wisdom is a gift of Spirit. Thus Aquinas: "He who knows the cause that is simply the highest without qualifications . . . is called wise without restriction, since he is able to judge and set in order all things by God's rules. He comes to such judgments through the Holy Spirit: *a spiritual man is able to judge the value of everything*, says Saint Paul, because . . . *the Spirit reaches the depths of everything, even the depth of God.*"[35] Aquinas's confidence is

---

35. Aquinas *Summa Theologiae* 2a2ae 45.1.resp; emphasis upon wisdom as supernatural gift is strikingly absent from the "public theology" essays of Ford on the topic, collected in *Shaping Theology* and *Christian Wisdom*.

striking. The Spirit makes it possible to judge and set in order all things by God's rules.

This is why theology asks the question of the place of the academy in the redemption of created intelligence with the expectation of a positive answer. Laments over the ruined state of the modern academy abound, some more immoderate than others.[36] Theology will certainly register the symptoms and feel a tug of conversion away from an institution in defect, because of the academy's capacity to embody and inflame the appetites of disordered intelligence. But to lament is not to despair but to grieve over the failure of some created reality to achieve its perfection; despair stultifies, whereas lament issues in truthful judgment. One initial judgment will be that to Christian faith the disarray of the arts of intelligence is not unexpected, because Adam's children can no more educate and inquire without vanity than they can govern without war. But even here theology should go further, having good reason to consider the academy as within the domain of God's redemptive rule, the domain not only of condemnation but also of forgiveness, vocation and sanctification. Recall Kuyper's derivation of three rules from the application of the principle of *palingenesis* to the cultural and scientific realm: "All existing things are in ruins . . . there is a means by which these can be restored . . . in part they are already restored."[37] Different institutions exist at different points in the history of redemption, differing circumstances evoking sharper or softer judgments. But in making such discriminations, theology is not at liberty to consider that the history of redemption has faltered, or all it will see will be decadence: the triumph of secular science, instrumentalization or irony. Theology may not demonstrate "too little confidence in the one who extends his dominion also over the kingdoms of this earth, nor expect too little by way of signs of this lordship."[38]

Such hopeful judgments do not arise from nowhere, but from minds and souls formed in patience by divine instruction. They apply a theology of intellectual virtue (and the vices by which it is opposed) derived

---

36. Among theologically-informed recent accounts, see Milbank, "Conflict of the Faculties"; D'Costa, *Theology in the Public Square*; Hauerwas, *State of the University*; MacIntyre, *God, Philosophy, Universities*. Howard's superbly drawn history *Protestant Theology* is deeply instructive for contemporary issues, as is (from a cultural-historical point of view) Clark, *Academic Charisma*.

37. Kuyper, *Principles of Sacred Theology*, 219.

38. Barth, *Church Dogmatics* IV/3, 122.

from exegetical and dogmatic reasoning, directed by contemplation and prayer, and attentive to the past through which we may imagine different and better ways of ordering the affairs of the intellect (thought is often set free by memory). All this, in turn, means that a condition for a Christian understanding of the humanities is the flourishing of theology.

Grasping this requires us to recover a conception of theology as more than simply one more discipline or faculty: as the encompassing ambience of the arts of the mind, through whose practices the natures and ends of creatures and their activities are brought to explicit awareness.[39] Theology inquires, not into one set of objects, but into all possible objects of inquiry relative to God as origin and end. This is why theology may be called the queen of the arts, though that appellation only makes sense against the background of a now lost understanding of the hierarchy of studies in which theology is the point at which the divine illumination of all things is made an object of contemplation.

Theology's vocation to articulate the encompassing context for intellectual inquiry is at present occluded. For a well-ordered theology which reads the history of the world as the history of redemption, there is nothing surprising about this state of affairs. Theology has long experience of the non-evidentness of its principles, and finds instruction in the gospel as to why this is so, and how to conduct itself in advance of a resolution. Composed in this way, theology can approach the matter of its place in the wider universe of letters with a measure of tranquility. Anxiety, belligerence or self-deprecation in view of the indifference or hostility of other disciplines are unnecessary and self-defeating. They concede too much to currently ascendant models of learning, reinforcing their projection of themselves as possessed of perennial validity; they encourage neglect of theology's contemplative practices and over-refinement of other skills in order to assimilate theology to profane science; they proceed as if theology's social home in the communion of the saints is deficient and in need of supplementation by the academy.

Theology can exist and flourish within or without the academy, and has done so in a large number of ways. No institutional locale is wholly

---

39. Theological enthusiasm for "interdisciplinarity" is a poor substitute for a theology of the life of the mind. Not only does it tend to generate material which is theologically jejune, and often mannered, opaque and artificial; it also assumes the very thing which ought to be in question, namely, that theology is *a* discipline. A sounder approach would be to subsume "interdisciplinary" engagements under theology's apostolic vocation.

adequate; each exposes theology to a set of vices as well as affording opportunities. What is required in all circumstances is a profound sense that
theology is moved, summoned and equipped by its object; prudence in
making arrangements about how to live in exile in the unfinished economy of redemption; and hope, for "we can take courage from the fact that,
in the life of the mind as elsewhere, there is always more to hope for than
we can reasonably expect."[40]

40. MacIntyre, *God, Philosophy, Universities*, 180.

3

The New Theological Humanism
and the Political Future

DAVID JASPER

THEOLOGY, I CONTEND, CAN never be pursued in isolation from everything else without great danger. On its own, like anything else, it quickly
becomes an obsession and a monomania. It cannot but be given articulation except in context, or manifold contexts, and it is thus, for its own
necessary good, an interdisciplinary exercise if it is to sustain any kind of
proper focus. Furthermore, theology is, in its very nature, an interpretative act rather than a statement—hermeneutics lies at its very heart—and
thus any theological claim can be no more than a considered option, a
responsible strategy that is continually to be tested in action that is not
singular but always, even in the most extreme reaches of the apophatic,
finally communal, political and ethical.

In this paper I lay no great claims to originality, relying heavily on the
work on William Schweiker and David Klemm in the field of what they
have recently termed "theological humanism." Perhaps at best I merely
seek to test what they propose, straying deliberately into fields of ethics
and political thought in which I have no particular training or academic
expertise, except a participation in the shared adventure of realizing our

humanity in all its integrity. The term "theological humanism" implies no conflation of its two elements. It is at once "theological *humanism*" and "*theological* humanism" in creative, imaginative and energetic interchange. At the same time "humanism," being notoriously difficult of definition is left embedded in a lineage which finds its complex roots in the Renaissance, and much more deeply, on the one hand, Socrates, and, on the other, perhaps, the scriptural claim that the Sabbath was made for man and not man for the Sabbath. Schweiker offers the simple proposal that "all humanists share the desire to respect and enhance the integrity of human existence."[1] That will have to do for now.

Theological humanism, I will agree, embraces a necessary, and necessarily developing respect for the wholeness and integrity of life which emphatically avoids the dangers of the extremes of, on the one hand, "overhumanization," and, on the other, "hypertheism." Overhumanization denotes the exclusive triumph of human power[2] in the shaping of our reality, which brings about, sooner or later, an inevitable foreshortening and over-definition of aims in materialist, economic or absolutist myopias. Specific ends will justify any means and thus result in grossly unbalanced distribution of goods, ecological disintegration and so on. Hypertheism, on the other hand, denotes a conviction that locates all human life and experience within a vision of God to the endangerment of responsible support for and recognition of the rich diversity of human life. What each extreme lacks is a proper sense of the *integrity* of life, which is lived neither exclusively on the *horizontal* plane of the purely secular, not the *vertical* plane of the obsessively religious, but in a rich and complex mutual acknowledgement of both in the pursuit of all human flourishing.

It was once remarked that "we live more profoundly than we can think." It is a timely reminder to academics. Yet thoughtful reflection necessarily follows the art of living and prompts the development of its artistry. Necessary to the well-being of our future is the admission that our grasp of the truth is fallible, a legacy, indeed, of Christian humanism which begins in the Bible, and is sustained through Clement of Alexandria, Erasmus and John Wesley who prefaced his Sermons with these words (looking back, no doubt, to St. Paul:

---

1. Schweiker, *Theological Ethics*, 203.
2. Klemm and Schweiker, *Religion and the Human Future*, 14.

> For, how far is love, even with many wrong opinions, to be pre-
> ferred before truth itself without love! We may die without the
> knowledge of many truths, and yet be carried into Abraham's bo-
> som. But if we die without love, what will knowledge avail? Just as
> much as it avails the devil and his angels.[3]

Yet this is not to deny the absolute imperative of reflexive thought, even to the theological dimension of thinking. If the two fundamental injunctions are that we love the Lord our God with all our heart, mind and soul, and then our neighbor as ourselves, the so-called "double love command" which is developed in Christian thinking as early as the *Didache*, probably written in the first century CE, there is a perpetual and necessary tension between them: for the love for God is a love of the absolutely "other" which engenders a reflexive and critical knowledge of self, and thus constructs a sense of neighbor which is rooted in the primary command and creatively so. The love of God is at the heart of the long tradition of reflexive philosophy of the self which stretches from Plato to St. Augustine and up to Paul Tillich in the twentieth century—a humanistic tradition that gives unremitting attention to the neighbor in his or her uniqueness and particularity rather than in abstraction or generalization.

By such reflexivity we move one crucial step beyond the epistemological against the background of the logic of perfection. In response to the double love command we are called not merely to think about thinking (in itself an important but poorly limited exercise), but to think about ourselves thinking in the face of the other: a genuinely reflexive mode of being which alone calls proper attention to the being of our neighbor. To think about ourselves thinking about thinking can only be achieved in a mode that must be described as rhetorical—one dangerous indeed if Plato is to be believed, though Aristotle was not quite at one with him in the matter of rhetoric. For, as Paul de Man once remarked, "rhetoric suspends logic and opens up vertiginous possibilities of referential aberration."[4] But another and more positive way of describing such possibilities, breathtaking in its implications as it hovers over the abyss of the unthought, is the opening up, in Anselm's familiar words from the *Proslogium*, of "that than which nothing greater can be conceived." But if Anselm was pursuing the *logic* of the idea of God as unsurpassable, the rhetoric of reflexivity

---

3. Wesley, *Sermons on Several Occasions*, vii.

4. De Man, *Resistance to Theory*, 17.

suspends logic, ensuring the impossibility of any conceivable reification of the yet unsurpassable God. Klemm and Schweiker expand on this idea thus:

> The "proof" provides a way to *criticize* ideas about God, since any idea that cannot endure the test of perfection cannot claim rightly to speak of the divine. In this way the proof might reduce us to silence and mystical awareness of God since, it would seem, every idea must always be deconstructed and surpassed. Yet the proof also shows, *constructively*, the human longing for the divine in and through degrees of imagined perfection. It shows us, what is more, the inseparability between God and the highest good.[5]

Perfection, then, can only be *imagined*, though that is enough, indeed essential—a deeply poetic act. It both acknowledges and utterly deconstructs the categories of transcendence and immanence as exclusive in a universal move appropriated by St. Paul in his speech on the Areopagus, that all people search and grope for God—"though indeed he is not far from each one of us. For "In him we live and move and have our being," as even some of our poets have said." (Acts 17:27–28). The words are probably to be linked to Posidonius, based on Plato.

But how does this relate to our theme of theological humanism and the political future? The reflexive move we have been considering is at once a move beyond self to the absolute, and infinitely regressive "other," and the deepest acknowledgement of the "self," a fragile, shifting and necessarily changeable realization of *soi-même comme un autre*, oneself as another. And the reference to Ricoeur's book of this name is crucial here in two respects. First there is his attention given to Nietzsche's *Course on Rhetoric*, based on a course taught in Basel in 1872–73, which "proposes the novel idea that tropes—metaphors, synecdoche, metonymy—do not constitute ornaments added onto a discourse that is by right *literal and nonfigurative* but instead are inherent in the most basic linguistic functioning. In this sense, there is no non-rhetorical "naturalness" of language."[6] Second there is Ricoeur's acknowledgement that "all my philosophical work, leads to a type of philosophy from which the actual mention of God is absent and in which the question of God, as a philosophical question, itself remains in a suspension that could be called agnostic." What Ricoeur seeks

---

5. Klemm and Schweiker, *Religion and the Human Future*, 65.
6. Ricoeur, *Oneself as Another*, 12. Emphases mine.

to avoid are what he calls "ontotheological amalgamations."[7] And yet God is not dismissed. Ricoeur's point is crucial because here we remain within the realms of rhetorical language and, though acknowledging the philosophical groundwork, move at the same time beyond that into the actual requirements of the ethical and the political spheres of human exchange and future possibility lived with integrity. It is to claim, without apology, a preference for St. Augustine's restlessness, which has its heart in the desire for God (the desire is all), over that of Descartes whose restlessness of thought denies God in the *cogito ergo sum*. "On this ground [that of Descartes] (affirms Schweiker), we learn not of our desire for goodness or God, but rather a sure and necessary philosophical foundation for claims to truth."[8] And thus we are back with Wesley's preference of love above truth in the tradition of Christian humanism, though we should include in modern thinking also Levinas, and before him Buber.

It is time to try this shadowy proposal for a theological humanism out in practice, and it is to the field of literature, and poetry in particular, that its characteristics begin to take on the sense of possibility. For it is here that theological thinking is tested, in an absolutely necessary interdisciplinarity, against the demands of human nature and experience, and it is in the promise and open-endedness of the literary text that the future, which depends upon the capacity for change and the avoidance of an ultimate fatalism, is explored and offered. Any story told and responsibly concluded in an achieved present is only the prelude to another story as yet untold and full of possibility, and (like the unconditional love of neighbor) guaranteed by the love of God that is at once and the same time anticipated and known. The classic expression of this is the final paragraph of Dostoevsky's *Crime and Punishment*:

> But that is the beginning of a new story, the story of the gradual rebirth of a man, the story of his gradual regeneration, of his gradual passing from one world to another, of his acquaintance with a new and hitherto unknown reality. That might be the subject of a new story—our present story is ended.[9]

Compare that with another famous ending—the last lines of *Paradise Lost*.

7. Ibid., 24.

8. Schweiker, *Theological Ethics*, 103.

9. Dostoevsky, *Crime and Punishment*, 559.

Som natural tears they drop'd, but wip'd them soon;
The World was all before them, where to choose
Thir place of rest, and Providence thir guide:
They hand in hand with wandring steps and slow,
Through *Eden* took their solitarie way . . .[10]

In each text by Dostoevsky and Milton there has been a crime and a punishment. But there has also been a growth in humanity and learning through love—human love. And there is the hope of redemption and a passage into another world. But, we might say, the new world inhabited already by Adam and Eve, full of choice and responsibility, of some regret for an idealized past (how well we know that ourselves), of companionship as well as solitariness—is a world utterly familiar to us. Here is how David Daiches (writing at a time when men were less sensitive to gender specific language) describes this world, reached at the end of a poem whose expressed purpose was to "justify the ways of God to men." He writes,

> Such is the mixed texture of our experience; such are the difficulties, contradictions, challenges, and rewards that await purposive man in the world. It is not the effortless peace of the Garden of Eden. It is something more interesting and more testing. And ultimately, to Milton, *so the poetry if not the argument tells us*, is more satisfying. Good comes out of evil not in the theological way of the *felix culpa*, the "fortunate fall," but more obliquely in the emergence of a world that in spite of everything is the world we want and need. *So God is justified, in a way that might perhaps have surprised him.*[11]

In Milton, the supreme poet of radical Christian humanism we find enacted the claim of theological humanism that "neither God's will nor human flourishing alone provides an adequate measure and orientation for human life . . . [but] that human beings are mixed creatures striving for wholeness and integrity."[12]

Creatures of hesitancies and regrets, capable of courage in the face of tears, we face a world in which change is not merely inevitable but absolutely necessary. Living more profoundly than we can think demands that

10. Milton, *Paradise Lost,* Book 12, lines 645–49.
11. Daiches, *God and the Poets,* 49, emphasis added.
12. Klemm, and Schweiker, *Religion and the Human Future*, Cover notes.

imaginative response to our experience of the neighbor which is honed upon the primary demand of love in a space of transcendence which avoids both overhumanization on the one hand, and hypertheism on the other. The imagination , thus understood, is crucial to our sense of moral responsibility, and is classically defined by the poet S. T. Coleridge as "the living Power and prime Agent of all human Perception, and . . . a repetition in the finite mind of the eternal act of creation in the infinite I AM."[13] Nor was Coleridge original, though no less perceptive, in his distinction between this primary imagination and the secondary, which "dissolves, diffuses, dissipates, in order to re-create; or where this process is rendered impossible, yet still at all events it struggles to idealize and to unify. It is essentially *vital*, even as all objects (*as* objects) are essentially fixed and dead." Coleridge's precision of language is typically presented and telling. Adam and Eve move out into the political spaces of the Bible with moral courage and the imaginative vision of "where to choose." The lack of balance or conclusion in the life lived more profoundly than thought or logic is, literally, vital, as is in literature both a sense of the tragic and of the humorous: the two masks which adorn the living theatre. Christian theology, born in the cradle of biblical literature, it has been suggested, finally avoids both. Calvin, we are told, only ever cracked one joke, and it was not funny. I am prepared to believe that (and, indeed, I once wrote a chapter in a book which I entitled "The Christian Art of Missing the Joke"). George Steiner has asserted that "Tragedy is alien to the Judaic sense of the world."[14] I am less sure of that, though the warning to the theologians—who do undeniably have a tendency to take themselves far too seriously—is useful.

We can never forget that Plato (though himself a great artist) banished the artists from his Republic—those meddlers, independent and irresponsible critics.[15] True, at one memorable point in the *Republic* he suggests that if a dramatic poet should try to visit the ideal state he should be politely escorted to the border. Iris Murdoch, characteristically, rallied to the artists' defense:

> The spiritual ambiguity of art, its connection with the 'limitless' unconscious, its use of irony, its interest in evil, worried Plato . . .

13. Coleridge, *Biographia Literaria*, I:304.

14. Steiner, *Death of Tragedy*, 4.

15. Murdoch, *Fire and the Sun*, 1.

> The pierced nature of the work of art, its limitless connection with
> ordinary life, even its defenselessness against its client, are part of
> its characteristic availability and freedom . . . Art cheats the reli-
> gious vocation at the last moment and is inimical to philosophical
> categories. Yet neither philosophy nor theology can do without
> it.[16]

It is only thus, with the artist, that we can dare to acknowledge that
human—indeed all—life is neither random nor determined, a humane acknowledgement at the heart of all genuinely moral and reflexive thought
that no less than quantum theory endorses in the behavior of elementary
particles. For just as theory can make extraordinarily accurate predictions
concerning the behavior of particles in the aggregate, it is powerless to
suggest the outcomes of individual events.[17]

And so it should be. There is always the exception that "proves the
rule." Theological humanism, pitched between the double love command,
acknowledges the balance to be maintained between the universal and
the particular, between the claims of divine order and the necessary freedom of the individual if we are to remain responsible, moral and consci-
entious within ourselves and before the other. But to be such is to remain
ever restless—the heart is restless until it finds its rest in God. In satirical
mode, Jonathan Swift in his *Gulliver's Travels* (1726) portrays the profound dilemma of the human condition in Gulliver's travels to and return from the country of the purely rational (and equine) Houyhnynms
who are indeed the truly "other"—rational creatures seen by Europeans
as mere "animals." Gulliver, as a human, is expelled from their land as a
threat to the delicate bonds of rational society, but he is, from thence-
forth, restless and never again capable of full integration into human society, beset as it is, above all by self-deception and aggrandizement, that
is, the sin of pride.

But we, unlike the fictional Gulliver, have never visited the land of
the Houyhnynms. And yet our hearts, too, are restless. For while we are
aware of the sublimity in the created order, both material and immate-
rial, there is an even greater cause for wonder; that is, the fact that we are
aware of it (reflexivity again). When, in the Conclusion of the *Critique of
Practical Reason* Kant famously remarks of the sublime:

---

16. Ibid., 86–87.

17. Klemm and Schweiker, *Religion and the Human* Future, 138.

> Two things flood the mind with ever increasing wonder and awe,
> the more often and the more intensely it concerns itself with them:
> the starry heavens above me and the moral law within me.[18]

What is even more remarkable by far is that the human mind is capable of reflecting on them—and also of reflecting upon that reflective capacity: that, in the words of Arthur C. Danto, "the universe, inner and outer, is open to something that is in itself unpictureable and perhaps even unintelligible, given the internal limits of human understanding."[19] To realize this reflexively is the basis for a genuine theological humanism and makes possible a hope for the future in wholeness and integrity.

In Heideggerian terms this could be described as learning to dwell poetically on the earth. One commentator on Heidegger has well summarized this:

> To dwell poetically on the earth as a mortal is to live in awareness of the godhead, the clearing, the blank but lightening sky. It is to live so as to measure oneself against that Nothing—that Nothing—that grants the possibility of the presence of and the Being of the things that there are. Within that clearing, as Heidegger puts it, brightness wars with darkness. There we struggle against particular ignorances and incapacities to bring forth truth.[20]

This is, in the end, not far from the concerns of theological humanism in its passionate struggle to bring forth the fruits of the Spirit in human action and in the face of human limitations. Just as Heidegger recognized that the achievement of Hölderlin was to turn poetic language back on its own founding power, so the reflexive turn which reflects upon thinking about thinking transformatively opens up a transcendence within. Thus, if for Heidegger the sacred is at work in the poetic act itself as a kind of knowing which is other than that of metaphysical thinking,[21] this is now carried into action in the future of human being. Furthermore, just as Heidegger avoids any decoding of the singularity of the text or poem which will tend to dissolve it into some universal "meaning" or system—so the process we have been pursuing insists upon the unique

---

18. Kant, *Critique of Practical Reason*, 127.
19. Danto, *Abuse of Beauty*, 159.
20. Edwards, *Plain Sense of Things*, 184.
21. Clark, *Heidegger*, 120.

and singular otherness of the other as a necessary part of the whole which calls forth our total attention.

In the end, however, theological humanism negotiates precariously in its avoidance of reification, its awareness of the godhead only within the impossibilities of imaginative thought, and thus engenders habits of thinking and acting that in love alone are open to the possibility of truth and beauty and goodness in the world: of joy that evokes compassion and generosity; of hope that provokes an openness to the future; of gratitude that articulates a loyalty to the tradition. It is a form of what my colleague in Glasgow, George Newlands, in his book on *Generosity and the Christian Future,* has termed "imaginative leaps of faith into the [. . .] future, not as a form of prophecy but as a way of inviting us to try to look at some basic issues from less familiar angles."[22] Such imaginative leaps require a constant revisiting and rethinking of images, metaphors and expressions that have guided the traditions of humanism in the West, and, for myself at least, specifically the Christian tradition: God as a transcendent deity— a "metaphorical cluster," to use Klemm and Schweiker's term, which has taken some hard knocks in the past two hundred years. God as light of the world, an image at the heart of the "natural theology" of the eighteenth century. The death of God (or "God as not God"), which moves in the twentieth century between the radical apocalypticism of Thomas Altizer to the humanism of Paul Tillich.

But, in the end, with all our history and accumulated imagery, we are creatures of the present and its future. What I have been trying to suggest, in a deliberate and interdisciplinary employment of the resources of literature, theology, ethics and so on, is a way of being that acknowledges the theological task of critique as a necessary expression of human freedom, but simultaneously moves beyond critique (which only becomes finally destructive of the very freedoms which it employs) and thus, in moving beyond, opens up a form of theology, and a way of "doing it" that is still largely unformulated in our schools and religious institutions. That is why the creative imagination is so utterly vital. Echoes of it are to be found in John Henry Newman's "illative" sense, in Friedrich Schleiermacher's hermeneutics, but perhaps above all in the chiastic sayings of the gospels themselves. It could claim to be a reclaiming of the tradition of biblical personalism which links the early creeds with Luther and the theology of

---

22. Newlands, *Generosity and the Christian Future,* 1.

Karl Barth, while dodging all final and exclusive affiliations. Within it we must each find our own path. For myself my preoccupation in the past few years and in my two most recent books, *The Sacred Desert* (2004) and *The Sacred Body* (2009)—two parts of an as yet unfinished work (of course)—has not been with the kind and form of theological project such as Radical Orthodoxy (as an example), but rather with the question of *how* on earth one can possibly *do* theology, or indeed "think theologically" in our time. It is, perhaps, as much a matter of style, a poetics maybe, as anything else. I finish with some words of David Klemm and William Schweiker in their recent "manifesto" for theological humanism which seem to me to resonate very closely with what I have been suggesting:

> This essay has sought to meet an *interpretive and practical challenge* of our age in a way that thwarts the celebration of power that can and does lead to the clash among peoples and also the wanton destruction of other forms of life. In this respect, an essay is a practical wager and not a proof. It is not a proof, because life is in the living and not in arguments. The wager is that by living theological humanism within religious traditions, it is possible to respect and enhance the integral relations of forms of life, natural, human and divine. That is the challenge and possibility of religion and the human future.[23]

---

23. Klemm and Schweiker, *Religion and the Human Future*, 174–75.

4

Historical Criticism, "Theological Exegesis," and Theology amongst the Humanities

JOACHIM SCHAPER

Historical (?) Criticism

NEAR THE UNIVERSITY IN which I teach there is a medieval cathedral with a large burial ground where you can find the graves of many former Divinity professors laid to rest in that churchyard in the eighteenth and nineteenth centuries. In several cases, their precise titles are mentioned, and, not unexpectedly, one finds more than one headstone referring to a deceased "Professor of Biblical Criticism." "Biblical criticism": an interesting term. It sounds slightly old-fashioned, has that eighteenth- or nineteenth-century ring about it. Remarkably, it is currently having a bit of a come-back. John Barton writes, in his book *The Nature of Biblical Criticism*, published in 2007:

> Biblical critics quite often present themselves as historians rather than as theologians, while opponents of criticism, or those who think the time has come to "move on" from it, regularly regard its historical character as the root of what is objectionable about it: biblical criticism, both agree, is history, not theology.[1]

1. Barton, *Nature of Biblical Criticism*, 31.

And Barton goes on to say:

> For many people working in biblical studies, this seems fairly obvi-
> ous. It can be seen in the preferred description of biblical criticism
> as the "historical-critical method." The use of this term, which
> has all but replaced "biblical criticism" in much academic writing
> about biblical study, points to the belief that a critical approach to
> the Bible consists in applying to it a method essentially at home
> in the study of history. For many, perhaps most, scholars it is axi-
> omatic that traditional biblical criticism has been dominated by
> historical concerns . . . On all sides it is agreed that history has
> provided the normative models studying the Bible since the rise
> of critical study in the European Enlightenment. Both those who
> attack biblical criticism and those who defend it generally do so by
> emphasizing its essentially historical character.[2]

So far, so good. I think that virtually everybody would agree with Barton's analysis. However, Barton then proceeds by calling into question the
whole notion of biblical criticism as an essentially historical discipline.
Indeed, questioning it is at the heart of his book. He separates the theory
and practice of historical enquiry from what he perceives to be the core
activity of the biblical critic. Barton postulates that the enterprise of biblical criticism is not in essence a historical enterprise. Let us once again
listen to Barton himself and his criticism of the term "historical-critical
method":

> The historical-critical method thus proves to be a less than ideal
> term for communicating what biblical criticism is about. In es-
> sence, criticism is neither historical nor a method. There has been
> a strong correlation with history, at least since the nineteenth cen-
> tury, and there has frequently been a tendency to speak as though
> criticism has methodological implications. But in itself the critical
> approach to the Bible is not a method but a series of explanatory
> hypotheses, driven by a particular attitude toward texts and tex-
> tual meaning. Though criticism certainly entails situating texts
> in the context of their origin, it does not necessarily involve the
> reconstruction either of historical events or of the history of the
> text's development. There are many examples of genuinely critical
> work that has little interest in either kind of history. And on the
> other hand, . . . there has been and is plenty of interest in history
> that is not at all driven by a critical mind-set.[3]

2. Ibid., 31–32.
3. Ibid., 67–68.

There are two points to be noted here: Barton claims that biblical criticism is an enterprise that is primarily defined by its central interest in the actual biblical texts—which most people would agree it is—*and* that that interest in the texts can lead, and does often lead, to critical work which is done regardless of historical interests and problems. He says that such non-historical critical work is nonetheless "genuinely critical."

Barton is certainly right in saying that "there has been and is plenty of interest in history that is not at all driven by a critical mind-set." The fact that today, to name just one example, many of the PhD students at the best universities of the United States who work on the history of ancient Israel are in fact fundamentalists speaks volumes. Ironically, there are few research students in Old Testament studies in the United States these days, apart from fundamentalists and ultra-conservatives, who show any interest in history. The result is that the history of ancient Israel is explored virtually exclusively by students who try to demonstrate that the Bible is what they call "historically reliable,"[4] but have no interest whatsoever in the methodological problems of doing history and no grasp of its complexities. So there is indeed "plenty of interest in history that is not at all driven by a critical mind-set." Whether Barton is right when he says that the enterprise of biblical criticism "does not necessarily involve the reconstruction either of historical events or of the history of the text's development," is another matter. I shall return to it.

"Theological Exegesis"

So there is much that is true in Barton's statement, but what about his central point—i.e., that "in itself the critical approach to the Bible is not a method but a series of explanatory hypotheses, driven by a particular attitude toward texts and textual meaning" and that biblical criticism is not historical in essence?

Before we can answer that question, we have to take a little detour and look at other current concepts of biblical exegesis and how they compare with Barton's view. His recent book on biblical criticism is one landmark in the current wider debate on the characteristics, methods and objectives of biblical interpretation. In recent years, historical criticism

4. For a British example of that approach, cf. Kitchen, *On the Reliability of the Old Testament.*

has been attacked from a number of angles, with critiques being formulated most notably by colleagues who follow a literary studies approach and by the practitioners of what is now commonly called "theological exegesis." It is the latter some aspects of which I would like to discuss now.

One of the best-known practitioners of "theological exegesis" is Richard B. Hays. In a programmatic article published in the first-ever fascicle of the *Journal of Theological Interpretation*, Hays writes, in his set of definitions of biblical exegesis as he would like to see it practiced, i.e., of "theological exegesis":

> Theological exegesis does not focus chiefly on the hypothetical history behind the biblical texts, nor does it attend primarily to the meaning of texts as self-contained works of literature, rather, it focuses on these texts as testimony. This means we need to learn to stand where these witnesses stand and look where they point. Insofar as we do this, we will learn to see *as* they see; . . . we will find our vision trained anew. If we read these texts as testimony, we will find ourselves constantly reminded that the Bible is chiefly about God, not about human religious aspirations and power struggles.[5]

Hays *also* states that:

> historical study is internal to the practice of theological exegesis. The reasons why this is so are themselves fundamentally theological: God has created the material world, and God has acted for the redemption of that world through the incarnation of the Son in the historical person Jesus of Nazareth. History therefore cannot be either inimical or irrelevant to theology's affirmation of truth. The more accurately we understand the historical setting of 1st-century Palestine, the more precise and faithful will be our understanding of what the incarnate Word taught, did, and suffered.[6]

So Hays accepts historical research as compatible with theological exegesis, indeed as "internal" to its "practice," but at the same time it is blatantly obvious that he assigns to history the function of supporting "theology's affirmation of truth." So history gets assigned, in Hays's universe, the function which, a very long time ago, philosophy was thought to have: that of handmaiden of theology.

5. Hays, "Reading the Bible," 13.
6. Ibid., 12.

The Marginalization of History

In his book, Barton takes issue with views such as Hays's. While he does not discuss Hays's contributions, he directly criticizes some recent works of R. W. L. Moberly and Christopher Seitz.[7] Taking up the gauntlet, Moberly has recently defended "theological exegesis" and has responded to Barton's view of the relation between biblical criticism and religious belief.[8]

Strangely, though, there is in fact one area in which Barton and the advocates of "theological exegesis" seem to agree. Their respective concepts have a central feature in common: historical enquiry is not seen as a constitutive part of the enterprise of biblical exegesis; rather, biblical exegesis focuses on the texts "themselves" without necessarily seeing them in the context of their historically reconstructed world of origin. Neither Barton nor Hays assign a *decisive* function to historical research when it comes to the core business of biblical criticism.

They have very different reasons for holding that view, though. Barton thinks he can arrive at the essence, so to speak, of biblical criticism by trying to isolate its core function that has kept it going through the ages. There were "genuinely critical" ways of interpreting Scripture before the enlightenment and the nineteenth-century fascination with history, he says, and there still *are* such non-historical and nevertheless "genuinely critical" approaches.[9] What he manages to do by stating the case thus is to establish a "broad church" of scholars seeing themselves as biblical critics without feeling they have to embrace certain concepts of history and historical methodology developed in the nineteenth and twentieth centuries. Barton wants to encourage biblical critics from being, as he nicely puts it, "in thrall to Troeltsch,"[10] i.e., to a historical method which, in Barton's opinion, is the result of a "severely reductionist view of historical study" which leaves "no way back to any kind of religious faith in the texts of the Bible."[11] "This," Barton continues, "is the difficulty that scholars in a more Anglo-Saxon tradition tend to feel, since they generally think that actual

---

7. Cf. chapter 6 of Barton, *Nature of Biblical Criticism*.

8. Moberly, "Biblical Criticism and Religious Belief," passim. I am grateful to Walter Moberly for making some of his recent publications available to me in electronic form.

9. Cf. above, n. 3.

10. Barton, *Nature of Biblical Criticism*, 47.

11. Ibid.

historical fact matters, even for faith."[12] Thus Barton acknowledges the contribution of Schleiermacher's contribution to hermeneutics,[13] as we shall see in detail later, but he rejects the further development of Schleiermacher's insights formulated by Ernst Troeltsch in the early twentieth century.[14]

Hays's reasons for holding the view that historical enquiry is not constitutive of the enterprise of biblical exegesis are different. His concept of biblical interpretation is focused, right from the start, on serving the church. His foundational statement is that

> Theological exegesis is *a practice of and for the Church.* We lavish our attention on the biblical texts because these texts have been passed on to us by the church's tradition as the distinctive and ir-replaceable testimony to events in which God has acted for our salvation. That is to say, theological exegesis regards these texts as *Scripture*, not merely as a collection of ancient writings whose content is of historical interest. A bare description of the ideational content of biblical writings ("the theology of Luke" or the like) is therefore not yet theological in the sense meant here. Theological exegesis . . . seeks to read the Bible as normative for a community.[15]

Hays does not envisage the fact that the sub-disciplines of theology, like Old Testament studies and New Testament studies, are subjects in their own right that are of massive importance not just in the context of church and theology, but of world history—and not just of the world history of religions, but of political and social history, etc. So it would make perfect sense to study the Old Testament, say, in the context of the study of the Ancient Near East and its contribution to world history—as was and is the case, in fact, in academic traditions other than our own. Similarly, every single sub-discipline of theology could be fruitfully treated in the context of purely historical and social sciences-orientated research. However, Hays, and his colleagues in the field of theological exegesis,

12. Ibid.

13. Originally published, posthumously, by Lücke in 1838. For a modern edition, cf. Schleiermacher, *Hermeneutik und Kritik.*

14. Cf., for example, Troeltsch, "Über historische und dogmatische": "Die historische Methode, einmal auf die biblische Wissenschaft und auf die Kirchengeschichte angewandt, ist ein Sauerteig, der Alles verwandelt und der schliesslich die ganze bisherige Form theologischer Methoden zersprengt" (730).

15. Hays, "Reading the Bible," 90.

choose not to. They view the sub-disciplines of theology as being somehow pre-ordained together to constitute the academic discipline of theology. Barton, by contrast, stresses the importance of practicing biblical exegesis in the context of the study of the humanities. However, he also marginalizes history, but for reasons very different from Hays's: Barton creates a dichotomy between literature and history, in the sense that he speaks of a literary and philological mode of interpretation as being constitutive for biblical criticism, as opposed to the study of history.[16]

Biblical Exegesis Inside and Outside the Context of Theology

As we have seen, however, the theological sub-disciplines could be practiced, and are being practiced, in other academic traditions than our own—in the context of historical and social-sciences research. Neither Barton nor Hays really address this fact. They both find a way of acknowledging the importance of history in very general terms, and they both find ways of marginalizing it. Both of them are suspicious of the implications of facing the fact that all theological sub-disciplines are *historical in nature.*

Unfortunately, both Hays and Barton avoid confronting the problems posed by historicism: Hays subjects the whole of historical research to the ultimate aims of a theological—or, more precisely speaking: a *dogmatic*—agenda, whereas Barton goes half the way, by taking Schleiermacher's insights on board and rejecting the consequences drawn by Troeltsch.

In so doing, both Hays's and Barton's approaches are, in their very different ways, examples of a major development in the academic study of the Bible in recent years. More and more exegetes shy away from facing the challenge of history as the central problem of biblical exegesis and generally theology. Ironically, though, the preoccupation with history that has so changed the humanities—and even the sciences—over the last two hundred years originates in Christian theology itself. Far from being an atheist or agnostic imposition on the humanities and their research methods, "historicism"—for want of a better term—is a product of Protestant theology. In a fine study, T. A. Howard demonstrates that the historical consciousness that has been regarded by so many theologians

---

16. Cf. Barton, *Nature of Biblical Criticism*, 123.

as corrosive of theology is actually itself deeply rooted in theology.[17] The breakthrough of a historical consciousness in the early nineteenth century is associated with a number of the towering figures of Protestant exegesis and theology of that period, among them Wilhelm Martin Leberecht de Wette and Friedrich Schleiermacher. It is the latter I would like to concentrate on.

Schleiermacher, critically interacting with the works of Friedrich August Wolf, Friedrich Ast, and Johann August Ernesti,[18] formulated his concept of hermeneutics as a science of understanding which is applicable to *any* text and thus went beyond the rationalism of enlightenment hermeneutics (of which Ernesti's *hermeneutica specialis* is a typical example), universalizing hermeneutics and opening the door towards a genuinely historical understanding. C. Helmer recently very aptly characterized Schleiermacher's concept of hermeneutics when she wrote that

> hermeneutics is the auxiliary discipline for the study of history. The historical object of hermeneutical study is twofold. The first task is to reconstruct the intersubjective context constituting the historical event . . . The second hermeneutical task is to reconstruct the unity underlying the author's speech . . . Hermeneutics is an "art" of infinite approximation that grasps the production of the new from the old through grammatical analysis, technical interpretation that studies authorial style and divination (which Schleiermacher always connects to comparison). *History is accessed by hermeneutics.*[19]

Schleiermacher thus attempts to formulate the rules for accessing history through the interpretation of texts. By the very nature of the enterprise, it would be self-contradictory to assume that there can be a Protestant hermeneutics, a Catholic hermeneutics, an Orthodox hermeneutics, an atheist hermeneutics or any such thing. Rather, there can only be—hermeneutics, because there is only one history. For the same reason, all texts are, in principle, of the same status and importance. We cannot have one hermeneutics for texts which some consider as holy, and another one for texts that are not so considered. It makes no sense to differentiate between a *hermeneutica generalis* and a *hermeneutica specialis*.

17. Howard, *Religion and the Rise of Historicism*, passim.

18. Moberly, "Interpret the Bible," 92–93, mentions and discusses Ernesti's views but fails to discuss Schleiermacher's hermeneutics.

19. Helmer, "Schleiermacher's Exegetical Theology," 237–38. Emphasis mine.

All texts are *historical products*, so for the purpose of understanding them by accessing their meaning though exegesis guided by hermeneutics, they all have to be treated as being on par. This is the truth which Moberly does not confront when he dismisses the "axiom" famously pronounced by Jowett—"*Interpret the Scripture like any other book*"[20]—takes it out of its context,[21] and fails to discuss the most mature and most systematic exposition of the insight which Jowett later pithily summarized: that exposition had been delivered by Schleiermacher in his *Hermeneutik*; Jowett is simply building on it, while failing to mention Schleiermacher in this context.[22] Jowett's supposed "axiom" is effectively just a convenient quip summing up what Schleiermacher had demonstrated. Isolating that quip, discussing its logic out of context, and dismissing it does not serve a meaningful purpose: whoever wants to rebut Schleiermacher's hermeneutics has to confront Schleiermacher.

This is where you may feel reminded of Hays's statement that "[t]heological exegesis does not focus chiefly on the hypothetical history behind the biblical texts, nor does it attend primarily to the meaning of texts as self-contained works of literature."[23] Rather, Hays wants to create a separate class of texts, a class of texts that, from the outset, are considered as being more authoritative than "texts as self-contained works of literature," i.e., a class of "texts"—biblical texts—"as testimony." And then he goes on to say: "This means we need to learn to stand where these witnesses stand and look where they point. Insofar as we do this, we will learn to see *as* they see; . . . we will find our vision trained anew."[24]

The obvious question is: How will Hays "learn to stand where these witnesses stand" without practicing the kind of historical reconstruction advocated by Schleiermacher, the kind of reconstruction derided by Hays as "the hypothetical history behind the biblical texts"? Does he think he will be able "to learn to stand where these witnesses stand" by reading the biblical texts in a vacuum, by using them as a kind of *perpetuum mobile*

20. Jowett, "On the Interpretation of Scripture," 377.

21. Cf. Moberly, "Interpret the Bible," 91–92.

22. Jowett, "Interpretation," 351 does mention Schleiermacher, but only with regard to his exegetical work on the New Testament. That seems strange, since Jowett's arguments on 377–78 are very reminiscent of Schleiermacher's *Hermeneutik*, which was accessible to Jowett: the text had in fact been published (posthumously) by Lücke in 1838.

23. Cf. above, n. 5.

24. Cf. above, n. 5.

of biblical interpretation? Is he unable to see that he is flatly contradicting himself?

Of course, every historical reconstruction is hypothetical. Historical reconstruction by its very nature is hypothetical. For the same reason, all textual interpretation is tentative, and, as Helmer says in a nice paraphrase of Schleiermacher's insight, "[h]ermeneutics is an 'art' of infinite approximation." There never is, and never will be, a final "assured result."

Hays, by contrast, seems to think that he has privileged access to the biblical texts if he approaches them with the right attitude, i.e. if he reads them "as *Scripture*" and "as testimony," as he puts it. There is no sense of the otherness of the text, no sense of the distance between us and texts that are roughly two thousand years old. By contrast, it was one of the great insights informing Schleiermacher's work that these texts are *alien* and that it is not *easy* to understand them. As a contemporary author puts it,

> The work of Schleiermacher constitutes a turning point in the history of hermeneutics. Till then hermeneutics was supposed to support, secure, and clarify an *already accepted* understanding . . . In the thinking of Schleiermacher, hermeneutics achieves the qualitatively different function of first *making understanding possible*, and deliberately *initiating understanding* in each individual case.[25]

And Barton rightly adds that

> Schleiermacher recognizes the *alien* character of whatever is written by another person to our own understanding; for him, successful interpretation is always achieved, not simply given. This is because it requires a penetrative grasp of the text, not mere openness to something whose meaning is obvious.[26]

Compared to Schleiermacher, Hays actually lacks a healthy sense of humility in the face of the ancient texts. He really seems to fancy himself, by virtue of being a Christian, as having privileged access to the understanding of the ancient texts he calls "*Scripture*." What hermeneutics, if any, inform his reading of the texts, then? Hays knows that he has to come up with more than just assertions and pious-sounding statements. So this is his hermeneutics:

25. Kimmerle, "Hermeneutical Theory," 107.

26. Barton, *Nature of Biblical Criticism*, 60.

> Learning to read the text with eyes of faith is a skill for which we
> are trained by the Christian tradition. Consequently, theological
> exegesis knows itself to be part of an ancient and lively conversa-
> tion. We can never approach the Bible as though we are the first
> ones to read it—or the first ones to read it appropriately. We know
> that we have much to learn from the wisdom of the people who
> have reflected deeply on these texts before us. Consequently, *theo-*
> *logical exegesis will find hermeneutical aid, not hindrance, in the*
> *church's doctrinal traditions.*[27]

One is tempted to say that, had certain sixteenth-century readers of
"Scripture" shared Hays's attitude, there would not have been a Reformation. Anyway: Hays feels that theological exegesis will have to offer something that does not just affirm well-beloved tenets of patristic exegesis
and Protestant scholasticism, not least because our forefathers were much
better at formulating their thoughts than their latter-day imitators will
ever be at imitating them. So he claims that

> Theological exegesis . . . goes beyond repeating traditional inter-
> pretations; rather, instructed by the example of traditional read-
> ings, theological interpreters will produce *fresh readings*, new
> performances of Scripture's sense that encounter the texts anew
> with eyes of faith and see the ways that the Holy Spirit continues
> to speak to the churches through the same ancient texts that the
> tradition has handed on to us. To put the same point in a slightly
> different way, the Spirit-led imagination, an imagination convert-
> ed by the word, is an essential faculty for the work of theological
> exegesis.[28]

This, of course, flies in the face of an exegetical practice of biblical
criticism grounded in Schleiermacher's concept of hermeneutics. Firstly,
and most obviously, a so-called "Spirit-led imagination" is beyond the
confines of academic discourse and therefore cannot seriously be ad-
duced in an argument that claims, like Hays's, to be scholarly. Secondly,
by saying that a proper interpreter of Scripture needs to have "an imagination converted by the word," he says that only Christians, and presumably only Christians of a certain disposition, can be proper interpreters of
biblical texts. Once again, this goes against the grain of all basic assumptions governing academic discourse within and across the disciplinary

27. Hays, "Reading the Bible," 15–16.
28. Ibid.

boundaries. Thirdly, although Hays claims that his method includes historical reasoning (as opposed to being led by it!), he lets his exegesis of the texts be governed, from the outset, by criteria that are extraneous to those texts: later doctrinal statements of the church, patristic and other readings of the texts in question, and so forth. What kind of historical method is *that*? Barton rightly comments on that kind of "theological exegesis" by stating that "[i]t is on the whole those who believe in 'moving beyond' criticism who are most prone to read their own theological systems into the scriptural text, and this is just what we should expect."[29]

". . . like any other"

Biblical criticism, then, is a historical subject "like any other," dealing with material that is fascinating not least because it is alien and because understanding it is not easy. Its methodology must be open to interdisciplinary scrutiny like that of any other historical discipline. It is part of theology as an overall academic discipline because its own history is that of a collaborator in the enterprise of serving the church. This is what Schleiermacher stated of theology: that it is constituted as an academic discipline by its purpose of serving the church. This may sound like the statement of Hays I quoted earlier. However, such an impression would be entirely misleading. While Hays speaks of theology as if it were something like a subject that is clearly definable in and of itself, like a fixed entity whose character is self-explanatory, Schleiermacher realizes that what we call theology is itself the product of historical contingencies. Theology is not a discipline in the same sense in which, say, medicine or classics are academic disciplines. As I pointed out earlier, all the sub-disciplines of theology could be explored in non-theological academic contexts. The only feature they have in common when they are practiced in the context of a theology faculty is that they are joined together to serve the church by educating its future ministers through equipping them with the specific array of knowledge which they will need in their future work. Schleiermacher puts it thus in paragraphs 5 and 6 of his *Brief Outline of Theology as a Field of Study*:

> §5. Christian theology . . . is that assemblage of scientific knowledge and practical instruction without the possession and applica-

29. Barton, *Nature of Biblical Criticism*, 165.

tion of which a united leadership of the Christian Church, that is, a government of the Church in the fullest sense, is not possible.

§6. When this same knowledge is acquired and possessed without relation to the government of the Church, it ceases to be theological and devolves to those sciences to which it belongs according to its varied content.[30]

Biblical Criticism, History, and the Humanities

Let us now return to our central question. What are we to make of Barton's claim "does not necessarily involve the reconstruction either of historical events or of the history of the text's development"? And is he right when he says that "in itself the critical approach to the Bible is not a method but a series of explanatory hypotheses, driven by a particular attitude toward texts and textual meaning"[31] and concludes that biblical criticism is not historical in essence?

Let us start with the first question. Although the work of the biblical exegete does not always involve the actual "reconstruction . . . of historical events" or of the histories of certain texts, the hermeneutics informing his or her exegetical work explores texts which are—"like any other" text—the literary products of unique historical circumstances, circumstances which need to be reconstructed and understood in order to have as full an appreciation of the text and its meaning as possible. Biblical criticism—or, in Schleiermacher's terminology, "exegetical theology"—forms part of "historical theology" and is therefore, in Schleiermacher's words, "part of the modern study of history; and thus all the natural divisions of that science are coordinate with it."[32] Any type of work in Biblical Studies is thus informed by and governed by historical objectives and historical methodology. History is not the handmaiden, as in Hays's definition of theological exegesis (or an optional extra, as in Barton's concept of biblical criticism), but it is right at the core of the enterprise of "historical theology" (to use Schleiermacher's terminology again) and thus also at the core of Biblical Studies.

30. Schleiermacher, *Brief Outline of Theology as a Field of Study*, 3–4.

31. Cf. above, n. 3.

32. Schleiermacher, *Brief Outline*, 69.

This is why, ever since the breakthrough of historical consciousness in the early nineteenth century, the questions raised by historicism have been inescapable.[33] The corrosive effects of the historical consciousness—the "relativism" which the current pope and his evangelical counterparts rage against and which, they feel, is threatening to undermine the practice of academic theology—came fully into view only in the twentieth century, in the work of Ernst Troeltsch and other heirs of Schleiermacher. This is why Barton tries to define biblical criticism while denying that the practice and the problems of history are at its core: he wants to exclude, by definition, the potential for further (perceived) corrosion in biblical studies by categorically excluding the so-called "severely reductionist view of historical study" that leaves "no way back to any kind of religious faith in the texts of the Bible."[34] However, Barton's position is a far cry from the biblical "criticism" endorsed by the pope and his evangelical equivalents. I shall say more about that in a moment.

As regards our second question, we have already more or less answered it. It remains for me to add that Barton's thesis that "the critical approach to the Bible is not a method but a series of explanatory hypotheses, driven by a particular attitude toward texts and textual meaning"[35] does not do justice to the critical approach. It is a method in the sense that the exegetical practice is guided by a hermeneutics which enables the exegete to reconstruct historical processes in which he or she will then be able to locate the texts that are under scrutiny. In Schleiermacher's words:

> §132. The full understanding of a discourse or piece of writing is a kind of artistic achievement and thus requires an "art doctrine" [*Kunstlehre*], or technology, which we designate by the term "hermeneutics."
> §133. Such a technology exists only insofar as its rules of interpretation form a system founded upon principles directly evident [!] from the nature of thought and language.[36]

The type of biblical criticism which results from this hermeneutics deserves to be called, and must be called, "historical criticism." After Spinoza and Schleiermacher, it is the only type of biblical criticism that

33. Cf. generally Murrmann-Kahl, *Die entzauberte Heilsgeschichte*.
34. Barton, *Nature of Biblical Criticism*, 47.
35. Ibid., 67–68.
36. Schleiermacher, *Brief Outline*, 70–71.

can properly be called scholarly. *Nota bene*: While Barton's concept of biblical criticism is in consonance with Schleiermacher's position, Hays's most certainly is not. The step Barton is not prepared to take is that taken by Troeltsch: to expose biblical criticism to the onslaught of historicism and to let biblical exegesis be purged by the radical insights won in the study of history. While Barton is not prepared to take that final step, Hays does not even start out on the journey. He repristinates a "theological" interpretation of biblical literature which is in fact dogmatic and strongly reminiscent of pre-Enlightenment approaches to "Scripture."

Historical criticism in the sense here established should of course be, and will always be, open to innovative approaches to the understanding of texts based on research in, say, anthropology, and other human sciences. That makes it no less "historical" and "critical;" on the contrary. But it must never let itself be governed by *dogmatically inspired* hermeneutical axioms. If it does, it ceases to be historical and critical. In fact, a hermeneutics governed by dogmatic axioms makes fresh and surprising insights impossible. No amount of "theological exegesis" of a dogmatic nature will be able to obscure that fact. In fact, such exegesis, through its results, often makes its own sterility painfully obvious.

To conclude: If biblical scholarship ceases seriously to engage with the historical circumstances which gave birth to the texts it seeks to understand, and to do so on the basis of a real interaction with contemporary historical theory, the humanities, and indeed the human sciences, all it will be able to produce is shallow interpretations of biblical texts to suit the theological flavor of the month. In order to remain an academic subject which will continue to be taken seriously, biblical studies—and the other subjects constituting theology!—will have to establish (reestablish?) a meaningful dialogue with history and the other humanities[37]—and, indeed, with the sciences.[38] It was a wise decision when the university reformers in post-1806 Prussia and founders of Berlin's *Friedrich-Wilhelms-Universität* established a theological faculty, yet denied it the dominant status it had been accorded in the mediaeval university system. In our time we need to reinstate theology as a subject that is able meaningfully to communicate with the humanities *and* the sciences, thus renewing the heritage of Humboldt, not squandering it—a theology that

---

37. Cf. Pannenberg, *Wissenschaftstheorie und Theologie*, 105–17, on Troeltsch's concept of theology as *Geisteswissenschaft*.

38. Ibid., 117–36.

can integrate Troeltsch instead of rejecting him and whose practitioners finally take the questions raised by historicism seriously by conceptualizing theology as a *Geisteswissenschaft* which is in dialogue with the whole of human knowledge.

5

Actuality in Theology and Philosophy[1]

SIMON OLIVER

IN THIS ESSAY, I will discuss a tendency in contemporary philosophy to prioritize the possible over the actual. This seems to be a very significant shift from pre-modern philosophy and theology which maintains the priority of actuality over potentiality. The clearest expression of this latter view can be found in Aristotle's *Metaphysics*:

> Now since we have distinguished the several senses of priority, it is obvious that actuality is prior to potentiality. By potentiality I mean not that which we have defined as "a principle of change which is in something other than the thing changed, or in that same thing qua other," but in general any principle of motion and rest; for nature also is in the same genus as potentiality, because it is a principle of motion, although not in some other thing, but in the thing itself *qua* itself. To every potentiality of this kind actuality is prior, both in formula and substance; in time it is sometimes prior and sometimes not.[2]

1. This essay is greatly indebted to a number of extremely fruitful conversations with my colleague Dr. Johannes Hoff of the University of Wales, Lampeter. Omissions and errors are entirely my own.
2. Aristotle *Metaphysics* IX.8.1049b4–15.

Aristotle further explains the sense in which potentiality might be temporally prior to actuality. He points out that a seed, which is potentially corn, is prior in time to the corn which it will later become. This is to say that something which is numerically identical (this *one* seed becomes this *one* ear of corn) features potentiality prior to actuality. However, there will always be something formally identical (this ear of corn has the same *form* as the seed which it generates) which is in act and which is prior to that which is potential. In other words, a seed, which is potentially an ear of corn, is generated by that which is actually an ear of corn. In the sense of "form," actuality is prior to potentiality.

In his commentary on this portion of Aristotle's *Metaphysics*, Aquinas makes clear that actuality precedes potentiality conceptually and with respect to knowledge. He points out that potentiality is always defined in terms of actuality, but actuality is not in turn defined by means of something else, but is only made known inductively.[3] For Aquinas, it is the actuality of the divine that establishes the priority of actuality over potency in both being and knowledge. Aquinas writes that, "Before the world existed it was possible for it to be, not indeed because of the passive potentiality of matter, but because of the active power of God."[4] Even if our knowledge begins in potency and passes to actuality,[5] it is always preceded by the actuality of God's own knowledge. Our motion from potential knowledge to actual knowledge is, for Aquinas, a deepening participation in the eternal actuality of God's self-knowledge.[6]

---

3. Aquinas, *Commentary on Aristotle's Metaphysics*, IX.7.1846.

4. Aquinas, *Summa Theologiae*, 1a.46.1 ad 1.

5. For example, I *potentially* know how to speak Portuguese and, by the motion of learning, come *actually* to know how to speak Portuguese.

6. Aquinas, *Summa Theologiae*, 1a.84.a5.responsio: "Secondly, a thing is spoken of as known in another as in a principle of knowledge; for instance, we might say that things seen by sunlight are seen in the sun. In this sense we must say that the human soul knows everything in the divine ideas, and that by participating in them we know everything. For the intellectual light in us is nothing more than a participating likeness of the uncreated light in which the divine ideas are contained." Aquinas goes on to explain that, besides the intellectual light which is in us, species taken from material things are required for knowledge. He therefore avoids the sense that material singulars are insignificant and that our knowledge is purely and exclusively a knowledge of eternal ideas. Nevertheless, material singulars have being (*esse commune*) by participation in being itself. They are genuine and potent secondary causes of our knowledge. This is explained in *Summa Theologiae*, 1a.14.a8.ad3. See also *Summa Theologiae*, 1a.15.

Modern philosophy tends to reverse this priority. It marks a point of distinction with theology which continues to prioritize the actual. How does philosophy prioritize potentiality? In a recent article, Michael Rea, in the course of discussing the application of analytic philosophical methods within the sphere of Christian theology, describes a critique of conceptual analysis which can be understood in terms of the prioritization of potentiality.[7] Rea points to the work of Bas van Fraassen. Although van Fraassen's contribution to analytic metaphysics in the form of his "constructive empiricism" has been very considerable, he has been forceful in his criticism of certain approaches to metaphysical issues. Put very briefly, van Fraassen argues that such metaphysics can result in the creation of "simulacra" which become the objects of philosophers' discussions. Rea cites a particular example from van Fraassen's work.[8] Imagine posing the question "Does the world exist?" Philosophers proceed to define the term "world" with considerable nuance and detail before claiming that the world exists if and only if the world *as they have defined it* exists. What makes the world of the philosophers a simulacrum is not the fact that it is postulated, but that "satisfying a philosopher's analysis of the concept 'world' is something very different from being a world."[9]

This tendency is reflected in much philosophy of religion. The philosopher identifies an apparently rigorous and clear, almost self-evident, definition of the term "God" (just read the opening six lines of Richard Swinburne's *The Coherence of Theism*) and proceeds to demonstrate the existence of this simulacrum, or, to put it another way, this idol.[10] "God" is postulated and defined in order to examine the *possibility* of this "God's"

7. It should be said that Rea does not express the matter in terms of actuality and potentiality. I take it that this portion of his very clear and helpful essay is more particularly concerned with the nature of conceptual analysis in metaphysics.

8. Van Fraassen, *Empirical Stance*, cited by Rea, "Introduction" in *Analytic Theology*, 23.

9. Rea, "Introduction," 23.

10. Van Fraassen's criticism in the realm of metaphysics and the philosophy of science is in some ways paralleled in the work of philosophers of religion as diverse as D. Z. Phillips and Jean-Luc Marion. Phillips, for example, spurred on by the example of Wittgenstein, points out that philosophers of religion ought not to discuss philosophical abstractions ("simulacra"), but rather take account of what the religious actually do and say—of the way religions "work" and the so-called "grammar of belief." See, for example, Phillips, *Religion and the Hermeneutics of Contemplation*. This is quite familiar and is often expressed in terms of a critique of the discussion of the so-called "God of the philosophers" which is, in fact, no one else's God.

existence. Kierkegaard famously pointed out this approach with reference to the following example which one can relate to debates concerning the existence of God:

> It is generally a difficult matter to want to demonstrate that something exists . . . The whole process of demonstration continually becomes something entirely different, becomes an expanding concluding development of what I conclude from having presupposed that the object of investigation exists. Therefore, whether I am moving in the world of sensate palpability or in the world of thought, I never reason in conclusion to existence, but I reason in conclusion from existence. For example, I do not demonstrate that a stone exists but that something that exists is a stone. The court of law does not demonstrate that a criminal exists but that the accused, who does exist, is a criminal.[11]

According to Kierkegaard, an enquiry into existence does not begin with the possibility of something's existence, but starts from an actually existing thing. Translated into theological method, we might say that enquiry into God does not begin with the creation of a simulacra whose *possible* existence we proceed to discuss, but rather with the *actuality* of some kind of encounter, whatever form it might take. The latter method is most obviously, but not unproblematically, exemplified in twentieth-century systematic theology by Karl Barth for whom theology begins not with the possibility of knowledge of God, but with the actuality of God's self-disclosure in revelation.

In this essay, I will focus particularly on the apparent prioritization of the potential (the possibility of God, or the possibility of knowledge of God) in aspects of the philosophical tradition. From where did philosophy's emphasis on "possibility" emerge? One might think that the stress on possibility is part of a tradition of general incredulity and doubt which focuses not on what we know, but "whether" or "how" we know what we know, and under what conditions knowledge is possible. In other words, it could be associated with modern philosophy's very particular concern with epistemology. Yet the doubting and incredulous stance which is characteristic of the priority of the possible over the actual might be reflected in a tradition which has influenced, and indeed characterized, so much Christian theology, namely the apophatic. Does apophaticism, whether in theology or philosophy, begin in reticent and skeptical fashion

11. Kierkegaard, *Philosophical Fragments*, 40.

by probing the *possibility* of knowledge? If not, in what sense is there a priority of the actual in such theology and philosophy? My discussion will begin with Nicholas of Cusa who, while being perhaps the final representative of Neoplatonic apophaticism in theological and philosophical enquiry, is nevertheless often interpreted as a proto-modern skeptic who is concerned first with the possibility of knowledge.[12] I will argue that in Cusa's discussion of wisdom he begins with the actuality of encounter, but does not offer any kind of positivistic theological knowledge which is characteristic of modern notions of God's self-revelation.[13] Rather, the possibility of creation—including human knowing—is an "actual possibility" in God's eternal nature. Moreover, the measure of our knowledge is not any series of concepts which we devise; it is the simplicity of God's knowledge.

Cusa is no skeptic concerned with the mere possibility of cognition, for he understands that knowledge, while beginning in "learned ignorance," is always partial but never "off-the-mark." The notion that knowledge is merely "representation" (rather than participation) introduces the sense of doubt and a concern with the possibility of knowledge. I will further locate the priority of the possible over the actual in the rise of theological nominalism characteristic of the work of, amongst others, William of Ockham. Here, in the focus on the possibility of divine deception alongside the notion of possible worlds that are mere reconfigurations of the individuals which compose the world we inhabit, we will see a characteristically modern variant of skepticism which is always concerned with what *might be* rather than with what *is*.[14] More particularly, I will suggest that Ockham's nominalism leads to the view that phenomena can be analyzed as abstracted from their created context in such a way that "idealized" phenomena or "simulacra"—which remain mere possibilities, not actualities as encountered in the world—become the subject matter of philosophy.

12. See Hopkins, "Nicholas of Cusa."

13. On the Hegelian background to the notion of "self-revelation," see Hoff's very important essay "Rise and Fall of the Kantian Paradigm."

14. The term "scepticism" has a technical and restricted definition in philosophy. For now, I use it in the broadest sense to refer to a radical incredulity that is concerned with the possibility of knowledge. Later in this essay, the distinction between scepticism and incredulity will become clearer.

What of theology, which apparently begins not with possibilities or simulacra, but rather with the actuality of God's self-donation? This aspect of the theological is the focus of an important analysis by Jean-Luc Marion who describes clearly the way in which philosophy, in its phenomenological guise, struggles to think of revelation even as a possibility.[15] Moving to this more recent analysis of possibility and actuality in theology and philosophy, I will suggest that theology reasserts the priority of the actual in all enquiry. Why? Because theology avoids the subject-object dualism by which conditions for possible knowledge are established in relation to knowing subjects. Instead, theology begins with creatures and the actuality of creation as it gives itself to be known in relation to an eternally actual creator.

Actuality and the Apophatic

The history of skepticism, extending from Pyrrho, Sextus Empiricus, and Diogenes Laertius in antiquity to Descartes in early modernity, is thought to have undergone a revival in the Renaissance as the influence of Aristotle diminished.[16] Such skepticism, broadly conceived, is concerned with the very possibility of knowledge. Is Nicholas of Cusa, writing in the first half of the fifteenth century, an early representative of modern philosophy, or does he preserve a more traditional view, one consonant with the theology and philosophy of the high Middle Ages? For Cusa, as with Plato, philosophy understood as the love of wisdom begins in the realization of what we do not know. However, this is not pure and unadulterated negativity, which simply rests in our ignorance. Why? Because the realization of what we do not know is—paradoxically—itself knowledge. But where can this knowledge of our ignorance come from? It emerges from the priority of the actual disclosure of being over the pure possibility of our knowledge which in turn provokes desire for wisdom.[17] Cusa

15. For example, see Heidegger, *Being and Time*, 63.

16. See Popkin, *History of Scepticism*. For a revised view of scepticism in the Middle Ages, see Lagerlund, *Rethinking the History of Skepticism*.

17. Much of what I have to say depends on an important distinction to which Sarah Coakley and Bernard McGinn have recently pointed, namely that between apophaticism on the one hand, and the tradition of negative theology, the *via negativa*, on the other. The Latin *via negativa* refers, of course, to the negation of our concept of God, and occasionally even to the negation of our negations in the Greek Dionysian tradition.

writes of this intense desire for wisdom in the form of a dialogue between someone with no formal education—the *Idiota*—and the apparently wise and learned *Orator*.[18] The *Idiota* points out that the *Orator* claims to be wise, but is in fact ignorant of his own ignorance. The two retire to a barber's shop to discuss the matter, whereupon the *Idiota* uses a number of characteristically Cusan examples to explain his position.

Wisdom, says the *Idiota*, proclaims itself in the streets and declares that it dwells in the highest places. So the *Idiota* looks to the streets, to the market place, and points out that one can see money being counted, goods being weighed, and oil being measured out. By the reasoning of counting, weighing, and measuring, human beings discriminate by means of a single unit. One is the beginning of number (all subsequent numbers are multiples of one), the smallest weight is the beginning of weighing, and the smallest measure the beginning of measuring. For the sake of argument, the *Idiota* takes the smallest weight to be the ounce, the smallest measure to be the inch. Every number is constructed by means of the one, every weight by means of the ounce, and every measure by means of the inch. But by what, asks the *Idiota*, do we attain to the one, to the ounce or the inch? Oneness is not attained to by number, because number is subsequent to the one. Likewise, the ounce is not attained to by means of weight, nor the inch by means of measurement.

What is Cusa's point here? It is that the composite cannot be the measure of the simple, or that what is subsequent to an origin cannot be the measure of its origin. Take the example of creation in Christian theology: the creative act cannot itself be a natural process, for natural processes are subsequent to creation and cannot "measure" creation. This is the basis for the Judaic, Christian, and Islamic conviction that God creates *ex nihilo*. As Cusa writes,

---

As Coakley points out, the Greek *apophasis* means "saying no," this being mirrored in the Latin tradition of the negative way. However, *apophasis* might also convey a sense of "revelation," from the verb *apophaino*, "to show forth" or "to display." So rather than resting in a mere negation of whatever we encounter, the apophatic tradition, beginning with *apophaino*, begins first with the actuality of a positive disclosure of being. So when I talk of the apophatic, I wish to emphasise not the unmitigated negativity in some strands of the *via negativa*, but the priority of revelation and disclosure in the apophatic. See Coakley, "Introduction," 539 n. 30 citing McGinn, "Three Forms of Negativity in Christian Mysticism."

18. Nicholas of Cusa, *De Sapientia*.

> ... the Beginning of all things is that by means of which, in which and from which whatever can be originated is originated; and, nevertheless, [that Beginning] cannot be attained unto by any originated thing. It is that by means of which, in which and from which everything that can be understood is understood; and nevertheless, it cannot be attained unto by the intellect.[19]

To put this in the parlance of Platonic metaphysics, Cusa is expressing the conviction that, for example, the Form of horse is not itself a horse.[20] Moreover, particular horses do not "measure" the Form "horse," but rather the reverse. Thus that which is the origin of measure is not itself a measure, that which is the origin of weight is not itself a weight, and that which is the origin of being is not itself *a* being.

Continuing his discussion of the wisdom which philosophy seeks, Cusa defines "supreme wisdom" in the following perplexing way: "that you know . . . how it is that the Unattainable is attained to unattainably."[21] This is a characteristically Cusan paradox. What does this mean? Cusa is pointing out that the means by which we attain knowledge, namely by comparison and measuring one thing in terms of another through a proportion, cannot be the means by which we attain that which is simple and the measure of all things. In other words, whatever means we use to attain knowledge of creation or the natural world, we cannot use those same means to attain knowledge of the origin of creation or the natural world. Why not? Because this would be to treat that origin as part of the order it is supposed to measure—in other words, as an object amongst other objects. In fact, in *De Docta Ignorantia* ("On Learned Ignorance"), Cusa goes further and states that wisdom is the realization that God is beyond all distinction—potency and act, motion and rest, lesser or greater, light and dark, maximum and minimum—and in God all opposites coincide.[22] Why? Because the absolute simplicity of God measures these spectra. It is not that God lies at the extreme end of, say, the act–potency or rest–motion spectrum. This would be to conceive God through a kind of proportionality, and such speech about God would in fact be speech about a creature. The crucial point for Cusa is that there cannot be a proportion

19. Ibid., I.8.

20. This interpretation of Plato's metaphysics of the Forms refers particularly to its later expression in the *Theaetetus*.

21. Nicholas of Cusa, *De Sapientia*, I.7.

22. See Nicholas of Cusa, *De Docta Ignorantia*.

between finite and infinite. The finite world is not simply a smaller version of the infinite. Rather, the infinite comprehends within itself all finitude because it is not itself just a very big finite thing.

The notion that opposites coincide in the simplicity of God is most clearly expounded in Cusa's *De Docta Ignorantia*. God is the "absolute maximum," exceeding all opposition, even the law of non-contradiction.[23] More particularly, God is beyond the Aristotelian distinction of act and potency, for God is what Cusa calls the *possest*, the coincidence of *posse* and *est*, of possibility and actuality, although he is deploying these terms in a quite unAristotelian way.[24] God is all that it is possible for God to be, and God contains within himself all real possibilities. No creature has realized all that it is possible for it to be, yet somewhat paradoxically that possibility is actual; that actual possibility—the *possest*—is God.

At first glance, it appears that Cusa is proposing something rather different to the Aristotelian notion of God as *actus purus*. However, it would be better to understand Cusa as refining in a very subtle way the Thomist priority of actuality over potentiality. For Cusa, one cannot, strictly speaking, speak of "priority" in God because this implies composition. He states,

> Therefore, absolute possibility, about which we are speaking and through which those things that actually exist are able actually to exist, does not precede actuality. Nor does it succeed actuality; for how would actuality be able to exist if possibility did not exist? Therefore, absolute possibility, actuality, and the union of the two are co-eternal.[25]

He goes on to explain that in creation, the actual and possible become distinct. This means that creatures feature potentiality, but that potentiality is defined with reference to a prior actuality *that lies elsewhere*, in another. In the end, all potentiality in creation is only real—that is, an "actual potential"—in relation to God himself. By contrast, Cusa maintains this division does not pertain to God. Within God's eternity is contained all that it is possible for God to be, yet that possibility is at once actual. God eternally actualizes himself. Cusa writes that,

---

23. Ibid., I.4.
24. Nicholas of Cusa, *De Possest*.
25. Ibid., 6.

I am speaking in absolute and very general terms—as if I were saying: "Since possibility and actuality are identical in God, God is—actually—everything of which 'is able to be' can be predicated truly." For there can be nothing that God [can be but] is not actually. However, the case of the sun is different. For although the sun is actually what it is, it not what it is able to be. For [the sun] is able to exist otherwise than it actually is.[26]

Once again, Cusa is claiming that God does not simply lie at the far end of a series of metaphysical spectra such as those between potency and act or motion and rest. This would be to conceive of God in terms that are too univocal with creatures. God is the "coincidence" of these opposites, for he comprehends or "enfolds" the very spectra themselves.[27] God is the trinity of absolute possibility, absolute actuality and the union of the two. This has implications not only for our knowledge of God, but for the nature of our knowledge in general. For Cusa, we attain knowledge by the comparison of one thing with another. Moreover, human perception is always from a certain perspective, and only God views each object from an infinite number of perspectives at once and therefore knows each thing as it is in itself. In *De Docta Ignorantia*, Cusa puts it this way:

A finite intellect . . . cannot precisely attain the truth of things by means of a likeness. For truth is neither more nor less but indivisible. Nothing not itself true is capable of precisely measuring what is true . . . So the intellect, which is not truth, never comprehends truth so precisely but that it could always be comprehended with infinitely more precision . . . Therefore, the quiddity of things, which is the truth of beings, is unattainable in its purity, and although it is pursued by all philosophers, none has found it as it is. The more profoundly learned we are in this ignorance, the more closely we draw near to truth itself.[28]

This has led some commentators to see in Cusa a proto-modern skepticism, particularly concerning empirical knowledge. Is this the case? What

26. Ibid., 8.

27. Ibid., 8: "Therefore, since the facts of the matter are such that God is Absolute Possibility, is Actuality, and is the Union of the two (and so, He is actually every possible being): clearly, He is all things, in the sense of enfolding all things. For everything that in any way either exists or can exist in enfolded in this Beginning. And whatever either has been created or will be created in unfolded from Him, in whom it is enfolded." Cusa's position is on the same trajectory as Aquinas. See *Summa Theologiae*, 1a.14.a9.

28. Nicholas of Cusa, *De Docta Ignorantia*, I.3; See also *De Sapientia* II.38.

we certainly do not find in Cusa is anything like the division between the phenomenal and the noumenal, or Locke's primary and secondary qualities. Our knowledge or perception of things is merely a partial knowledge which can be infinitely perfected. Most important, however, is Cusa's claim that our knowledge is not the measure of things, but is rather itself *measured*. First, the intellect is measured by what it knows, but ultimately it is measured by God's simple and eternal knowledge. This means that potential human knowledge is measured by a prior actuality: the actuality of that which is known, whose potential is, in turn, a sharing in the actuality of God's knowledge, which is God's eternal self. This is in contrast to much modern philosophy which begins, as in Kant, with the *a priori* "conditions for the *possibility* of knowledge." So under this modern philosophical scheme, what measures human knowledge is not some prior actuality which gives itself to be known and which has its ultimate origin in the eternally simple source of being, but rather the pre-established conditions under which knowledge is deemed *possible*. In short, human knowledge becomes its own measure, whereupon it becomes idolatrous; what we see in our knowledge is merely ourselves.

Cusa's notion that our knowledge is partial and, while not "off the mark," always subject to ever-greater perfecting, is indicative of a more general Neoplatonic tradition of which he is one of the last representatives. That tradition used the metaphor of illumination in speaking of human knowledge. In Plato's dialogue *The Republic*, Socrates famously describes knowledge and the nature of the Good metaphorically with reference to the illumination provided by the sun.[29] He points out that the sun provides light, warmth, and therefore sustenance to the creatures and objects around us, and also illuminates the world to make things visible and therefore knowable. This becomes a metaphor for the illumination provided by the Good within the visible realm that we inhabit. For Plato, the Good makes things knowable, and it is by participation in the Good that things come to be and are sustained. Crucially, we can participate in the Good with more or less intensity. Moreover, fact and value are not in any way dissociated: something is knowable—and something *is*—to the extent that it is good. My intellect can be more or less intensely illuminated by the Good, and the visible realm that I attempt to know will be

---

29. Plato *Republic* VI.508a ff.

more or less knowable according to the intensity of its share in the Good. So knowledge can be more or less bright.

This tradition had a broad influence on Christian belief and practice leading up to the high Middle Ages. To believe in God was not to believe in just another object within our metaphorical visual field, but to believe that our knowledge is made possible by something wholly other to which creation points—that there is something actual which precedes our knowledge's possibility. Yet this belief and knowledge is not thought to be untrustworthy and therefore a source of skepticism, bur rather partial and susceptible to ever greater illumination and clarity of vision. As Cusa put it, our knowledge is capable of ever greater precision. Most importantly, true wisdom is thought to begin in realizing the dimness of one's own perceptions of that which gives itself to be known.

Representation, Deceit, and Ideal Knowledge

How is this tradition of knowledge as illumination superseded in modernity in such a way that potentiality comes to have priority over actuality? I will consider two important shifts in late mediaeval thought: the understanding of knowledge as representation, and theological nominalism.

Claims about the nature of the univocity of being in the thought of John Duns Scotus have lately been subject to contention. What is less debatable is the proposal that Scotus anticipates a particularly modern form of epistemology when he teaches that knowledge is a form of representation rather than illumination.[30] What does this mean? Imagine I am gazing at a tree. According to the view that knowledge is merely representation, my knowledge of a tree is rather akin to my mind taking a snapshot of the tree as if my mind were a camera.[31] Whereas for an earlier tradition the form of the tree would come to reside in the intellect in such a way that there is an intimate connection between knower and known, for this later tradition what I know is not the tree itself, but *only a representation*

30. The most scholarly treatment to date of this aspect of Scotus's thought is Olivier Boulnois, *Être et Représentation*. Of course, the best-known recent critique of the representational theory of knowledge is Rorty, *Philosophy and the Mirror of Nature*.

31. In his discussion of representational knowledge, Rorty uses a different metaphor: human knowledge is akin to the reflection of images in a mirror. Philosophy's task is the polishing of the mirror in the hope that representations become clearer with respect to their objects.

of the tree. This is significant for two reasons. First, representations can be the cause of mistrust. In other words, my representational knowledge of the tree can be called into doubt because it is only a representation—a picture or snapshot, if you like. Understood in this way, the knowledge that comes from our senses can be the object of suspicion and doubt, and hence knowledge as representation is often regarded as the beginnings of a peculiarly modern form of skepticism. A corollary of this provides the second reason why knowledge as representation in Scotus is important. Because knowledge is now somewhat problematic, the focus for philosophy shifts from *what* we know (in which ontology [the what] and epistemology [the knowledge] are intertwined) to *how* we know what we know. This therefore marks the invention of an autonomous and particular variant of philosophy which has become of almost exclusive concern in the modern period, namely epistemology—the study of "how" or "whether" we know what we know. With knowledge understood as representation, created beings are known without reference to a transcendent and simply are as they *appear* to be to us in our representation of them. We do not know things in themselves (however falteringly or partially), but only *representations* of those things. In some forms of modern philosophy, the central project therefore becomes exclusively epistemological: the assuaging of skepticism and radical doubt by the attainment of certain or foundational knowledge.

Further developments in theology and philosophy contribute to the history of skeptical enquiry and the concomitant prioritization of the possible over the actual. The first concerns the possibility of divine deception, which leads beyond mere incredulity. This is occasioned in part by William of Ockham's much-debated view of intuitive and abstractive cognition.[32] By "intuitive cognition," Ockham means the immediate perception of an individual to which we are present by means of one or more of our senses. Importantly, this includes a judgment concerning whether or not the thing exists. Unlike earlier theories, an act of "abstractive cognition" (which, broadly speaking at the risk of over-simplification, concerns imagination or recollection) does not necessarily concern the formulation of universal concepts from particulars. Instead, such cognition refers to abstraction from existence and non-existence. An act of

---

32. See, for example, Ockham *Quodlibetal Questions* (Quodlibeta Septem), V.5. This aspect of Ockham's epistemology is discussed in Gilson, *Unity of Philosophical Experience*, ch.3, and Panaccio and Piché, "Ockham's Reliabilism."

abstractive cognition (such as a memory) does not contain within itself anything sufficient to cause me to assent to a proposition (for example, that my memory of my friend wearing a black coat last night is true).[33] For the moment, we are particularly concerned with Ockham's view that we can have intuitive cognition of non-existent individuals. This is not to say that we have an intuitive cognition that something exists when in fact it does not exist. Rather, Ockham allows the possibility that one can have an intuitive cognition of something that does not exist, and part of that cognition is the (correct) understanding that what one intuits does not exist. This is not brought about naturally, as in the case of an intuitive cognition that something does exist (for example, the desk at which I am working), but rather by divine intervention. Ockham said that, "In this question I propose two theses. The first is that by God's power there can be an intuitive cognition of an object that does not exist. I prove this, first, through the article of faith, 'I believe in God the Father Almighty.'[34]

As Panaccio and Piché suggest, the reasons why Ockham held this very unusual thesis are complex, but particularly concerned with the possibility of intuitive cognition of non-existents suggested because of an emphasis on divine omnipotence and focus on the sovereign freedom of the divine will as distinct from the divine nature.[35] However, one important consequence of Ockham's thesis concerning the intuition of non-existents is that it affords a particular epistemological status to possibilities. In other words, I know non-existing things—which must nevertheless be *potential*—in the same way that I know existing things: by the certitude of intuitive cognition.

The notion that we can have intuitive cognition of non-existents is, of course, not indicative of skepticism. However, when the possibility of divine "intervention" in human cognition is entertained in this way, it does raises a possibility which was to appear with particular force in skepticism, particularly leading to the philosophy of Descartes: the view that God could deceive us.[36] To understand why this is particularly important

33. A more detailed and nuanced description of Ockham's distinction between intuitive and abstractive cognition can be found in Karger, "Ockham's Misunderstood Theory." On the debate concerning the interpretation of Ockham on these issues, see also Karger, "Ockham and Wodeham," and Stump, "Mechanisms of Cognition."

34. Ockham, *Quodlibetal Questions*, VI.6. See also *Ordinatio* I.

35. Panaccio and Piché, "Ockham's Reliabilism."

36. Ockham, *Quodlibetal Questions*, V.5: "Nonetheless, God can cause an act of

in the history of skepticism, it is necessary to distinguish skepticism from mere questioning or incredulity. Take the case of a stick that is dipped into a bucket of water. It appears as if the stick bends or becomes crooked. Referring only to my sight, this is what I would believe is the case, although I can doubt very much that this is the case, partly because I can put my hand in the water and feel that the stick is still straight. However, with reference to something else in my "cognitive world," namely an accumulated knowledge of optics and the effect of water on perception, I can prove that my initial perception that the stick is crooked requires amendment or nuance. The point about this process of reason is that I can use one aspect of my perception and understanding (optics and water) to correct another aspect of my perception and understanding (the crooked appearance of the stick). This is how the usual process of inquiry and general incredulity operates in any intellectual enterprise. What makes divine deception different is that it calls into question *every* aspect of my perception and understanding in such a way that I cannot use one part to correct or amend another. The result of this emphasis on divine deception—the idea that God could annihilate the world while preserving my perception of that world—is that the reality of the world is indistinguishable from the possibility that it has been annihilated while my perception of that world is preserved. In principle, therefore, there is no way to end one's incredulity in the case of such skepticism; possibility reigns.

However, Ockham's nominalism and his so-called "principle of annihilation," articulated in the context of the discussion of the intuition of non-existents, marks, as Amos Funkenstein has shown, the radical shift from the theological cosmology of Aquinas and that which will be articulated by Cusa a century or so after Ockham.[37] Ockham maintained that, "every absolute thing that is distinct in place and subject from every other absolute thing can by God's power exist when that other absolute thing is destroyed."[38]

For Aquinas and Cusa, any existing singular is part of an intricate and delicate system of reference, which, crucially, forms a whole. This had been the conviction expressed in Platonic and Neoplatonic cosmologies

---

believing through which I believe a thing to be present that is [in fact] absent. And I claim that this belief-cognition will be abstractive, not intuitive. And through such an act of faith a thing can appear to be present when it is absent."

37. Funkenstein, *Theology and the Scientific Imagination*, especially 135.

38. Ockham, *Quodlibetal Questions*, VI.6; Ockham, *Philosophical Writings*, 26.

extending back to the *Timaeus*: the cosmos forms a *uni*verse. One could only understand a part with reference to the other parts and, ultimately, the whole. For Ockham, by contrast, the parts of the universe were "self-standing" and comprehensible in their singularity. One part could be annihilated without consequence for the remainder. As Funkenstein remarks, while, for Aquinas, God could create other worlds (and thus they are "possible"), each of those worlds forms a coherent whole such that one part belongs intrinsically within that whole. For Ockham, every individual thing is "immediate to God" in such a way that the individuals composing the world we inhabit could be reconfigured in an infinity of possible ways to form possible worlds. Unlike earlier thinkers, Ockham could therefore conceive of possible worlds that are mere re-configurations of the world we inhabit. For Aquinas, this makes little sense. The individuals of this world are constituted in their identity by their very place in the whole. Take them out of that context and they are no longer what they were.

The consequence of Ockham's nominalism and principle of annihilation which concerns us immediately is the notion of "idealized experiments." If individuals are immediate to God and therefore intelligible in their individuality divorced from any wider context within creation, this makes it thinkable to "annihilate" all but those phenomena one wishes to consider. One could therefore conceive of a particular phenomena in nature, say the motion of a body removed from any particular context, and consider only that motion. Thus one can imagine an "idealized" or "pristine" motion which is stripped of any complexity or context. A clear example of such an "ideal" is Isaac Newton's reference to a single body in motion through a vacuum.[39] All other aspects of creation—the context, for example, of motion—have been removed or "annihilated." Newton uses such an "idealized moving body" to formulate his three laws of motion. No such motion has ever pertained, for all "actual" motion that we observe occurs within an intricate context that furnishes it with meaning. For Newton, natural philosophy as represented in the idealized thought experiments of the *Principia Mathematica* is not concerned with the world as it is actually received, but an idealized "possible world" represented by phenomena divorced from their context. In such circumstances, natural philosophy's starting point is not the world as it is encountered, in all

---

39. For a more detailed discussion of Newton's understanding of motion in relation to idealised experiment, see Oliver, *Philosophy, God and Motion*, ch. 6.

its complexity, but an approximation that is but a possibility or "simu-lacrum." It is a "possibility," a construct arrived at through annihilation.

In returning to Cusa, it is possible to see the further importance of this development in relation to the priority of the possible over the actual. For Cusa, it is the eternal simplicity of divine self-knowledge which "measures" our knowledge and ensures its veracity. This is to say that it is the actual which measures the possible. In a natural philosophy that is concerned with idealizations, it is the reverse: the possible measures the actual. For Newton, for example, it was the possible (idealized) motion of a single body in a vacuum that is used as the measure of all actual motions. This in turn can be translated into the method of philosophy of religion that begins with simulacra. An "idealized" possible being, which we name "God," is used to measure and interpret the actual world. Either the simulacrum we call "God" is shown to be a bad measure, in which case it is disposed of in favor of another possibility (certain forms of atheism or scientism), or we alter and nuance the simulacrum so that the world becomes measurable by its standards (fundamentalism). Either way, the possible measures the actual.

Phenomenology and the Possibility of Revelation

Has philosophy attempted to progress from its confinement within ideal possibilities which form approximations to the actuality of the world? Twentieth-century philosophy in the form of phenomenology represents, in part, a wholesale rejection of representational knowledge and an attempt to return to "the things themselves." There is a sense in which this form of philosophy strives to begin with the actuality of the givenness of the world to human consciousness. In a recent essay, Jean-Luc Marion asks whether such an approach to philosophy can offer more to theology, given that the former tends to prioritize conjecture and possibility while the latter concerns actuality.[40] He discusses what he takes to be a core aspect of religion and theology, namely revelation, and asks whether philosophy can at least admit the possibility of revelation. On the face of it, there is a clear difficulty: revelation entails an authority transcending experience manifesting itself experientially. Under the principle of sufficient

40. See Marion, "Possible and Revelation."

reason (Kant's "religion within the limits of mere reason"), Marion concludes that revelation is rendered impossible. Marion states,

> The emergence of the principle of reason forces metaphysics to assign each being its concept and its cause, to the point of dismissing any beings irreducible to a conceptualizable cause as illegitimate and hence impossible. It is therefore no fortuitous coincidence that the thinkers of the *causa sive ratio* also disqualified the possibility of miracles and revelation in general. In this sense, religion remains admissible only by renouncing revelation in the full sense.[41]

This suggests that philosophy of religion will establish the conditions for the possibility of revelation a priori, in advance of revelation's actuality. This neutralizes revelation, for it will subject revelation to established conditions of reason in such a way that it becomes no revelation at all. Once again, we are left discussing chimera or idols. If revelation remains, it does so as moral law or as irrational and fanatical, breaking the conditions of its own possibility.

Marion asks whether the phenomenological method can open the possibility of revelation and thus provide some relationship with theology. However, the Kantian transcendental method, which attempts to delineate "the conditions for the possibility of knowledge," still, for Marion, haunts phenomenology as conceived by Husserl.[42] For Kant, the possibility of knowledge is conditioned by the formal condition of intuition and concepts. This is the lens through which phenomena are received. The world is never received as it actually is, but under the conditions for the possibility of knowledge.[43] Nevertheless, by referring to the sheer "givenness" of phenomena, the Kantian limits of the possible are extended. Genuinely to return to the things themselves means that our intention (that is, what we intend or surmise in the face of a particular experience which marks the limits of the possible) is subsequent to the fact of being given to consciousness, which testifies to the necessity of receiving phenomena as they give themselves, not according to conditions of possibility. So Marion writes, "By thus lifting the prohibition of sufficient reason,

41. Ibid., 2.
42. See Marion, "Saturated Phenomenon."
43. See Kant, *Critique of Pure Reason*, 238 (A218/ B265).

phenomenology liberates possibility and hence opens the field possibly even to phenomena marked by impossibility."[44]

What philosophy of religion tends to close, phenomenology of religion could open.[45] However, Marion suggests that there are still problems with the phenomenological method. Put very briefly, he is concerned that this approach to philosophy continues to establish a horizon, which, while not rendering revelation impossible, will nevertheless subject revelation to "conditions of possibility." He cites two in particular: the *I* and the horizon. The first, the *I*, concerns the method of reduction. Phenomenology involves a reduction of the everyday lived experience of the world towards the intention of a conscious subject—a transcendental subjectivity. Marion's concern is that whatever is received in revelation remains constituted by this "I." In other words, there remains a subject-object relation: the subject constitutes the phenomenological object in such a way that the *I* forms another condition of possibility for revelation. Yet "The I has not the slightest idea, notion, or expectation regarding who or what is revealed."[46] The notion of "reduction" seems to preclude, or at least radically limit, revelation. Similarly, phenomenology, according to Marion, "presupposes a horizon for presenting the phenomena it reduces and constructs."[47] In the case of Heidegger, this horizon is Being under which "God" is thought. Heidegger asserts that "the holy [*das Heilige*], which alone is the essential sphere of divinity, which in turn alone affords a dimension for the gods and for God, [the sacred] comes to radiate only when being itself beforehand and after extensive preparation has been cleared and is experienced in its truth."[48] In other words, God can only be made manifest within a particular space, which is measured by Being rather than by God himself.

We are left, therefore, with phenomenology delineating the possibility of revelation in advance of its actuality, which, according to Marion, in effect neutralizes the possibility of revelation. It renders revelation "impossible" in such a way that revelation takes on an "extrinsicist" character:

44. Marion, "Saturated Phenomena," 5.

45. Ibid., 7.

46. Ibid., 9.

47. Ibid., 10.

48. Heidegger, "Letter on Humanism," 258, cited and quoted in Marion, "Possible and Revelation," 11. Marion remarks that the transcendental method of Rahner is subject to precisely this horizon of Being with respect to revelation.

it arrives "outside" the established conditions of possibility for experience. Under such circumstances, revelation is simply reduced to the bizarre, the weird or the unintelligible.

Marion's answer to this aporia of revelation comes in the form of his concept of the "saturated phenomenon," of which revelation is the most acute kind.[49] Put briefly, a saturated phenomenon can be distinguished from the everyday experience of an ordinary object in the following way. According to Husserl, intention is always in excess of intuition. In other words, I see the mug on my desk from just one of an infinite number of perspectives as the mug gives itself to be known. My intuition is limited by a single perspective. But what I "intend" is the mug in its entirety: its countless uses, the infinite circumstances in which it might be viewed, and so on. This is to say that the object is constituted by the transcendental subject, namely by the intention. By contrast, the saturated phenomenon is the reverse; what is given in intuition exceeds intentionality. The intention which is contributed by the *I* is overwhelmed by what is given by the phenomenon concerned. For example, in viewing Christ dying on the cross what I intend is the execution of a first-century Jewish man; what is given in intuition is the incarnate Son of God dying for the sins of the world. For Marion, the *I* is *constituted by* the saturated phenomenon, whereas in ordinary experience the *I* constitutes the intuited object. To put this is Cusa's terms as discussed above, human knowledge becomes *measured* by the actuality of God's givenness, rather than being the *measure* that constitutes possibility.

This very brief discussion of Marion's position suggests the way in which phenomenology's continued prioritization of the possible and its concomitant inability to think revelation outside of its own conditions of possibility is overcome: philosophy becomes subject to the prior actuality of God's givenness in revelation because, through the saturated phenomenon, revelation establishes its own horizon in constituting the *I* who receives that revelation. In essence, Marion is talking the language of grace with respect to theology and philosophy. However, there remain two concerns. First, revelation has been defined with reference to a particular kind of phenomena, the saturated, and then again a particular kind of saturated phenomena. This leaves behind a residue of so-called "ordinary phenomena" which we might think belong to the philosophical

49. See Marion, *Being Given*, 199–247.

enterprise. Meanwhile, theology deals with a delineated subject matter in the form of revelation understood as a variety of saturated phenomena. Secondly, and related to this first concern, philosophy in the guise of phenomenology remains within the dualism of subject and object; there is always a suspicion that the *I* will in some way continue to mark the horizon of possibility unless the whole of human consciousness, including the reception of ordinary phenomena, is rendered subject to a prior actuality. Can these concerns be assuaged? The division between subject and object is peculiar to modernity and is alien to pre-modern theology. Instead of this dualism, theologians such as Aquinas typically refer to "creatures" and creation. Moreover, as we saw above with respect to idealized "possible" phenomena, creation forms a unity in which each part is constituted by its relation to the whole. There is little sense in which an *I*, as an isolated individual consciousness, can constitute a condition of possibility for the experience of objects in the world. Rather, because the "*I*" is more fundamentally a creature embedded by necessity in creation, it is constituted by the prior actuality of that creation. Moreover, the actuality of that creation is more than any person could imagine. On this view, there is a sense in which all phenomena are, to some degree, saturated. Why? Because what we intuit in *creatures*, rather than *objects*, will always exceed our mere intention because the creature, precisely in being created, always already implies the radical otherness of the creator.

Marion's scheme of the saturated phenomenon distinct from ordinary phenomena leaves with it the sense of an "ordinary nature" that is not graced. There also remains a parallel dualism in the form of subject and object. By reconfiguring this scheme in terms of creation, all phenomena can be described as "saturated" in Marion's sense in such a way that the whole of creation becomes, to some degree, revelatory and in excess of our attempts to grasp it or subject it to *a priori* conditions of knowledge—to possibilities rather than actualities. This becomes more reminiscent of the Cusan scheme described above in which we begin with the actuality of creation as it gives itself to us, *and as it constitutes us by that gift*. That actuality remains in excess of our ability to grasp it, and yet our grasp is not "off the mark" in a way that would suggest skeptical doubt. This entails, however, beginning the philosophical and theological task with *docta ignorantia*: learning that the actuality of creation exceeds us infinitely and yet, in its givenness from an eternally actual source, is the starting point of all our enquiry.

6

Keeping the Faith: Christian Philosophy as a Square Circle and a Wooden Iron

LAURENCE PAUL HEMMING

THE NORTH AMERICAN THEOLOGIAN Thomas Guarino recently posed the question "To what extent can some current modes of secular thought serve as a medium for theological reflection?" Another North American theological thinker, Rusty Reno, making passing reference to John Paul II's encyclical letter *Fides et Ratio*, replies on his behalf to say: "formulating a satisfactory answer is imperative."[1] This essay asks: What can we possibly mean when we say we will "formulate a satisfactory answer"—satisfactory to whom, and by what standard? On what ground will the formulation be made? And who experiences this imperative, and how does it address them, and from whence? Or, turning to Guarino himself, how is "secular thought" to be measured, and by whom? What does it mean to think about thinking in this way? In the statements of both men, thinking is taken as an independent measure of the self who thinks, such that in the first instance, there are different kinds of thought which (might) lie before us, and in the second, any given self can voluntarily choose or adhere to any one or other of these kinds as he or she wills or selects.

1. Reno, citing Guarino, in "Theology's Continental Captivity."

In this trivial moment of journalistic *reportage* all the impasses of theology's contemporary entanglement with philosophy can be seen to be enacted. For we are here teaching, and repeating endlessly, that we will *choose* what is to be thought and how, while at the same time deciding for ourselves (we "clever" theologians) how secularity is to be thought, and so sitting in judgment on what—I can only presume—we think ourselves to be *ourselves* entirely uncontaminated *by*. In this we exhibit the arrogance of the subjectivity of the modern subject, free in all respects with respect to all things, critically distinguishing in this complete freedom between the good and the bad, between right, wrong, good, and evil, as these things fall easily into our hands, and disdaining to very hell all those who do not recognize what we ourselves see so easily; and not heeding, not even once and for a moment, the Dominical command "Judge not, lest you yourselves be judged!" We, who know, know what is best, and that is what we think.

The Encyclical *Fides et Ratio* was itself an extraordinary exercise in thought. For it confessed that thinking itself has a history, *is* historical, and at the same time the Encyclical consistently instrumentalized thinking to the theological and social task. So we learn early on that "the Church can do no other than have a high esteem of the duty of reason in pursuit of those aims through which the life of man is rendered more worthwhile."[2] With this social and historical instrumentality, philosophy is in the Encyclical continually relegated to the task of assisting theology to do its work, even though, we are told, "the Church does not have a philosophy of her own, nor does she select one to the detriment of the others."[3] Philosophy is guided, the Encyclical says, "by a course plotted by reason," and is at the same time and at its best (citing a document of Pope Paul VI's on priestly training, *Optatam Totius*) "a perennially valid philosophical heritage."[4]

The Encyclical attempts to locate this constancy in "the perennial *novitas* of the propositions of St. Thomas Aquinas,"[5] as that one who best synthesizes philosophy and theology into a unity. How to translate that word *novitas*? Newness? Immediacy? Originality? Novelty? What is at

---

2. John Paul II, *Fides et Ratio*, §5.

3. Ibid., §49.

4. Ibid., §49.

5. Cf. ibid., §43.

issue here is a most fundamentally metaphysical thought: at one and the same time what is *latest* and most immediate to the human subject is itself and always *ever-same*, "the" *perenne*, the "everlastingly" and constant—constant presence. Here, we would have to say, constant presence as the *divine* presence. But taken in what way? As philosophical presence? As therefore that which can be reached *de ratione*, rationally? Or is it reached theologically, in respect of faith?

For if John Paul II answers Guarino's and Reno's question—that there is a thinking that "serves as a medium for theological reflection" and that responds to the imperative "that we formulate a satisfactory answer"—the Pope at the same time formulates the answer to the question "why is there an imperative at all, and how does it manifest itself?" in a particular way. The Encyclical characterizes the imperative in the following manner: acknowledging the present crisis which brings the *need* before us in the following (all too historical) terms. There were, says the Pope, "some idealists [who] strove in various ways to transform faith and its elements—even the death and resurrection of Jesus Christ—into dialectical structures" and who, together with those who opposed them (atheists and positivists), provoked a crisis of rationalism, such that "something akin to nihilism has arisen."[6]

The tracing of this crisis to a series of events of the nineteenth century, as the Encyclical in fact does, and to a precise group of thinkers, and so to the historical character of this development of reason itself, fails entirely to illustrate how this history *befell*, and goes on befalling, the humanity whose history it is. The "idealists" in question are in fact none other than the singular Hegel himself. Referring to his system of speculative idealism as the work of a plurality is a mark of the Encyclical's implicit understanding that Hegel did not "initiate" this situation of thought, but was responding to what had already occurred, as an event in being itself.

The intensely voluntaristic language of all the theologians I have quoted so far, including John Paul II, a language of what *must* be done, and what group did what to bring this imperative to the fore, yet brings us all the more sharply up against the imperative itself. For we explain motivations, and we understand actions, not as mere choices (if we really want to understand them), but at the deepest level of the "from whence" individuals themselves *spring* in their thinking, and so as what they

6. Ibid., §46.

understand is in some way *binding* and ineluctable for them. Binding, not just for themselves, but as much for themselves as for those whom they address and who are to hear what they have to say. Binding, therefore, in life as a whole, in thinking through the whole, binding in thinking as such. In acknowledging the historical character of thinking itself, John Paul II already acknowledges the influence of Hegel, perhaps even despite himself, in that it is Hegel who introduces into philosophy its historicality. The historical character of philosophy is not, however, Hegel's "achievement," but rather Hegel's own response to the "crisis of rationalism" to which the Encyclical refers. It is in this respect that we have to attend to, so that we can understand, the "speculative Good Friday," an idea which Hegel introduces with his essay *Faith and Knowing (Glauben und Wissen)* of 1802–03, developed further in the final sentence of the *Phänomenologie* as the "Calvary of absolute Spirit."[7]

Taking up a sentence of Pascal's *Pensées*, that "nature is such that it *indicates* everywhere a God *lost* as much within man as outside man,"[8] Hegel speaks of the "godlessness" (*Gottlösigkeit*—literally, God-losingness, not just the prior absence, but the very departing of God) of the *once* historical, *now* speculative, Good Friday, through which "the highest totality, in its entire earnestness and out of its deepest ground, at the same time can and must rise from the dead in the all-embracing and happiest freedom of its form."[9]

Hegel describes the singularity of finite subjectivity, of what it means to be *living* through the godlessness of "nature" as it passes over dialectically to become absolute spirit, absolute (infinite) *Geist*, subjectivity as such. In this sense, Hegel's is as much a philosophy of "becoming" as Nietzsche's, and on the same metaphysical basis. Hegel argues elsewhere that "God . . . can only be grasped through living,"[10] the very activity of coming into the full happiness of *form (Gestalt)*. We could be tempted, as theologians, to read these passages theologically, and indeed they are in a certain way guided by an understanding of God founded in and driven by the history of Christianity: however, they are above all else a description of a prevailing metaphysics. Nor are they any less philosophical than

7. Hegel, *Phänomenologie des Geistes*, 531. "Schädelstätte des absoluten Geistes."

8. Hegel, *Glauben und Wissen*, 123ff., citing Blaise Pascal, *Pensées*, 441.

9. Ibid., 124.

10. Cited by Heidegger, *Hegels Phänomenologie des Geistes* in *Gesamtausgabe*, 142, citing Hegel, *Hegels theologische Jugendschriften*, 318.

Nietzsche's own proclamation of the death of God, and not less than Nietzsche's own writing do they announce the *end* of metaphysics. In this sense, Hegel writes *from out of* a metaphysical situation, rather than *writes a theological metaphysics.*

How are we to reconcile what I have suggested is a crisis, yielding an imperative, that is best brought to description by Hegel, with John Paul II's perennial philosophy, most exemplified by St. Thomas Aquinas? In St. Thomas's theological thinking there is an orientation to the *all*, the totality of being of the particularity of the individuality, which John Paul II alludes to and presumes in the horizon of *novitas* which he says characterizes the propositions of St. Thomas (and why therefore we should refresh ourselves in them). For St. Thomas the totality of time is made present to God, such that each moment that is had successively for us is simultaneously co-present to the single act of God's being, such that in God they are not differentiated sequentially (even though God knows what sequence they are in for us).

In St. Thomas a doctrine of salvation gets extended *back* from a purely theological discourse (redemption) to a philosophical one—what it means to know particular things, and therefore both what is distinct and what is identical in how *we* (and so each given *I* in his or her particularity) know(s) them when compared with how *God* knows them. St. Thomas concentrates on how the human soul is taken up through the perfection of its intellect, into the divine intellect, in final deiformity (or damnation, but St. Thomas is really here only interested in the redeemed). We should note a parallel with Hegel's concern: not faith and reason so much, but faith and *knowing* (*Wissen*): what it means to *know* in particularity and as absolute knowledge (when we "know as God knows"). St. Thomas interprets the statement of St. John's first letter ("we shall be like him, for we shall see him as he is") in such a way that the redeemed, divinized, and so deiform creature is so, not because he *sees* God, but because he now sees *as God himself sees.*[11]

There is not the time to pursue this adequately now, but Hegel radicalizes a possibility that opens up only with the distinct configuration of God and the self in Descartes' account of subjectivity, which at the same time explains Pascal's own position (on the absence of God in nature and in the subject). For whereas for Aquinas the soul is always perfected

11. Cf. Aquinas, *Summa Theologiae*, Sup., Q. 92, art. 1, corp.

through, in, and by the world—and so, strictly speaking, there is no "interior" (ideal) subjectivity—in Hegel the assimilation of the particularity of the subject into absolute spirit *as* the movement of time is the way in which particular, specified "times" (the countable moment, Aristotle's τὸ νῦν) are *through the very activity of living* synthesized to absolute time which is at the same time the totality of time *as* infinity. Here the godlessness of nature is "sublated" by infinity itself.

Martin Heidegger notes in this respect that for Hegel (and in direct contradistinction to Heidegger's own thought in *Being and Time*) "being is the essence of time, being that is, *qua* infinity."[12] This genealogy, from Descartes through Pascal to Hegel is central in any understanding that the "crisis of rationalism" named by John Paul II is in fact far wider-reaching that simply an effect of German Idealism in the nineteenth century. At the same time, what Hegel describes is the very befalling of the imperative: it is how history befalls the humanity whose history it is. For the movement of spirit into absolute spirit is at the same time the overcoming of the dread "earnest" of suffering, and so of the very interiorization of the effect of godlessness in a nature evacuated of God. This is the emergence in its very *self* of the pressing *imperative* of the method of doubt *as* an imperative. The method of doubt is methodologically *necessitated by* the present situation of the being of being human.

Descartes states at the very opening of his *Principles of Philosophy* that "it is necessary for the one seeking the truth, once in his life—insofar as he is able—to doubt all things,"[13] This "it is necessary," although asserted on the basis of Descartes' commitment to method, nevertheless should be heard with the full force of the imperative we heard at the beginning of the paper, and which I have been seeking to bring to description all the way through. Descartes says that it is not possible to know what *is needed to be known* (it is not possible to take knowledge into certainty—one might paraphrase St. Thomas here by saying, "know as God knows") without already once having doubted: doubt is the precursor of the securing of what is binding for man *as binding*. It is this binding-character of the present situation which Reno, Guarino, John Paul II, and everyone else has been after from the start. Descartes adds "indeed the

---

12. Heidegger, *Hegels Phänomenologie des Geistes* (GA32), 209.

13. Descartes, *Principiorum philosophiæ* in Descartes, René, *Œuvres publiées*, vol. 8, 5.

doubtful should be considered false."[14] From the very outset, therefore, Descartes takes up a position which is not world-indicating, but world-denying—world-effacing—in order to establish what is "most certain and easy to know": what is therefore binding.[15] What is most certain and easy to know, however—even while supposing "that there be no God and that there are no bodies, and even were we ourselves not to have . . . indeed any body at all"[16]—is the cognition that "*ego cogito, ergo sum* is of all things the first and most certain."[17] This securing of the self, as then secured by God, makes possible the securing of (the) world. Only a self and a world made Godless could be secured on this ground, but the tragic aspect, the baleful misery (the speculative Good Friday of the place of the skull, this Calvary-in-general) is "made happy" by sublating the world *to* the infinite. Sublation (*aufheben*) means at one and the same time uplifting, fulfilling, preserving and at the same time *cancelling*—the *negation* of the particular in its assimilation to the infinite: Hegel's analogue of St. Thomas's solution to the problem of time in God, but understood from *within* the being of being human.

If we return to the notion of godlessness as it is raised by Pascal, inasmuch as we trace it to Cartesian philosophy, we would be better and more historically accurate to understand it arising from out of the same ground of which Descartes himself also argues. For the origins of Pascal's claim have more to do with the debates in and around the consequences of Suárez's metaphysics as foundational—more so than Aquinas's, to the present *philosophical* situation. Heidegger's own comparison of Aquinas and Suárez in a 1929 lecture argues that "for the development of modern metaphysics . . . Aquinas, and Medieval philosophy in the sense of High Scholasticism, are important only to a lesser extent . . . direct influence was exercised by the Spanish Jesuit Franz Suárez."[18] A central argument of Suárez, himself developing the interpretation of Aquinas he received at the hands of Cajetan, was the existence of a "pure nature" apart from God, on which God can choose to act.

14. Ibid.
15. Ibid.
16. Ibid., 7.
17. Ibid.
18. Heidegger, *Die Grundbegriffe der Metaphysik*, 77.

The *philosophical* elucidation of a nature apart from God on the one hand, and a nature which can be reclaimed into God on the other, proceeds in not one, but two directions, which arise on the basis of the *same* metaphysical ground—the "godlessness" of philosophy. Again the issue here is not who "thinks up" or "does" philosophy in a particular way, but rather what *befalls* philosophical thinking (how humans think *despite* ourselves, in any given historical epoch)—and in what sense the imperative that has persisted with us since the beginning of this paper manifests itself as a *demand*. It is here that we can see emerge what can be called a "Christian philosophy," as the counter-movement to "materialism," "secularity," and every form of the proclamation of the death of God which itself functions as a way of describing the whole of being. This "Christian philosophy"—of which Hegel's is only the highest form—is the Christian "believer's" response to all that culminates in the West with first Hegel's own, and then Nietzsche's, proclamation of the death of God.

Nietzsche (and Marx) in this sense invert Hegel, while taking up the godlessness of which he speaks and first brings to a full metaphysical description. It is the *same* godlessness, however—that radical de-divinization of nature and man alike that we can trace at least as far back as Suárez (and some have even attributed to Socrates and Protagoras).[19] This godlessness, flight of the gods, call it what you will, at one and the same time transforms a mere and ordinary word found frequently in St. Thomas, *'naturaliter,' 'natura'* ("the" natural, naturally), into a *technical* term of thinking. In the wake of godlessness something like "nature as a whole," "nature as such," and "human nature" are brought into being as regions of specification and enquiry: we would have to say, as objects. Brought into being does not simply mean "are": being as a whole is also denoted here. With respect to being as a whole the imperative demand that the object-character that the terms "nature" and "human nature" *make*, indeed *press* and *force* on us, has to be understood: something *has* to be resolved in a new way that was *as yet unresolved*, and out of a situation that both *did not pertain before* and at the same time can be widely seen *now* (and so to *have emerged*). Widely seen really means "experienced": what "befalls us," despite ourselves.

By "experienced" I therefore mean again what I spoke of earlier as "what is binding for man in thinking." The essence of rationalism has

19. Although for a discussion of the accusation of atheism in the latter, see Hemming, *Postmodernity's Transcending*, 210ff.

been a kind of ahistoricism, which manifests itself in claims like "one and one equals two in all possible worlds and at all possible times," or that the law of the excluded middle is a *necessary* truth of thinking. Arithmetical "truths" of this kind are easy to "prove" and so "experience" as binding. The sillier aspects of recent postmodern attempts to question this binding-character even in arithmetic, however, do point to something deeper.[20] The formula "one plus one equals two" is only a *formula*: that it *is* recognizably binding does not explain *why* or *how* it is binding, and yet the Greeks, for instance, knew that there was a "why" and a "how" (and that there is a "why" and a "how" does not mean the "consensus is broken" or that the binding-character is lessened, despite even Wittgenstein's claims on this point).[21] The law of the excluded middle is a metaphysical position which, as such, can at least be enquired into. This does not make arithmetical truths somehow contingent or relative, but it does show them to have a history, that they are part of the being-historical of man. It is precisely in this light that Hegel's own "Logic" has to be understood. Moreover, Hegel's description of dialectical reasoning is illustrative of the extent to which arithmetic can be understood to have an ontological basis, in this case grounded in the transcendent structures of the subjectivity of the subject. The dialectical interpretation of the "principle of identity" where A=A is negated to mean A=*not*-A because A overcomes A, and so A comes to be (be-comes) more than A, and yet remains in some sense determined *from out of* A is precisely the connection between the supposedly merely copulative "is" of A *is* A, but now thought as a *temporal* determination. A exceeds A means, in being A (in being *known* as A), inasmuch as A *is*, it *is, with respect to (the) infinite.*

Put another way, inasmuch as A, knowledge of A yields: *that there is infinity.* This is not mere postmodern trickery: precisely not. It is the binding character, the so-called "experiential" "proof" of life and being. At the very end of Hegel's *Phänomenologie*, we find Hegel asserting: "the nature, moments and movement of this knowing have thus resulted in this, that it is the pure being-for-itself of self-consciousness; it is I . . . this and no other I."[22] Therefore "it must on this basis be said, that nothing comes to be known [*gewußt*] as existing, which is not in *experience*, or

20. See for instance the chapter on Kristeva in Sokal and Bricmont, *Intellectual Impostures*, 37–47.

21. Wittgenstein, *Bemerkungen über die Grundlagen der Mathematik*, 37ff.

22. Hegel, *Phänomenologie des Geistes*, 523.

as it might also be expressed, which is not *felt* to be true, as an inwardly revelatory eternity, as sacralities from the exercise of faith, or whatever other expressions are required."[23] It is what, after Hegel (the "after" being heard in the widest possible sense, thus, even through his inversions in Nietzsche, Marx, and so forth) makes all philosophies of becoming possible.

The inversions of the metaphysical situation that emerge from this comportment to the newly found *thingliness* and object-character of "nature" arise out of the *single* event of the absence and departure, the closure, of the divine. Faith, taken up into metaphysics, means figuring the divine in the being that I am (the living being that I am). I *manifest* dialectically the being of absolute subjectivity in specific subjectivity, in the subjectivity of my own subject.

Why is it that Hegel calls his principal work a *phenomenology* of *Geist*? We see that the proper object of the enquiry is the self, but the self taken in a particular way. Thus what appears, the phenomenon, is not what actually *is* but rather what indicates the being of something else: the infinite. It is the *being* (living) "here" of the absolute concept ("there"), of absolute self-consciousness for itself. What appears does so for the sake of making manifest something that it itself is *not*, that is to say something that is other than itself, whilst at the same time manifesting what it is not in virtue of what lies already *in* what is not as what is *really* to be seen in what is manifest "here and now." Thus this is a phenomenology only insofar as it makes what the self in its self-appearing appears *for*, which is the immutable and permanently self-subsisting, the absolute concept as such, *being*. Hegel says that "being no longer has the significance of the abstraction of being"[24] but as "rest [is] of itself as absolute-restless infinitude" where the "differentiation of movement is resolved . . . the simple essence of time which in its itself-self-sameness has the pure form of space."[25] The pure absolute strictly speaking has no time, but *as* time, or "temporalized," it gives time to the appearances. It is the condition for the differentiation that movement *is* itself (A=A to A=/A such that A overcomes the A that it is). Thus the movement in question turns out at the same time to be the movement of all phenomenal (i.e., appearing) things,

---

23. Ibid., 525.
24. Ibid., 123.
25. Ibid., 123 f.

and the movement in which the self actually knows *it*self and so in some sense also *is*.

We are accustomed to understand Hegel as an up-building, a constructive straining forward for an infinite horizon. Here, however, we see that what in fact allows the straining-forth, the constructive activity of the dialectic to undertake the work of becoming, is the way that motion unfolds not as a forward-moving, but as it were, *backwards* so that the phenomenal appearances disclose something which is already-there, already present, and so strictly speaking ("ideally") "already present," and as an "already" is *past*. The striving forwards that is the self proceeding from consciousness into self-consciousness is the proceeding forwards down this passageway of the *transcendens*. In fact, however, the proceeding forwards is towards, and in synthesis of, the making-apparent of what is already there, being *as* the absolute concept. In this sense, the synthesizing processes of sublation appear to proceed, but actually operate in the manner of receipt, i.e., they operate backwards. The essential structure of the motion is, therefore, circular—which is why it is possible for the direction of the motion to be mistaken: it only *appears* to be a forward motion in becoming, it *really is* a backward motion in making becoming, the appearability of what as appearance is only appearance *for*, appearance *of*, being as such. To lay down a marker for a conclusion I have not yet written for this paper, it is this problematic character of the order of motion of the appearances that has turned me again and again to the question of analogy and the so-called *analogia entis*.

Although there is not the space to show why, in fact this is properly and strictly in accord with the peculiar temporal structure of the *cogito* which Descartes develops in the *Meditationes*. The *cogito* secures itself as finite substance *against* what it doubts, and then proceeds to secure itself upon what is already *infinitely* there, and so already lying present. Thought, for Descartes and for Hegel, stretches forward to discover and so disclose—which means give appearance to, allow to appear phenomenally—what is already *prior* in its presence: God. It is for this reason that Heidegger is able to say with absolute correctness that "For Hegel the formerly, the *past*, constitutes the essence of time" and "for Hegel being (infinity) is also the essence of time."[26] In fact both Nietzsche's "will to power," as not the "willing of a subject" but rather the willing *from out of*

26. Heidegger, *Hegels Phänomenologie des Geistes* (GA32), 211.

which subjectivity appears at all, and Marx's "end" of history each operates from out of precisely the *same* temporal metaphysics, made possible only in the wake of the Cartesian subject, where inasmuch as time discloses the whole of being, "being is the essence of time."

The very tracing of the genealogy of this understanding of the movement of subjectivity into (absolute) spirit as the annihilation of the particular for the sake of the all is itself a prevailing metaphysical situation, an imperative that (for Hegel) befalls present humanity. In this genealogy, however, we can also see how it becomes possible to move beyond the voluntaristic language of "what Hegel did," or how we avoid the trap of judging for ourselves "to what extent can some current modes of secular thought serve as a medium for theological reflection?" (and thus avoid congratulating ourselves for having "formulated a satisfactory answer") so that we can understand the extent to which Hegel himself provides us with a genuine phenomenology, a formal indication of being in its appearances. This genuine phenomenology, this description of how things manifest themselves, also shows how what Hegel describes prevails even now (even in places where Hegel is no longer read or where no direct influence of his could be traced) such that what he describes performs and refigures—to use Hegel's own word, 'lives'—the movement Hegel himself describes.

I do not wish to trace the complexities of the commentary of Henri Cardinal de Lubac in this debate between grace, nature, and the "supernatural," for once again and for the most part, they are motivated by an essentially theological concern. What does interest me, however, for the relationship between philosophy and theology, is how a certain reading of de Lubac, which would consider itself to be quite uninfluenced by Hegel, unfolds in the very way Hegel describes.

The Catholic theologian Hans Urs von Balthasar makes the claim that de Lubac's work is to be interpreted from a suspended place "in which he could not practice any philosophy without its transcendence into theology, but also no theology without its essential inner substructure of philosophy."[27] This perpetual collapse of theology into philosophy is then driven to its most extreme form by John Milbank in his recent small book on de Lubac.[28] And yet Milbank only pushes to an extreme

27. Balthasar, *Henri de Lubac*, 12.
28. Cf. Milbank, *Suspended Middle*, 39ff.

what can without doubt be found as a tendency in de Lubac's own work, consistent with a view de Lubac himself expressed.

De Lubac, in attempting to describe the relationship between theology and philosophy, concluded (in an article from 1936): "Every philosopher of today, provided he be perspicacious enough to pass beyond positivism and enter truly into philosophy, is, whether he wishes it or not, and perhaps in just proportion to his perspicacity, a Christian philosopher."[29] Milbank cannot resist accusing de Lubac of being to a certain extent incoherent on the relationship between grace and nature, and yet he describes de Lubac's understanding of the relation between the two thus: "If creation implies both autonomous being and entirely heteronomous gift, while grace implies a raising of oneself *as* oneself to the *beyond* oneself, then the natural desire of the supernatural implies the dynamic link between the order that constitutes spirit, such that this link is at once entirely an aspect of the Creation and entirely also the work, in advance of itself, of grace which unites human creatures to the Creator."[30]

Milbank's presentation of an understanding where there really never is a "pure nature" because it is always sublated into unity with the Creator (into the infinite) both describes the dialectical movement of Hegel's thought and—"crucially" (as Milbank himself might say)—*evacuates* any notion of a "pure nature" (either as world or the being of being human) of Divine presence. But the evacuation of divine presence from "nature" is precisely what precipitated the *imperative* of the dialectical movement in the first place—which, I would suggest, posits the possibility of the *repetition of the dialectic*, both as the infinite proceeding of the particular into the infinite, and as an endless, one might (provocatively) say "eternal," recurrence of the *same*—the same *as* dialectical structure *in itself* (what in Descartes we would identify as the "mathematical"). Dialectical reason *as* constant presence.

In speaking of Milbank, von Balthasar, and de Lubac, I do not intend to single any of the three out—it would be entirely possible to trace this structure at work in any number of other twentieth-century and contemporary theologians. My point is that they exhibit in an exemplary way the metaphysics that prevails in almost all dogmatic or systematic theology at the present time—this is how the "imperative" befalls those given the

29. de Lubac, "Sur la philosophie chrétienne," esp. 251.
30. Cf. Milbank, *Suspended Middle*, 39. Emphasis original.

gift of faith. More sharply put: this is the meaning of John Paul II's assertion of the *novitas*—the immediate temporal horizon—of the imperative, for a (correct) interpretation of St. Thomas forces the understanding of Thomas into a present godlessness, which he himself would have been unable to bear.

It is here that I wish to explain, to some extent at least, my own motivation. For Martin Heidegger's response to Hegel's "being is the essence of time" was, in speaking of Hegel in relation to his work *Being and Time*, to argue "therefore the thesis: *The essence of being is time*—is the exact opposite of that which Hegel sought to demonstrate in the whole of his philosophy."[31] However, the reverse in question is not *simply* a reversal, in the manner of Marx and Nietzsche (an inversion), for although Heidegger speaks frequently throughout his philosophical work of the "godlessness of philosophy"[32] (and especially in relation to the history of philosophy after St. Thomas Aquinas and up until Kant), the imperative which he believes to have befallen *philosophy itself* is not the degree to which it can be put into the service of theologians such that "a current modes of secular thought can serve as a medium for theological reflection," but rather to ask all over again and make thematic the question of being, as a question about beings as a whole, the "all." This very questioning, received as an imperative, separating God and being, "requires wholly new distinctions and delimitations."[33]

It is here that I want, as a theologian, to sound caution. The title of my paper, as may already be familiar, is taken from Martin Heidegger's 1927 lecture *Phenomenology and Theology*,[34] in a figure he repeated in his 1935 lecture course *Introduction to Metaphysics*, where he says that "a 'Christian Philosophy' is a wooden iron and a misunderstanding,"[35] and five years later when he says "square and circle are at least compatible in that they are both geometrical figures, while Christian faith and philosophy remain fundamentally different."[36] In addressing what is said

31. Heidegger, *Hegels Phänomenologie des Geistes* (GA32), 209.

32. Cf. Heidegger, *Geschichte der Philosophie von Thomas von Aquin bis Kant*, 7.

33. Heidegger, *Seminare*, 437.

34. Cf. Heidegger, *Phänomenologie und Theologie* in *Wegmarken*, 66.

35. Heidegger, *Einführung in die Metaphysik*, 6. "Eine 'christliche Philosophie' ist ein hölzernes Eisen und ein Mißverständnis." This is often translated as "a square circle," a figure more familiar to English speakers.

36. Heidegger, *Nietzsche II*, 132.

here as in some sense a novelty, we would do well to be reminded (as Mark Jordan does indeed remind us) that "for [St.] Thomas, membership in a school of philosophy does not befit Christians. [. . .] Thomas speaks about philosophy, of course, as a habit of knowing necessary for an educated believer [. . .] I cannot find that the epithet *philosophus* is ever applied by Thomas to a Christian."[37]

37. Jordan, *Alleged Aristotelianism*, 6. For the repetition of the point, see Jordan, *Rewritten Theology*, 169, passim.

7

Theology and Legal Theory

DAVID McILROY

Introduction

JOHN MILBANK'S AUDACIOUS BOOK *Theology and Social Theory*[1] challenged us to think of theology as social theory, criticizing secular social theories and exposing the ontologies of violence, the assumptions
of original discord, which lie at their heart. One can perhaps imagine a
parallel volume entitled *Theology and Historical Theory*, taking on historical materialism, the Whig view of history, and other secular historical
metanarratives and contrasting them with Christian understandings of
the purpose and unfolding of history. But what about the idea of *theology
as legal theory?*

The relationship between theology and law has long been recognized as important, yet potentially antagonistic. As long ago as the twelfth
century, Stephen of Tournai said: "the theologian and the lawyer . . . have
different preferences, for one delights in what is bitter, the other in what is
sweet. If I write about the law the theologian will be displeased. If I write
about theology, the lawyer will tear his hair. They must make allowances

---

1. Milbank, *Theology and Social Theory.*

for one another."[2] Nonetheless, as John Witte points out: "law and religion stand in a dialectical harmony, constantly crossing over and cross-fertilizing each other."[3]

The relationship between theology and legal theory is explored in this paper which asks three questions:

1. Is theology legal theory?

2. If not, is it nonetheless the case that Christian theology has a legal theory?

3. What is the relationship between Christian theology's legal theory and the philosophy of law?

Is Theology Legal Theory?

Milbank's claim that theology is sociology is based on his assertion that Christian ecclesiology is true sociology. Also weight bearing in his claims for ecclesiology is Milbank's account of the Eucharist as participation in atonement.[4] Can a Christian theology be identified in which legal theory is similarly intrinsic to the theological project? Not in the East, in which the predominant motif for sin is that of sickness, and therefore salvation is about being made well as a consequence of the actions of the Great Healer.

But what of the West? Paul's letters to the Romans and the Galatians speak a lot about Law, and if Paul is read as giving penal substitutionary atonement pride of place that might lead to us concluding that the particular brand of Reformed theology which asserts penal substitutionary atonement as its test of orthodoxy offers us theology as legal theory, a theology which is inextricable from and inexorably an outworking of the legal theory which is at its heart.

And yet, we should pause before we draw such a conclusion too quickly. Stephen Holmes pointed out in a recent article in the *Scottish Journal of Theology* that penal substitutionary atonement in its theological, as opposed to its caricatured, forms, depends primarily not on an understanding of law, but on claims about God as gracious and loving.[5]

2. Stephen of Tournai, *Die Summa des Stephanus*, 1.

3. Witte, *God's Joust*, 458.

4. Milbank, "Second Difference," 226, 232; *Being Reconciled*, 41, 154.

5. Holmes, "Can Punishment Bring Peace?" 112.

Given that God is loving and given that God is righteous, God chose to act in Christ to reconcile the world to God through the atoning death of Christ. A God who cared merely about the absolute moral law could cheerfully condemn the whole human race to hell.

Augustine, in the *Enchiridion*, presents us with the problem in these terms:

> Would it not have been just that such a being who rebelled against God, who in the abuse of his freedom spurned and transgressed the command of his Creator when he could so easily have kept it, . . . who by an evil use of his free-will broke away from his whole-some bondage to the Creator's laws—would it not have been just that such a being should have been wholly and to all eternity deserted by God and left to suffer the everlasting punishment he had so richly earned? God would certainly have done so, if he had been only just and not also merciful. He intended that his unmerited mercy should shine forth the more brightly in contrast with the unworthiness of its objects.[6]

Atonement, however understood, therefore depends on the Christian claim that God is, fundamentally, love. Theology reduced to legal theory is not Christian theology; it is no longer an enquiry into the nature of the Christian God. A theology whose fundamental presupposition is about certain laws in the universe might lead to Deism, to a blind watchmaker God; it might lead you to believe in the Auditors of Reality of whom Terry Pratchett writes in his *Discworld* novels;[7] it might lead you to the affirmation of *karma*,[8] but it would not lead you to exploring and reflecting upon the mystery of the Christian God.

We turn then to the second question: if Christian theology is not fundamentally legal theory is it nonetheless true that Christian theology has a legal theory?

Does Theology Have a Legal Theory?

The answer to this question is yes. Christian theology does have a legal theory, or to be more precise, a legal theory is part of the best and most

6. Augustine, *Enchiridion*, ch. 27.

7. The Auditors of Reality appear in Pratchett's *Reaper Man*, *Hogfather*, and *Thief of Time*.

8. O'Donovan, *Ways of Judgment*, 113.

comprehensive systematic theologies.[9] Both the narrative of Scripture and the theological questions raised within it force reflection on the relationship between Christianity and law. This is evident not just from the atonement, but also in terms of Christianity's understanding of the meaning of the Torah, creation, the Fall, and the Last Judgment.

Torah

Every theologian attentive to the Bible has to form a view as to the proper relationship between the Hebrew Scriptures and the New Testament and hence between the Torah and the teaching and work of Jesus. Christianity would not be what it is without Moses and the tradition that gave Judaism and Christianity the Torah. Christianity and its relationship to the Law of Moses is at the heart of the gospels and the New Testament epistles. As we can see from the book of Acts, the precise nature of that relationship has been both controversial and problematic even since the early Church. Every Christian theologian has to decide what to do with the Torah, and even the decision to ignore it is a significant decision. Whether they reach a wholly negative conclusion about law like Marcion and Nygren[10] or a wholly positive conclusion like the theonomists, or one of the more mainstream views on the relationship,[11] the intrinsic connection between the two Testaments means that the theologian's choice has important ramifications.

The Torah is, however, only one of a number of moments in salvation history where theological issues and questions of law overlap or seem to arise together.

Creation

In the Genesis narrative, God gave Adam and Eve a commandment in the Garden (Gen 2:17). Being related to God and, as God's rational creatures,

---

9. Strauss has similarly argued that "an understanding of the nature and place of law within human society" is a "general philosophical concern," in "Justice, legal validity," 65–66.

10. Nygren, *Agape and Eros.*

11. For a selection of such possibilities, including the theonomist approach, see Strickland et al., *Five Views on Law and Gospel.*

capable of conscious response to God, human beings are subject to God's commands. This is a basic feature of our being. There are important nuances to how this is understood. Is it best to think of these commands in terms of natural law? And, if so, is natural law "an intuitive sense of what is right and wrong, just or unjust, divinely implanted in men's hearts" or "a divine law inscribed in the very nature and structure of the universe in such a way that it can, in part, be read off by the minds of rational creatures?"[12]

Are alternative descriptions preferable? Should we talk in terms of creation ethics, instead of natural law, in order to make it clear that rather than starting with the world and seeking to derive moral imperatives just from the way the world is, we start with God's revelation and in the light of that look at God's creation and seek to identify "moral imperatives that are both divine commands and also good sense?"[13] Or should we adopt Bonhoeffer's suggestion and speak about the divine mandates, thereby holding a balance between creation and culture?[14]

There are nuances here, and the nuances have importance both at the level of systematic theology—how we understand God's law to be given in creation relates to our doctrine of the economic Trinity—and at the level of practical theology—the way in which God's law is understood to be given in creation will affect the ways in which Christians present their arguments about ethical and political questions in the public square. We will return to these questions in the final section of this paper.

Fall

Closely related to questions about how the natural law is given by God in creation are questions about the extent to which human beings' ability to discern God's law has been affected by the Fall. In addition to that question, there are also questions about the nature of the Fall itself. Is the curse of death that afflicts humanity the natural consequence of human beings' disobedience to God or is it an actively imposed divine penalty? Does the law of sin and death operate as a natural law, like the laws of motion, which move the planets through the space, or is it a divinely pronounced

12. Anderson, *Law, Liberty & Justice*, 16.
13. Barclay, "The Nature of Christian Morality," 129.
14. Lovin, *Christian Faith*, 131; Bonhoeffer, *Creation and Fall*.

judgment? What does either answer, and the complicated variations on each, say about understandings of God's grace and God's wrath?

Atonement

How does the death of Christ relate to God's law and human laws? There is a sharp intersection between the two at the cross. The chief priest pronounces Jesus guilty of blasphemy (Matt 26:65; Mark 14:64) but Pilate declares Him innocent of any crime (Matt 27:19-24). Jesus bears the curse of those who broke God's law (Deut 21:23; Gal 3:13) but is vindicated by His resurrection from the dead (Acts 5:30; Rom 4:25; Eph 1:20). The relationship between the law and the cross is perplexing and paradoxical.

I have already indicated that penal substitutionary atonement sees the death of Christ in legal terms.[15] But ideas of law, understood as the order that God has given to the world, are present in older theories of the atonement too. For both Athanasius and Anselm, it would be unthinkable that God's redemption of the world should be anything other than a restoration of God's ordering of the universe God has created. "For Athanasius universal order would be undermined if God went back on his word concerning the consequences of human sin: 'you must not eat from the tree of the knowledge of good and evil, for when you eat of it you will surely die' (Gen 2:17). For Anselm universal order would be undermined if God did not act to maintain and satisfy his own honor."[16]

The Last Judgment

Questions about the nature of the Last Judgment are inextricably linked to visions of Heaven and Hell. The nature and duration of Hell, the existence of purgatory, and the possibility of universal salvation are all bound up with the model of the Last Judgment we adopt. Is God's final judgment pure retributivism, paying back sinners without mercy for the evil they have done to others? Is the final judgment God bringing to light the truth of human lives, the cumulative effect of a lifetime of choices either for God and others or for ourselves?

15. This need not be the overarching narrative, however; see McIlroy, "Towards a Relational and Trinitarian Theology of Atonement."

16. Colwell, *Living the Christian Story*, 94–95.

Can we reason from certain practices of human judgment, be it retributive, rehabilitative or restorative, to divine judgment by means of a variation of the *analogia entis*? If we reason by analogy from penal retributivism, does that lead to seeing God as a wrathful God administering a judgment by works? If we reason by analogy from rehabilitation does that result in the doctrine of purgatory? Where does restorative justice take us? Does it lead to universalism, to purgatory, to both, or does it make a restored relationship with God in Christ the basis of the Last Judgment?

Or, is God's judgment wholly different from human judgment, as Moltmann suggests in *The Coming of God*?[17] What degree of equivocation is appropriate in speaking of God's judgment by reference to human judgments?

The Elephant Trap: Seeing State Law, Biblical Law, and God's Law in Unequivocal Terms

Reflecting on the Last Judgment raises a question which we need to be alert to throughout our examination of law as a motif in the Bible. Most of the time, the Bible is not talking about state law as we know it. Such law is to be found in the edicts of Nebuchadnezzar and Pharaoh and in the decrees of the Persian and Roman empires. Most of the time, however, the Bible is concerned with the *Torah*, and that is not primarily state law but rather a moral code, a way of life.

Joan Lockwood O'Donovan opens her *Theology of Law and Authority in the English Reformation* with the claim that "From a theological perspective, it is arguable that all public disagreement is about authority and law, divine and human, whatever may be the ostensible issues."[18] Because of their common reference to ideas such as "law," "justice," and "authority," it would be easy to assume that academic theology and jurisprudence were talking about the same thing. The reality is, however, that as George Bernard Shaw once commented about the relationship between Britain and America, theology and law are two countries divided by a common language. To give just one example of this, Bernard S. Jackson and Jonathan Burnside have demonstrated that what Israelites in the millennium

---

17. Moltmann, *Coming of God*, 142, 250.

18. Lockwood O'Donovan, *Theology of Law*, 1.

before Christ understood by Torah and how it functioned is radically different from the Roman and mediaeval understandings of law.[19]

It seems to me that there are grave dangers of distorting the message of the Bible if we proceed from a particular understanding of law and punishment and use that as the grid through which we read the Bible. Doing so, in effect, sets up that particular theory of law and punishment as the canon, the measure of what God's justice *must* look like. Instead, theological reasoning should proceed from the vision of God and of God's justice revealed in Scripture and use that to inform and reform theories of law and punishment.[20]

It should be clear from the preceding discussion the extent to which questions relating to law are raised by attention to salvation history. It should also be clear that answering those questions will provide a lot of the material for articulating a Christian theory of law. We turn now to consider our third question: the relationship between theology's legal theory and the philosophy of law.

What Is the Relationship Between Christian Theology's Legal Theory and the Philosophy of Law?

There are at least five thinkers whose thought would be worthy of sustained attention at this point. Luther's Reformation effected not just a religious but a legal revolution, explored in detail by John Witte in *Law and Protestantism*.[21] John Calvin's training as a lawyer is evident in both the structure and the substance of his theology. In relation to both Luther and Calvin it would be instructive to draw out from their theologies the approach to law that is inherent in them.

I want, however, to look at two other Christian thinkers whose theories of law are not merely closely integrated with their theology but are in fact made explicit. The two thinkers are the Dutch neo-Calvinist Herman Dooyeweerd and the Dominican friar, Thomas Aquinas. Had space

19. Burnside, *Signs of Sin*; Burnside, "Criminal Justice," 237; Jackson *Studies in the Semiotics of Biblical Law.*

20. I regard Jonathan Burnside's work on restorative justice as exemplary in this field. See Burnside and Baker, *Relational Justice.* Another thought-provoking interpretation of justice from the Christian perspective is Marshall's *Beyond Retribution.*

21. Witte, *Law and Protestantism.*

permitted I might also have examined the thought of Hugo Grotius as a third example.

Herman Dooyeweerd

Herman Dooyeweerd's greatest achievement was his systematic Christian philosophy. Dooyeweerd's philosophy of law, expounded in his *Encyclopedia of the Science of Law*, is but one aspect of his comprehensive and explicitly Christian philosophy.[22] Both mainstream legal theory and theology have had trouble digesting Dooyeweerd. Legal theory's difficulty with Dooyeweerd is that his is an explicitly Christian philosophy. Dooyeweerd makes it plain at the outset that it is founded on the central meta-narrative of creation, fall into sin, and redemption by Jesus Christ in the communion of the Holy Spirit.[23] He maintained that "The central theme of the Word-revelation, [is] that of creation, fall into sin, and redemption by Jesus Christ in the communion of the Holy Spirit. And it is this very core of the divine Revelation which alone reveals the true root and center of human life. It is the only key to true self-knowledge."[24] Theology's difficulty is different in nature. It arises from Dooyeweerd's denial that he was doing theology at all and from his insistence that theology was only one discipline of thought among many and did not enjoy a privileged position.

Dooyeweerd's philosophy claims first that positive state law, whether made by legislators or by judges, is a manifestation of what he calls the "juridical aspect" of reality, one of the fourteen or fifteen aspects of reality which can be theoretically distinguished but which are God-given and which co-inhere in the real world.[25] In speaking in such a way, Dooyeweerd has already made a key philosophical choice, to regard state law

---

22. Sadly only one volume of Dooyeweerd's five volume *Encyclopedia of the Science of Law* has been translated into English so far and the *Encyclopedia* itself does not fully incorporate all the insights of Dooyeweerd's mature thought. Even more problematic, the volume which has been published has been the subject of a sustained criticism as to the adequacy of its translation by Friesen, "Dooyeweerd's *Encyclopedia of the Science of Law*." Online: http://www.members.shaw.ca/hermandooyeweerd/Translation.pdf.

23. Dooyeweerd, *Encyclopedia of the Science of Law,* 1:47–49, 58–61; *In The Twilight of Western Thought*, 35, 41, 64, 111, 125, 136, 144, 186.

24. Dooyeweerd, *In The Twilight of Western Thought*, 186.

25. Dooyeweerd, *Encyclopedia of the Science of Law,* 1:13–21.

as exhibiting significant continuities with privately made rules, such as those of families, clubs, and churches, which make it proper to consider them under the same category. There is therefore something in common between the Torah, *nomos*, as spoken of in both Testaments, and the rules and regulations adopted by contemporary polities. Importantly, faith is identified by Dooyeweerd as another one of these aspects of reality.

Second, Dooyeweerd insists at the outset of his *Encyclopedia* that the aspects are abstractions and subtractions from reality, they are devices adopted for the purpose of theory. Because what we are theorizing about is reality, however, it is not possible to think only about the juridical aspect of reality without regard to its other aspects. On the contrary, when looking at reality from the perspective of the juridical aspect it is necessary to have regard to such of the other aspects of reality as are relevant in the particular case in question.[26] Because reality is seamless, theoretical thought in one discipline must always take account of the implications of theoretical thought in other disciplines.

Third, it follows from what has been said above that it is not enough to relate legal theory solely to the other aspects of reality which appear immediately to our senses or proximately when we reflect. Legal theory must be related ultimately to God, and it is not enough to offer a merely generic theistic grounding for legal theory, it is imperative to relate legal theory to the actions of the God who has revealed Godself in Christ Jesus.

Nonetheless, Dooyeweerd argues, the relationship between Christian philosophy or legal theory and God's self-revelation is not via theology.[27] There are three reasons why Dooyeweerd is insistent on this point.

The first is that spiritual life and spiritual death are a matter of our response to God, not of the correctness of our theology. "[T]he true knowledge of God in Jesus Christ and true self-knowledge are neither of a dogmatic-theological, nor of a philosophical nature, but have an absolutely central religious significance. This knowledge is a question of spiritual life and death."[28] Dooyeweerd wants to maintain that the child who has "accepted Jesus into his heart" or the little old lady who has lived her life knowing that she is a forgiven sinner, redeemed by Christ and made part of his church by the Holy Spirit, know God and therefore know

26. Ibid., 1:20. Strauss, "Justice, legal validity and the force of law," 73–74.

27. Dooyeweerd, *In The Twilight of Western Thought*, 113, 135.

28. Ibid., 146.

themselves, whereas an academic theologian of impeccable orthodoxy may be dead in his sins.[29]

Second, Dooyeweerd wants to maintain that the ground-motive, the basic conviction, the worldview of creation, fall into sin, and redemption by Jesus Christ as the incarnate Word of God, in the communion of the Holy Spirit, is not somewhere we think to but somewhere we think from. It is, as it were, the Archimedean point from which we view the world.[30] Dooyeweerd claims that "This spiritual basic motive is elevated above all theological controversies and is not in need of theological exegesis, since its radical meaning is exclusively explained by the Holy Spirit operating in our opened hearts, in the communion of this Spirit."[31]

The third reason we might term "the Galileo problem." As is well known, Galileo was condemned by the Inquisition for showing how his astronomical work contradicted the view that the earth was motionless at the centre of the universe. Dooyeweerd points out how Aristotelian metaphysics was incorporated both into Catholic Thomism and into Protestant Scholasticism, with the result that challenges to the philosophy of Aristotle were perceived as challenges to theological orthodoxy and dealt with as such.[32] Dooyeweerd had his own, ad hominem, reason for insisting that philosophy or other scientific enquiry was not subject to the veto of dogmatic theology but accountable only to the basic presuppositions of the Christian worldview. During the early years of his tenure as Professor at the Free University of Amsterdam, his colleague Vollehoven and he were the subject of an enquiry into their theological orthodoxy by the Calvinist hierarchy at the University. Distinguishing philosophy on Christian foundations from dogmatic theology enabled Dooyeweerd to preserve his own academic freedom of enquiry.

Nonetheless, Dooyeweerd recognized that dogmatic theology and Christian philosophy remain interrelated.[33] Dooyeweerd would have agreed with Harold Berman's insight that "the compartments into which we have divided the world are not self-contained units, and . . . if they are

29. Ibid., 146, see also 60, 125, 135–36.

30. There are echoes here of Stephen Williams' account of Christ as the truth in response to Nietzsche in chapter 9 of *Shadow of the Antichrist*.

31. Dooyeweerd, *In The Twilight of Western Thought*, 146.

32. Ibid., 158–61. The other example Dooyeweerd uses is of the 6 days of creation: see, 149–51 and *Encyclopedia of the Science of Law*, 1:32.

33. Dooyeweerd, *In The Twilight of Western Thought*, 129–30.

not opened up to each other they will imprison and stifle us."[34] Dogmatic theology and Christian legal theory impact on one another and draw on one another, but concepts taken from the one must be used with care, analogically.[35] Indeed, Dooyeweerd argues that the connections between the aspects of reality are such that structural analogies, what he calls "analogical moments" "give expression to the inner coherence between [each] aspect and all the other modes of experience within the temporal order."[36]

Dooyeweerd's project was to establish the integrity of different scientific enquiries but at the same time to insist that each must be conducted in the light of Christ. In my view, while there is much to admire in the audacity of Dooyeweerd's project and the intricacy of its execution, important aspects of his conception require revision. One of the most pertinent questions which has been asked about Dooyeweerd's thought is whether his identification of faith as a separate aspect of reality holds or not.[37] Dooyeweerd's distinction between dogmatic theology and the basic Christian worldview is far from watertight. After all, Dooyeweerd does not just speak of creation, fall, and redemption but specifically of fall into sin, of redemption by Jesus Christ and of the communion of the Holy Spirit. There is already a reading of the biblical text taking place here; there is already an interpretation of the Christian story. Dooyeweerd's distinction between theology and the basic Christian worldview works only if theology is defined narrowly, so as to separate out both being alive in Christ[38] *and* the fundamental Christian metanarrative and seeing *both* as fundamental to and therefore different from the enquiry into revealed truth.

There is also a clear and ineradicable debt to a particular theology at the heart of Dooyeweerd's philosophy. Dooyeweerd places cosmonomic law at the center of his theory because of the prominence of God's law in Reformed theology,[39] he identifies retribution as the core of the jural aspect of reality because of Calvinist exegesis of Rom 13:1–7,[40] and if not

34. Berman, *Interaction of Law and Religion*, 18.

35. Dooyeweerd, *In The Twilight of Western Thought*, 148–50; Witte, *God's Joust*, 458–59.

36. Dooyeweerd, *In The Twilight of Western Thought*, 149.

37. See Olthuis, "Dooyeweerd on Religion and Faith," 28–29.

38. Rom 6:11; Eph 2:5; Col 2:13.

39. Dooyeweerd, "De staatkundige tegenstelling," 5.

40. Dooyeweerd, *New Critique*, II:129, 134. The translator of Spier's *An Introduction*

the whole of his theory of the aspects, at least his decision to identify faith as a particular aspect of reality, is an application of Abraham Kuyper's idea of sphere sovereignty.[41] As Albert Wolters puts it: "It is not too much to say that Dooyeweerd first began to elaborate his systematic philosophy in an attempt to provide a more general ontological foundation for Kuyper's principle of sphere sovereignty."[42]

Importantly, Kuyper claimed to find sphere sovereignty in Scripture.[43] It was not, for him, a philosophical idea but a theological principle. Dooyeweerd's entire Christian philosophy therefore hinges on the application of a principle of theological origin, discerned through the sort of theorizing in dogmatic theology which Dooyeweerd argued was exterior to Christian philosophy. This leads to the paradox that Dooyeweerd's very contention that dogmatic theology's place alongside Christian philosophy as merely a special science inquiring into one of the aspects of reality itself depends on an account of reality given in a particular dogmatic theology.

Even more than these particular examples, the fundamental problem is Dooyeweerd's idea of the ground motive as impeccably revealed by the Holy Spirit. I indicated that Dooyeweerd had three concerns that led to his insistence on this point. As to the first, the distinction between spiritual life and theological truth, Dooyeweerd is surely right that our relationship to Christ may be one thing, and our understanding of that relationship and articulation of it quite another, even defective to the point of heresy.

On the second point, that the basic Christian ground motive is not in need of theological exegesis, Dooyeweerd's contention seems to be straightforwardly false: the ground-motive is *not* solely pre-theoretical. The relationship between creation, fall, and redemption has been categorized in a number of different ways in Christian theologies.[44] The

---

to *Christian Philosophy*, at 89–91, 215, opts for the term "judgment" instead, which seems less susceptible of misunderstanding than "retribution."

41. Dooyeweerd, *A New Critique of Theoretical Thought*, 1:102; "Kuyper's wetenschapsleer," 217.

42. Wolters, "Intellectual Milieu," 7.

43. Kuyper cited 1 Cor 15:23 as showing that Scripture recognises things according to their different kinds: see Henderson, *Illuminating Law* 131–33. Spier acknowledges that there "are no particular texts which literally enunciate" the idea of sphere sovereignty, but he maintains that "it runs as a continuous line throughout the Bible": *An Introduction to Christian Philosophy*, 46.

44. A point made by Olthuis, "Dooyeweerd on Religion and Faith," at 36–37.

questions which arise about how we are to understand, creation, fall, re-demption by Jesus Christ, and the communion of the Holy Spirit seem to be both so pregnant in Dooyeweerd's identification of the ground-motive and potential answers so fruitful in terms of answers for theology, phi-losophy, and law that it seems, frankly, obtuse to draw a rigid distinction between the ground motive on the one hand and theology on the other.

As for the "Galileo problem," insisting on the ground-motive as above theological enquiry does not appear to be necessary to resolve it. Would it not in fact have simply been enough for Dooyeweerd to stress that dogmatic theology is an inherently fallible human enterprise and therefore must always be open to correction from outside itself? After all, the God with whom we are called into relationship is a God of surprises, who transcends our attempts to confine God within the bounds of human rationality. Just as medieval metaphysics needed to be open to the pos-sibility of correction from physics, so contemporary theology ought to be ready for a mutual exchange with law.

Thomas Aquinas

I turn now to Thomas Aquinas. Dooyeweerd was critical of Aquinas, blaming him for introducing into the Church the ground-motive of au-tonomous nature and supra-natural grace which displaced the biblical ground-motive of creation, fall, and redemption in theoretical thought, whether philosophical or theological.[45] Since de Lubac, there is, however, a significant question mark over whether it was Aquinas who was respon-sible for this innovation.[46] This is important, because Dooyeweerd him-self acknowledged the *nouvelle théologie* as a positive move away from the unbiblical dualism of nature and grace and towards the biblical ground-motive of creation, fall, and redemption.[47]

---

45. Dooyeweerd, *Encyclopedia of the Science of Law*, 1:61–63; *In The Twilight of West-ern Thought*, 43–45, 65–66. Dooyeweerd's criticisms are followed by Taylor in chapter 4 of *The Christian Philosophy of Law, Politics and the State*, a chapter which is notable for its lack of reference to the primary texts.

46. de Lubac, *Catholicism*; de Lubac, *The Mystery of the Supernatural,*.

47. Dooyeweerd, *In The Twilight of Western Thought*, 141. Marlet argued in *Grun-dlinien der kalvinistischen* that Dooyeweerd's negative reading of Aquinas was heavily dependent on the work of R. K. Sertillanges and read back into Aquinas too much of the dualism present in later scholasticism.

I want to argue, against Dooyeweerd's reading, that in Aquinas's treatise on law there is in fact to be found a developed account of the biblical ground-motive of creation, fall into sin, and redemption by Jesus Christ as the incarnate Word of God, in the communion of the Holy Spirit, which has significant implications for Christian legal theory.[48] The *Prima Secundae* of Aquinas's *Summa Theologiae* finishes with a treatise on law and grace in which Aquinas tells us how God the Father has ordered the world to the Son[49] and is bringing about His purposes through the work of the Spirit.[50] This great piece of sustained theologizing about law has not been recognized as such because, despite its location within an explicitly theological treatise and despite its clear line of theological argument, it has habitually been truncated by legal scholars into an application of Aristotle's *Politics* to the theory of law. It is, however, as Nicholas Sagovsky has recently described it, a piece of "theological jurisprudence."[51]

Read as a whole, in unabbreviated form, in Aquinas's treatise on law, human law is situated within a grand (meta-)narrative, a particular account of the story of God's dealings with humanity, in which Aquinas sweeps from creation, the providential work of the Spirit in revealing God's laws through nature,[52] to the law of Moses (the Old Law),[53] and on to the significance of the death and resurrection of Christ, and the regenerating work of the Holy Spirit (the New Law).[54]

Aquinas's account is thoroughly theological, and human law is discussed in relation to it. Aquinas's most significant, though by no means only, departure from Aristotle is his denial that human rulers are competent to ensure the virtue of the communities that they govern.[55] True virtue comes only through the indwelling power of the Holy Spirit who conforms us to Christ-likeness. Given the limits on their powers, all human rulers can achieve is shallow justice, a concern with worldly goods,

---

48. This section of the essay is a shorter version of chapter 4 of McIlroy, *Trinitarian Theology of Law*. The essential argument is also set out at "A Trinitarian Reading of Aquinas's Treatise on Law."

49. Aquinas, *Summa Theologia*, I-II, 93.1 ad.2; 93.4, resp., ad.2.

50. Aquinas, *Summa Theologia*, I-II, 93.6 ad.1.

51. Sagovsky, *Christian Tradition*, 113.

52. Aquinas, *Summa Theologia*, I-II.94

53. Ibid., I-II.98–105

54. Ibid., I-II.106–114

55. Finnis, *Aquinas*, 222–52.

and a protection of the freedom in which true virtue may flourish.[56] The primary function of human law is restraining the wicked; promoting defined forms of the good, while important, and on Aquinas's account, predating the Fall, is only secondary.[57]

If this theological reading of Aquinas's theory of law as precisely a theology of law is unfamiliar to lawyers and others, it is because in an academic perspective, which long ago rejected his theology, it is the idea of natural law which has proved the most tenacious. The impression that Aquinas's idea of natural law was his most valuable, or if you are a fideist, his most pernicious contribution, is, however, a false one. It is not Aquinas's idea of natural law that has endured. The content and indeed the basic conception of natural law has changed radically in subsequent intellectual history from the way in which Aquinas used and deployed the idea.

The failure to attend to the salvation-historical dynamic in Aquinas's treatise on law and grace has led to distortions in the understanding of the place of natural law in his theology. I have argued elsewhere[58] that in Aquinas's scheme natural law serves the same purpose it does in the Apostle Paul's Epistle to the Romans, on at least one plausible reading of that most scrutinized and hotly disputed of books. Aquinas is attempting to answer the question: how can God be just in condemning human beings for their ignorance of God and of God's laws? If, as certain forms of Christian negative theology and Islamic thought were later to hold, God is totally unknowable, then the logical implication would be that human ignorance about God's nature is not only explicable, but also excusable and, in fact, inevitable.

Against this, Aquinas's argument is that everyone knows enough about God's nature and God's requirements for God to be justified in the conclusion that all have sinned and fall short of the glory of God. No one loves God and worships God *as they know they ought to*. No one obeys God's will and follows God's laws *as they know they ought to*. Given this state of affairs, everyone is in need of the Savior Christ Jesus. Such a theological account of natural law is a long way away from arguing that

---

56. Gilby. *Principality and Polity*, 130; Finnis, *Aquinas*, 237–38.

57. Gilby *Principality and Polity*, 179–80, 306; *Between Community and Society*, 327; Finnis, *Aquinas*, 228–31.

58. McIlroy, "What's at Stake in Natural Law?"

unaided reason can deduce the moral imperatives of human life from a self-evident, universally applicable reading of nature as it now is.

The Shape of Christian Legal Theory

Aquinas's departures from Aristotle and Dooyeweerd's insistence on the importance of the biblical motifs of creation, fall into sin, and redemption by Jesus Christ, lead to the following theological claim: only Christianity grounds the conceptions of authority, justice, and of natural right or natural rights which we need to conceptualize law. In other words, a right theory of the function and purpose of human law is dependent upon a theology that is attentive to the actions of the triune God.

To Alexander Pope's claim that the proper study of mankind is man, theology responds that a proper study of human beings must recognize that human beings are God's creatures. To fail to recognize this dimension of human life is to miss what Jacques Maritain called the priority of the spiritual.[59] The consequence of such a failure is that our thinking, our theories about human life, human activities, and human institutions, becomes disordered.[60]

A Christian legal theory should point to the following data. The world was created by God and was created good. This is a truth which Reformed theology, at its worst, does not do enough with (a criticism which applies all the more to Jansenism). The realities of relationship and of work, which do so much to shape human lives, are God-given.

This good world is, however, seriously marred and flawed. As G. K. Chesterton once quipped, "original sin . . . is the only part of Christian theology which can really be proved."[61] The doctrine of the Fall is important. Christianity can explain how the world is because its explanation accounts for the world as it is, both at its best and its worst.

The context of creation and fall identifies two of the basic realities with which human law has to reckon. It has to promote and create space for those things in human society which are good, and it has to restrain

---

59. Maritain, *Primauté du Spirituel.*

60. This is at the heart of O'Donovan's moral theology, as it lay at the heart of Augustine's arguments regarding love: O'Donovan *Resurrection and Moral Order*, 85–86, 249; *Problem of Self-Love in St. Augustine*, 79, 159.

61. Chesterton *Orthodoxy*, 10.

those things which are destructive of human society. A Christian legal theory would not be complete, however, without reference to the redemption of the world through the death and resurrection of Christ and the promise of the *eschaton*. Because Christ has already "put the world to rights," human legal institutions are freed from the pretension of having to do so. Their function can be seen to be important, but limited.

The Christian message has some serious implications for law. If the Law of Moses had enabled people to be perfectly law-abiding, would Christ have needed to come? The question is central to the Christian message, because behind it lies the acknowledgement that all have sinned and fall short of the glory of God. No one can be right with God through perfect, unerring obedience to law, whether human or God-given. No one but Jesus is capable of that. Moreover, the Christological hymns of the New Testament teach that in the Second Person of the Trinity all things hold together (Col 1:15–20; Eph 1:10, 19b–23; Phil 2:5–11). Christianity claims that the Son is the one who fulfils our humanity and makes sense of the universe.

Jurisprudence, the technical name for the philosophy of law, is as prone to fads as any other academic discipline including theology. One of its central questions is *what is law?* In the twentieth century, Hans Kelsen sought to ground law, to base it upon a *Grundnorm*, and Herbert Hart refined that idea by positing a rule of recognition which conferred the status of law on particular norms in a given jurisdiction. But beyond that technical answer, what grounds law? What makes sense of the heteronomy into which we are born as human beings and subject to which we live our lives? Christian theology answers that human law is ultimately grounded on Christ, and on him alone. In him, law, like every other facet of created and human life, holds together and is sustained. Law takes its subordinate place in God's ordering of the universe in the light of the person and work of Christ.

Law is not, therefore, for Christians a means of achieving perfection or establishing the perfectly just society. These assertions already give a Christian theology of law a radically different direction from Islam and Judaism.

Grounding and Interacting without Dominating:
The Relationship of Hospitality between a Christian
Theology of Law and Legal Theory

We can build on the insights of Dooyeweerd and Aquinas to develop a conception of how Christian theology might speak into all academic disciplines, offering an understanding of them in the light of the lordship of Christ, without, however, dominating and controlling those disciplines. The Christian metanarrative, which we do not just examine theoretically but which we find our own place within, should ground Christian legal theory. A Christian legal theory should be more than merely theistic; it should be unashamedly rooted in the Christian metanarrative. As we reflect theoretically on that metanarrative we engage in dogmatic theology. Such dogmatic theology should inform legal theory and vice versa.

To say that theology provides the foundation for legal theory is not to argue that all legal theory is disguised or anti-theology. I am not contending that all legal theory is, in reality, a transmogrified or secularized theology, in the manner in which Carl Schmitt argued that all political theory was in truth political theology.[62] What I am, however, arguing is that there is what Jacques Derrida recognized as a "Mystical Foundation to Authority," the sub-title to his 1989 lecture at Cardozo Law School[63] and that the foundation of law is, as Jacques Ellul argued, theological.[64] Legal theory has a legitimate, semi-autonomous discourse about *how* law functions, which is proper to it. That is not to say that theology has nothing to say on such questions, but it is to say that such questions are not all directly theological.

Having said that, though, theology does claim to provide the foundation for *why* law functions. The three Abrahamic faiths all root obedience to human rulers in obedience to God. Followers of those religions obey human rulers for God's sake and argue that all human beings obey laws because the human institution of law is, in the last analysis, mandated and authorized by God. However, precisely because of its understanding of the work of Christ, Christianity argues, against Islam, that government's role in enforcing righteousness through law is limited.[65]

62. Schmitt, *Political Theology*.

63. Derrida, "Force of Law."

64. Ellul, *Theological Foundation of Law*.

65. McIlroy, "Role of Government."

In this way, to take up Milbank's analysis again, accounts of the origins and foundations of human law which posit some basis for human law other than God are anti-theologies; that is to say, they usurp the rightful place of theology in legal theory, by seeking to offer an account of human law's authority otherwise than by reference to God.

I have argued elsewhere, however, that Christians account for the action of God in politics in terms of both ontology and grace.[66] Theology does not just offer an explanation for the ontology of law, it also has the potential to offer explanations of the ways in which sinfulness is manifest in law which mistakes its ontological foundation. Moreover, and here there is perhaps most work to be done, Christian theology may affirm that human law is sustained by the action of the triune God, is used by God for God's own purposes, and that to an extent and even when law does not recognize or even explicitly rejects its dependence on the Christian God.

The place of theology in relation to the natural sciences was under threat so long as God was understood as "the God of the gaps"; in other words, if a causal explanation could be found in terms of what theologians would call secondary causes, God did not need to be invoked, and so God was relegated to the function of standing as a cipher for that which could not yet be explained.

This view of God has lost both scientific and theological credibility.[67] In scientific terms, the hope of the quest for the so-called "theory of everything" is that it might be possible one day to provide explanations in terms of secondary causes for *how* everything in the universe fits together. In theological terms, it is only those untutored fundamentalists who refuse the help of doctors and medicines on account of their being secondary causes, preferring to rely on prayer and direct divine intervention alone.

Instead, Christian theology points to God to explain *how and why* the universe came to be in the first place, in terms of the will of the Father, and *why* it operates at all, namely because it coheres in the Son and is enlivened by the work of the Spirit. Moreover, Christian theology has

---

66. McIlroy, "Idols and Grace."

67. As Gunton points out, "Our God's action is not immediate but mediated action. Immediate action would overwhelm and depersonalize, if not worse; recall the story of Moses wishing to see God's glory (Exod. 33:19–23). The incarnation provides our chief model of mediation. God's actions in Christ are sovereign and achieve their end, but they respect our createdness and personhood." *Father, Son and Holy Spirit*, 80.

been rightly reminded by Jürgen Moltmann that the Spirit is at work in the world, moving it from the future, towards the *eschaton*, when God's divine verdict on human laws and judgments will be given.[68]

If this is a plausible theological account of the work of God, as being behind and working through the secondary causes which science observes, then how much more so is such an account necessary and viable in relation to the humanities, to those subjects which study human beings, those beings made, according to Christian theology, by God and capable of love towards or rebellion against God.

None of what I have said above implies the dissolution of legal theory into theology. Again Dooyeweerd is helpful. His science of law identifies law as a proper subject for enquiry, the enquiry into the juridical aspect of reality, which has its own proper focus and integrity. Christian theology should complement, critique, and inform such enquiry but it does not overwhelm it, substitute its own methodology, or render it redundant. If Christian dogmatic theology of the kind I have shown Aquinas was doing not only has implications for legal theory but can in fact be said to have a legal theory, it is nonetheless not the whole of legal theory. You cannot answer all the questions of the philosophy of law simply by reading a work of systematic theology.

Integrating legal theory within a wider Christian perspective therefore demands that proper account be taken of law's autonomy. The problem of the autonomy of law presents itself in two different dimensions. On the one hand, law is autonomous in that it is made by human beings, not by God. It therefore participates both in the rebellion of humanity against God and yet also in the providential purposes of God by which that rebellion does not lead to total annihilation of human society and of the human race. This creates a dialectic at the heart of Christian legal theory which cannot be synthesized but only resolved at the Last Judgment.

On the other hand, law is autonomous in that it has its own special internal logic, or to put it another way, its own special morality. A good lawmaker does not legislate for the community in the same way that he would make his own personal moral decisions. A good judge does not apply the law solely by having regard to her own moral compass; instead she is called upon to apply the law faithfully, to render judgments that are consonant with the existing legal framework. This may, on occasion,

---

68. Moltmann, *Theology of Hope*, 212, 223.

require her to decide a case in a manner contrary to her own moral instincts. There is, therefore, a virtue, which Aristotle calls legal justice.[69] There is a discipline to the practice of law which Luther calls station ethics. There is a function of just judgment which Oliver O'Donovan identifies and makes dominant in his Christian political and legal theory.[70]

The Task Ahead

Milbank's claim in *Theology and Social Theory* is that the Christian understanding of society is both more attractive and more compelling than its secular alternatives. *Pace* the important debates about whether the Christian hope is exclusivist, inclusivist, or universalist, the Christian Church claims to stand as *pars pro toto* for humanity. Both because our world finds its meaning in Christ and also because Jesus Christ is the exemplar of humanity—because he entered fully into the human condition—to speak into the world in the light of Christ is to illuminate the fundamental realities of the world in which we live.

The task for Christian theologians and Christian legal theorists, and above all for those like myself, who pretend to be both, is to articulate that case with all the intellectual and rhetorical powers at our disposal. Just as Milbank claims that the Christian vision of society is one which knows society better than secular society knows itself, so the claim would be that Christian legal theory has greater attractiveness and explanatory force than its secular alternatives.[71]

In saying that, I recognize that anyone familiar with my work would suspect me of offering an *apologia pro vita sua*. My two books to date have been *A Biblical View of Law and Justice* which offers a canonical theology of law[72] and *A Trinitarian Theology of Law* which is its counterpart as a systematic theology of law. My next project is a Christian philosophy of law, offering, for those without theological inclination or training, a glimpse of the beauty and truth of the Christian understanding of the task of secular law. This book will seek to work out in practice a vision of

---

69. Aristotle, *Nicomachean Ethics*, 1136b34–35.

70. O'Donovan, *Desire of the Nations*, 37–40, 233; *Ways of Judgment*, 5–7.

71. On this theme, see the conclusion to Witte, *God's Joust, God's Justice* entitled "Challenges of Christian Jurisprudence," 450–65.

72. McIlroy, *Biblical View of Law and Justice*.

theology as legal theory, a vision which shows how human law and legal institutions make most sense when understood from within the metanarrative of God's dealings with humanity, a metanarrative which tells the story of humanity's creation, fall into sin, and redemption by Jesus Christ in the communion of the Holy Spirit.

8

Against Eschatological Over-Determination: Can Social Science Contribute to Theology?[1]

CHRISTOPHER CRAIG BRITTAIN

THE PRESENT STATE OF the debate over the relationship between theology and social science is not healthy. In the 1970s, when Latin American Liberation Theology and European Political Theology were at the peak of their influence, numerous theologians developed an enthusiastic, if sometimes also rather naïve, embrace of Marxian social science. Their motivation was largely driven by a concern to uncover how theological discourse was ideologically distorted by its social context. But the momentum of the trend has now contributed to the development of a diametrically opposed attitude, particularly in the form of John Milbank's sweeping claim that all social theories are themselves anti-theologies in disguise.[2] His book *Theology and Social Theory: Beyond Secular Reason*, articulates a forceful defence of Christian theology as the "queen of the sciences,"[3] against the claims and methodologies of "secular reason" and

1. Some elements of this paper have previously appeared in chapter three of Brittain, *Weight of Objectivity*.

2. Milbank, *Theology and Social Theory*, 3.

3. Ibid., 38.

social science. He argues that "secular discourse" represents a "pagan theology," or an "anti-theology," constituted by its opposition to orthodox Christian theology.[4] Social science's authority is not based upon a more accurate or reliable description of society, Milbank claims, but merely on an acceptance of equally unfounded assumptions about the world; assumptions which he roots in "pagan" mythology.

Theological engagement with social-scientific disciplines like sociology has yet to recover from Milbank's claim that theology has no need of social theory. His basic position has received considerable support among theologians sympathetic to communitarian and virtue approaches to theology. Stanley Hauerwas, for example, adopts Milbank's suggestion that "the pathos of modern theology is its false humility,"[5] and suggests that the choice to be made is whether one advocates "a theology that has given up on its ability to tell us the way the world is and a theology that confidently and unapologetically proclaims the ways things are."[6] Hauerwas develops this position in his recent book *The State of the University*, in which he argues that "theology is a knowledge" that must be rightly represented in the curriculum of the university. Theology is not a subject among subjects, he suggests, but involves having "our knowledge shaped by the radical character of the Gospel."[7] Here Hauerwas dismisses social-scientific disciplines and secular political concerns by appeals to ecclesiology, which he advocates with characteristic flourish in slogans like: "I don't need a foreign policy; I have a church" or "justice is a bad idea for Christians."[8]

Such statements are, of course, rhetorical in nature and intend to challenge what Hauerwas considers to be a deeply ingrained reflex towards natural theology in contemporary Christian thought and church life. But the tone and the implications of these claims are problematic. This paper argues that such casual dismissal of secular disciplines in the name of defending the distinctiveness and priority of theological concerns are ill advised and, ultimately, unhelpful to theology. For in their concern to avoid what they consider to be the reductionism of social

4. Ibid., 3.

5. Ibid., 1.

6. Hauerwas, *With the Grain*, 21.

7. Hauerwas, *State of the University*, 3, 7.

8. Hauerwas, *After Christendom*, 45–69.

science, theologians like Milbank and Hauerwas construct a reductive account of the church. The over-determined authority of social context and measurable empirical data that they oppose are replaced by an over-determined eschatological realization of the fullness of the Kingdom of God. Their alternative to social science is based on an implied possession of the fullness of the Gospel.

Although both Hauerwas and Milbank offer compelling warnings against how easily the agenda of theology can be manipulated or annexed by social scientific methodologies, their replacement of sociology with theological concepts does little to enhance an understanding of contemporary ecclesial life, present challenges to the church's mission, or help us reach a fuller attentiveness to the movement of the Spirit in our time. After offering a criticism of Milbank's ideas about social theory, the discussion will begin to sketch out an alternative way to conceive of the relationship between theology and sociology as a fruitful, mutually critical dialogue, with some reference to David Martin and Theodor Adorno. The limitations of rational choice theory's treatment of religion will then be criticized from a theological perspective, to illustrate that the engagement between theology and social science need not be a one-way conversation. Theological criticism can contribute to the scrutiny of social reality, and help social science attend better to the object before it.

Milbank on the Policing of Theology

Milbank's project is largely based on the argument that theology has become marginalized in contemporary Western culture and academia because it has surrendered to the norms of secular epistemology and the authority of science. He suggests that theology has adopted a "false humility" before the secular, and so he intends to "restore in postmodern terms, the possibility of theology as a metadiscourse."[9] To achieve this requires a critique of the authority of secular social theory, as well as a portrait of Christian theology as a completely distinct form of knowledge from that of modern reason.

The claims Milbank makes about Christianity as a basis upon which to reject social theory are sweeping, yet his argument offers little by way of detailed historical analysis or explanation. His genealogical account of

9. Milbank, *Theology and Social Theory*, 1.

the emergence of secular reason out of the Christian tradition operates at the level of assertion. Milbank states that initially "there was the single community of Christendom."[10] At such a time, there was not a recognized split between a sacred and a secular realm. Theology's discourse was considered the authoritative source of knowledge about both the divine and the world of daily life. Exactly when this unified community was firmly established remains unclear in Milbank's text,[11] but its hegemonic authority was challenged sometime after the late Middle Ages, and was permanently undermined with the outbreak of the Reformation.[12]

Initially, the forces that challenged the unified Christian community are treated by Milbank as outside invaders. He suggests that the Reformation, for example, was not the product of forces emerging out of the Christian tradition itself. Instead, this challenge to the "sealed off totality" of Christendom "instituted an entirely different economy of power and knowledge."[13] Subsequently, however, Milbank argues that Christian society became secularized, not because this was inevitable or desirable, but because it failed "to preserve the rule of the Gospel."[14] According to him, ecclesial authorities gave into legal formalism, rational instrumentalization, bureaucratization, and sovereign rule even *before* these were adopted by the more "secular" political powers outside the Catholic Church. Thus it remains unclear throughout this genealogical account of church history whence this new "economy of power" emerged from, and what forces contributed to its development.

Secular theories about the nature of society, Milbank suggests, are based on a certain "reading" of the world which assumes that society is founded upon contracts between autonomous self-constituting subjects, in order to escape from the chaos of the struggle for self-preservation found in a state of nature (Hobbes). Society, he argues, is thus assumed

10. Ibid., 9.

11. This understanding of a single community of Christendom fails to mention the conflicts between rival sects and authorities in the early church, the conflicting theologies that made the Council of Nicea necessary, the Pelagians and Docetists, the split in the Church between East and West, the rival Popes, and other fierce conflicts and regional differences within the Church prior to the Reformation.

12. Ibid., 10.

13. Ibid., 9.

14. Ibid., 16.

to be a regulative instrument to prevent the outbreak of a primordial violence.[15] His point is to suggest that this is merely a metaphysical assumption, a myth, in which the central character of the narrative is unlimited power. Milbank argues that similar assumptions are present throughout the entire traditions of political economy and sociology. When the contractualist assumptions of Hobbes were jettisoned, they were replaced by the primacy of self-interest (Smith, Hume), which continued to define itself against Christian "charity." What develops during these cultural shifts does not represent the development of a more accurate understanding of society, continues Milbank, but simply a change in "social imagination."[16]

Rhetorical Narrative over Social Theory

Milbank's critique of the sociological tradition is based upon his assertion that "no social explanations can be sought beyond the unfounded *mythos* which a particular society projects and enacts for itself."[17] Every culture, he argues, possesses its own privileged metaphorical systems, "which govern how it understands what underlies the tensions of reality."[18] Secular reason and social theory[19] choose to privilege certain patterns of behavior that replace the once dominant Christian understandings, but these are no more cognitively valid or well-founded than those replaced. All thought "depends upon contingent theoretically unjustifiable assumptions" or "local narratives." It cannot transcend the limits of local human experience by means of a universally valid reason. If this is so, Milbank continues, then the question becomes not so much which "narrative" is true, but which encourages a more attractive view of the world.

15. Ibid., 12–13.

16. Ibid., 32.

17. Ibid., 64.

18. Ibid., 179.

19. Milbank employs the term "social theory" to include any theoretical or empirical attempts to understand social action and experience in historical and naturalistic terms. By relying on "secular reason" (rational argumentation that assumes a "methodological atheism" seeking a universalizable explanation for historical events and action), Milbank argues that "social theory" is founded upon ungrounded assumptions about ultimate reality, based upon an "ontology of violence." There are, of course, many different "social theories," but Milbank uses the term in the singular, since he wants to challenge the very possibility of an objective theory of society, and the legitimacy of any understanding of the social that is not based on Christian theology.

This critique of secular argument assumes that theoretical inquiry is undermined when restrained by the rules of logic. Among those who advocate a "rhetorical turn" in philosophy, the assumption is made that "all scholarly discourse is rhetorical in the sense that issues need to be named and framed, facts interpreted and conclusions justified."[20] Within moral theory and theology, this point is frequently developed further. Martha Nussbaum argues that "stories . . . contain and teach forms of feeling, forms of life."[21] Emotions, she claims, are not "natural stirrings" but constructs that rest upon certain beliefs. If this is true, then feelings can be modified by modifying beliefs. Nussbaum concludes, therefore, that "criticism of emotion must be, prominently, an unwriting of stories."[22]

This is precisely what Milbank attempts to do: to un-write the story told about society by secular social theories, and reassert a Christian version of the narrative, with a completely different plot. In his articulation of the "radical imagination of peace within the Christian mythos,"[23] he is influenced by the work of Alasdair MacIntyre, who argues that an ethical society requires the revitalization of some coherent value scheme and that some particular tradition is essential in order to ground those virtues that make a just society viable.[24] Furthermore, MacIntyre often suggests that Christianity is one of the traditions that best nurtures the renewal of virtue which he advocates. At this point Milbank's position parts company with this version of neo-Aristotelianism. He criticizes MacIntyre's position for its suggestion that the dialectical examination of one's starting point helps to establish virtue more securely in relation to reality.[25] In other words, MacIntyre is faulted for trying to validate his preferred narrative (Christianity) through argumentation.[26]

Milbank argues to the contrary that "the practice of virtue [is] much closer to a rhetorical than a dialectical habit of mind."[27] Dialectics inevitably becomes a form of foundationalism, he states, constantly sliding towards universalism and metaphysics. As soon as one begins to speak

20. Simons, "Introduction," 9.

21. Nussbaum, "Narrative Emotions, 218.

22. Ibid., 223–26.

23. Milbank, *Theology and Social Theory*, 331.

24. MacIntyre, *After Virtue*.

25. Milbank, *Theology and Social Theory*, 328.

26. Ibid., 339.

27. Ibid., 328.

in terms of the legitimation of the objective "Good," he suggests, one is on a slippery slope towards secularity and empty universalism. He states that "specific content seems to be a matter of rhetoric."[28] Thus, when it comes to discussing the phenomenon of a conversion from one tradition to another, Milbank argues, against MacIntyre, that the conversion is not legitimated on the basis of criteria found within one's prior tradition, nor from any outside source. Instead, "what triumphs is simply the persuasive power of a new narrative."[29]

Confrontation with Science

These presuppositions lead Milbank into a confrontation with the nature of science, whose goals of objectivity and logical argument he opposes directly. He is highly critical of the authority granted to science in modernity for the legitimization of knowledge. "Natural science itself," he claims, "possesses no privileged access to truth." Its achievement is "merely that of instrumental control.[30]

To illustrate some of Milbank's presuppositions about science, it is instructive to turn briefly to *The Rhetoric of Science* by Alan Gross. Gross concludes in his analysis of the rhetorical nature of scientific texts that there is no more objectivity in modern science than in medieval theology.[31] Although the study demonstrates that rhetorical statements are at times influential within the scientific community, and that rhetoric is employed during fierce disputes between schools of thought and methods of experimentation, Gross's suggestion that there may be nothing left of science "not the result of prior persuasion" is overstated.[32] Scientific discovery, he argues, is simply a matter of invention, and what are considered facts and what importance is granted to them are rhetorical issues, so that "only through persuasion are importance and meaning established."[33] Because objectivity is "a carefully crafted rhetorical invention," and because Gross believes that Aristotle's decision to grant logic and mathematics

28. Ibid., 329.
29. Ibid., 346.
30. Milbank, *Theology and Social Theory*, 71.
31. Gross, *Rhetoric of Science*, 84.
32. Ibid., 3.
33. Ibid., 4.

particular authority "was itself rhetorical," he concludes that "scientific knowledge is not special, but social; the result, not of revelation, but of persuasion."[34] *Theology and Social Theory* makes similar claims. There "are no facts, only interpretations,"[35] and scientific experimentation "begins by the formulation of data."[36]

Both Gross and Milbank dismiss the authority of science because they assume that falsified scientific theories serve no purpose. Because they can point to a history of erroneous scientific claims, and because it is possible to provide examples of the use of rhetorical persuasion by individual scientists, they conclude that false scientific theories do not serve to advance knowledge in any way—that their failure is entirely meaningless—and, thus, changes within science only serve to undermine its legitimacy. Such a view enables Milbank to judge scientific disputes to be nothing other than rhetorical arguments. What are the implications of such a position for epistemology, and for a discipline like sociology?

The social anthropologist Ernest Gellner is willing to admit that, at one level, all scientific data and evidence are saturated with interpretation, but he also insists that this cannot be taken to prove the validity of relativism, or the failure of science. Whereas what he calls "third-person" claims assert opinions about things that are assumed to be accurate, "first person" claims can only make such assertions by presenting evidence. While both types of claims may be biased by subjective interpretation, in "first-person language, everything is on trial."[37] Science hopes that its claims, however biased and distorted by interpretation and rhetoric, can develop increasingly reliable knowledge because its statements are open to being challenged by others, and it must use evidence to defend itself against opposing claims. Gellner's basic argument against positions similar to that of Milbank is surely correct:

> it seems doubtful to me whether a well-entrenched dogmatism, well equipped with self-maintaining circular devices [e.g. all is rhetoric and narrative], can ever be budged, as long as it is allowed to insist on 'realist' third-person language. It is only the switch to a first-person language, which suspends the authority of the lan-

34. Ibid., 15–16, 20.
35. Ibid., 281.
36. Ibid., 270.
37. Gellner, *Relativism and the Social Sciences*, 21.

> guage in which the dogmatism is articulated . . . which can break
> through a well-fortified, well-entrenched dogmatism.[38]

Yet Milbank suggests that one cannot criticize a position within a particular tradition from the perspective of a more generalized "language." Causal explanation for social events, claims Milbank, can only point to preceding conditions "at the point where they have already been superseded by the new circumstances."[39] Max Weber, he argues, can only seek explanations for social phenomena because he "clings to the notion of an "interior" subject," whose motivations can be compared with external events. Such assumptions, for Milbank, amount to the acceptance of certain problematic presuppositions, such as an autonomous, self-serving interior subject. But these assumptions are for him based only on the "story" of the Enlightenment. As this is for him self-evident, Milbank quickly concludes that the "narrative relation [is] more fundamental than causal explanation."[40]

This perspective allows Milbank to dispose of many problems with which the social sciences wrestle. The issue of the complex relation between society and the individual is brushed aside, for the antinomy is simply "mediated by narration," which has "no room whatsoever for social science."[41] Outside social forces do not determine social action and events, "deep levels of practice" do; certain "forms of life" rooted in particular narratives.[42] Social scientific theories are considered nothing more than narratives that determine the meaning of human history "by telling a story with certain emphases, and to insinuate that certain precedent conditions for events really constitute sufficient . . . causes."[43] One can only describe human beings, Milbank suggests; one cannot explain their actions.[44] The social scientific concepts "explanation" and "understanding" are both rejected as "positivist" for seeking objective truths about social reality.[45] Instead, to understand or explain a social phenomenon

---

38. Ibid., 23.
39. Milbank, *Theology and Social Theory*, 83.
40. Ibid., 83.
41. Ibid., 71.
42. Ibid., 89.
43. Ibid., 249.
44. Ibid., 260.
45. Ibid., 264.

"is simply to narrate it."[46] He concludes, "theology can evade all and every social scientific suspicion."[47] Any threat to theological claims by secular social theory is "at an end," for secular reason itself is merely another ungrounded narrative, and a heretical religion in its own right. What remains of society are multiple, equally ungrounded, local narratives.

"My narrative, right or wrong!" could be one description of Milbank's position, although it would be hard to have any basis upon which to label anything "wrong" in such a view. Narratives are stories, "forms of life," based on ungrounded assumptions or myths. There are no standards with which to judge what might constitute a more legitimate form of narrative.

An issue Milbank skirts is the problem of historical shifts in attitude and knowledge. Given the power he grants to narrative as a "form of life," shared custom becomes the generator of communal ideas and beliefs. There exist no norms or standards outside one's cultural conventions, with which to judge such conventions. While this idea is invoked in order to respect differences among cultures, it forecloses on self-criticism of one's own assumptions about the world. On what basis would one decide that former belief was, in fact, erroneous? Why would someone change "narratives?" To do so, within Milbank's schema, could only be considered a heresy, which is exactly what he labels anything outside the boundaries of orthodox Christianity (boundaries that are themselves often vague). Conversion, as observed in Milbank's criticisms of MacIntyre, can only be the result of "rhetorical persuasion," but this vague concept does not really explain anything.

A criticism Gellner levels against Ludwig Wittgenstein is relevant here: "If only Luther and Voltaire had been told how language functioned, they would not have striven to reform the conceptual custom of their time. If you believe that you will believe anything."[48] If each community simply creates its own standards and forms of legitimation, and all such forms are equally valid, then it is impossible to understand why some members of communities begin to challenge the assumptions of their cultures.

---

46. Ibid., 267.
47. Ibid., 260.
48. Gellner, *Relativism and the Social Sciences*, 174.

Practice and Subjectivity

Milbank's assumptions about the centrality of narrative are intertwined with his understanding of social knowledge as being the continuation of ecclesial practice. While criticizing Wayne Meeks' historical analysis of the social composition of the early Christian *communities*,[49] Milbank states that: "What is incomprehensible is the implication that the social aspects of Church life have some degree of causal determinacy over beliefs. The problem here is: how is one even to think of the being of *this* society in abstraction from its beliefs?"[50]

There is, he insists, no "society" before the text: "why should one assume that behind a logic that appears to us irrational and alien, must be concealed a reality of action which we will more readily comprehend?" In medieval societies, he claims, political and economic practices were infused by religious norms, and so one cannot search for determinative factors for social behavior beyond the "deep level of practice" that social actors were engaged in.[51] Similarly, he argues that in Islamic societies the social order is actually "inside" the religion, and so "the idea of a 'social factor' dissolves away into nothingness." The metaphorical system established by a given narrative, he suggests, provides a seamless regulation of social activity. People who inhabit a particular narrative will believe and act in a certain given way. Milbank would have his reader believe that to search for any deeper explanation for social action is folly.

Milbank's argument at this point is influenced by George Lindbeck's *The Nature of Doctrine*. Lindbeck's book represents what he calls a "cultural-linguistic approach" to understanding the normative role of Christian doctrine for communal belief and practice. Religion, he argues, is like a language, a "form of life" or culture, and doctrines are the authoritative rules of discourse, attitude, and action, which function like a grammar structures a language.[52] Lindbeck claims that a religion is a "comprehensive interpretive scheme" that embodies a certain myth, which is also heavily ritualized. It structures human experience by shaping the entirety of one's life and thought, functioning, Lindbeck says, likes a Kantian *a*

---

49. The use of the plural ("communities") highlights the lack of consensus that existed within early Christianity, a problem that Milbank's argument ignores.

50. Milbank, *Theology and Social Theory*, 120.

51. Ibid., 89.

52. Lindbeck, *Nature of Doctrine*, 18.

priori. Doctrines offer a set of acquired skills, an idiom, which makes the construction of a "reality" possible. As such, a religion is "a communal phenomenon that shapes the subject."[53] By being immersed in such a cultural world, one learns to discriminate the rules "intuitively," and the particular symbolic system becomes the precondition for experience, for "we cannot identify, describe, or recognize experience *qua* experience without the use of signs and symbols." Drawing upon Wittgenstein, Lindbeck develops this point to assert that one's religion goes so far as to shape even pre-experiential life.[54]

One can see how Milbank's argument that a social order is "contained" within a religion coincides with Lindbeck's perspective. But, as in Milbank's case, Lindbeck's theory begins to break down when it comes to describing subjectivity. After arguing that the biblical text "absorbs the world," Lindbeck addresses the question of who qualifies as linguistically "competent" in order to determine which statements and rules are to be considered doctrinal and normative.[55] He is quick to admit that "membership in mainstream communities does not guarantee competence." Among most Christians, he laments, the "official language . . . has not become a native language, the primary medium in which they think, feel, act, and dream."[56] Such people, he argues, are not competent to qualify as part of the *consensus fidelium*, and are unable to judge what "authentic Christianity" is, and what is not. Instead, one must look to "saints" in the community, who have so interiorized the grammar of their religion that they are reliable judges.

What, then, of the great impact that narrative is supposed to have in moulding the subject (even its pre-experiential life)? By Lindbeck's own admission, many Christians are unable to agree on even primary doctrinal issues. The Christian narrative only shapes its subjects when these same subjects have already submitted to the authority of experts who inform the membership of the doctrinal rules they must submit to. It is not so much the power of the narrative that moulds the subject, but the subject's prior acceptance of the power of ecclesial authority to legislate the "form of life" required of its adherents. Most people, Lindbeck admits,

53. Ibid., 32–33.
54. Ibid., 36–38.
55. Ibid, 118.
56. Ibid., 99–100.

do not do so. Both he and Milbank exaggerate the extent to which human identity, thought, and action are constituted by a unified narrative. Nothing so seamless is actually available. Most human beings, in fact, are not moulded by one single narrative. Subjectivity occurs at the intersection of many orientations and influences. Put simply, in the terms of "narrative theology," people often live out of more than one "story."

An Over-Determined Role for the Church

In his insistence that theology does not require the mediation of the social sciences, Milbank states that, "theology is just another socio-historical gaze, just another perspective alongside other gazes."[57] He has denied the legitimacy of secular reason because it merely surveys religious phenomena on the basis of its own heretical *mythos*, and so he concludes that its gaze is no more valid than any other. "In the 'new era' of postmodernism," Milbank proclaims, "the human has become subordinate to the infinitely many discourses which claim to constitute humanity, and universality can no longer pose as the identical."[58] One would think that in the relativistic society Milbank describes, the best one can do is simply continue to narrate one's "local narrative" and be content to parry off universalist assaults by deconstructing their opposing claims to legitimacy. However, Milbank resists such a conclusion: "to ascribe to it a merely partial interpretative power, would undo the logic of the incarnation. For why would we claim to recognize the divine *logos* in a particular life, unless we had the sense that everything else was to be located *here*."[59]

The Christian life is a form of practice that embodies this reality, states Milbank. The Christian mode of action is a definite form of practice, a certain enactment of virtue. By imitating the shape of Jesus' life, one achieves a non-violent "pattern of existence" that contrasts and challenges the rule of secular pagan power.[60] This pattern of life depends on the acceptance that "there is a 'right,' and in this sense a 'natural' way for human beings to be." By situating oneself within the Christian narrative, a "habit" is acquired; a unique model of practice, which alone is "capable

---

57. Milbank, *Theology and Social Theory,* 247.
58. Ibid., 260.
59. Ibid., 246.
60. Ibid., 396–97, 400.

of standing as an alternative to nihilism."[61] Milbank assumes that the specific content of this authentic pattern of life is obvious to any reader of the Christian Bible, ignoring any hermeneutical and historical-critical problems of interpretation. He thus fails to address the fractured reality of the church and the wide variance of beliefs and practices contained within it. As such, his theology does not address some of the primary problems faced by contemporary churches.

A similar dynamic is present in Stanley Hauerwas's version of this Milbankian rejection of social science. In his own non-foundational approach to theology, Hauerwas argues that all truths discovered through other academic disciplines "must be tested and judged by the truth known through revelation."[62] To resolve the problem of the elusiveness of the full self-evident nature of the content of this revelation, Hauerwas, like Milbank, turns to the church as being the source of practices which shape the knowing subject, as well as the proper site in which to encounter the Christian narrative story: "knowledge can be rationally sustained only by a politics called church."[63]

But Christians are all-too familiar with the elusive nature of the purity of this vision of the church. Hauerwas's concept of the "politics called church" often appears on the ground to resemble the politics found in all spheres of social life. The church's capacity to produce a different (read "better") human being than the world outside the church is far from self-evident, and one need not list the endless series of mistaken and ideological assumptions held by Christians in the past to highlight the finite and tragic limits of Christian knowledge and understanding of the world. Milbank and Hauerwas bestow upon the church a function and responsibility that serves to replace the need for all other academic disciplines found in the modern university.

The work of Milbank, as well as of Hauerwas, do illuminate ways in which social science is often far from objectively neutral, and they offer important cautions against making theology subservient to a description of the world based on observing so-called "facts" about the "real world." But their sweeping and simplistic rejection of social science is only possible by covering over the problems of social life with an over-determined

---

61. Ibid., 326, 338, 332.
62. Hauerwas, *With the Grain*, 236.
63. Ibid., 239.

deployment of eschatological concepts like the invisible church, the Kingdom of God, and the fullness of the Gospel. The alternative Christian practices and habits that their theology depends upon to shape the very being of the individual can only do so in a complete manner when such divine achievements are established here on earth as they exist in heaven. The present patterns and manifestations of ecclesial life do not enable the contemporary Christian to step out of the very this-worldly dynamics which social science intends to describe and explain. The full distinctiveness of Christian practice and virtue lies ahead of us. While it is true that, thankfully, the church does enjoy a foretaste of this reality, and has benefitted from a long history of partial witnesses to this fullness, it cannot trade on the future promise of God's fullness to evade wrestling with the complexities involved in reflecting on and responding to contemporary social existence. For theology to maintain a critical lens on the explanations offered by social science does not demand that it argue that these explanations cannot and do not offer important insights into the behavior of contemporary Christians.

Social Theory and Theology: David Martin

Sociology's concern to explain human patterns of behavior in social terms need not, contrary to the claims of Milbank and Hauerwas, expel theology from the real. That it sometimes is employed to do so cannot to be denied, but it is also true that this is not always a bad thing for the church to have to contend with this challenge. Social scientific investigation can serve as a corrective to human bias and limited assumptions. Such issues plague the reflections of theologians and Christian believers as much as they do other human beings, and so the church can benefit from the self-reflexivity that may come from attention to the hypotheses and methodologies of social science. Having itself described by external observers can help the church achieve a deeper, and potentially more faithful, grasp of its own present reality.

To affirm this is not to reintroduce sociology as a discipline positioned to provide theology with a "grand narrative" about the true nature of reality, which will then police theology's capacity to reflect on the truthfulness of God. That would be to replace theology with social science, rather than to create a dialogue between two distinct disciplines.

If sociology has the potential to critically confront the assumptions and claims of theology, the same must be said of theology towards sociology if there is to be a meaningful conversation. To begin to bring this into view, the very different nature of the two disciplines will now be highlighted.

The British sociologist (and Anglican priest) David Martin distinguishes between sociology and theology in the following manner: sociology represents the "science of the possible," in the sense of identifying patterns that limit and constraint human behavior in specific social contexts, inhibiting some achievements while encouraging others. Theology, by contrast, he describes as "the symbolization of the ineluctable and the promissory."[64] Milbank and Hauerwas might balk at this choice of words, which clearly does not directly emphasise the agency of God, but the primary point of Martin's statement is to argue that what theology brings to the study of society is an attention to what lies beyond immediate apprehensions and achievements.[65] As such, this emphasis is not so far as one might initially assume from the basic concern voiced by Hauerwas when, in *With the Grain of the Universe*, he links theological knowledge with the practice of prayer.[66] Theology involves attentive concern for that which eludes human assumptions and capacities. The already-existing givens before the individual are not taken by theological reflection to be the fullness of reality. Good social theory should also be looking for dynamics and patterns beyond the immediately given. This is Martin's point, and a good deal of his own work in sociology of religion is focused on exploring how existing social structures frustrate and interrupt the concerns and logics of Christian language and ideals.

Rather than explore Martin's reflections on this matter in more detail, which focus on how sociology might serve theology, it is more useful for the purposes of the present discussion to remain with the question of what contribution *theology* can make to sociology, given the criticism directed thus far against Milbank's attitude toward sociology. Contrary to his view, theology and sociology can engaged in a fruitful dialogue. Neither a defensive rejection of the other, or a mere pillaging of resources without any mutual engagement, this dialogue has to do with the basic value judgments and claims which inform the interpretation

---

64. Martin, *Reflections on Sociology and Theology*, 245.

65. Ibid., 46.

66. Hauerwas, *With the Grain*, 10.

of sociological research, and perhaps more substantively, with a critical scrutiny of assumptions made by sociology about the nature of reality.

To illustrate this point, some reference to Rodney Stark's rational choice approach to religion may serve as an example. Stark's work offers a useful point of reference because it has a prominent position in the sociology or religion, but also because his work is not infrequently employed uncritically by theologians and church leadership . As such, his example also serves to warn against conceiving of the use of the social sciences as an immediate and straightforward pillaging of the Egyptians (recalling Bernard Lonergan's metaphor for the relationship between theology and social science).

Theology contra Rational Choice Theory

The advocates of Rational Choice Theory in social scientific methodology intend to overcome a perceived "disparity in development" that exists between natural and social science.[67] They do so on the basis of adopting mathematical models from economic theory and applying them to the analysis of social action. This approach is understood to bypass metaphysical assumptions about human nature and behavior, as well as holistic theories about the nature of society at the macro level, by focusing on strategic and instrumental decisions by individuals in social interaction. The perspective develops a voluntaristic theory of action, emphasizing the role of calculation and the achievement of expected outcomes in human behavior. Rational choice theory argues that intended consequences motivate human choice in social interaction, more than environmental conditioning, repetition of custom, or essential attribute.

The applications of rational choice theory in the study of religion by Rodney Stark are based upon the following premises about human activity:

1. human beings act rationally, weighing the costs and benefits of actions, and make choices with the intention to maximize the benefits of their actions;

2. the ultimate human preferences (or needs) used to assess costs and benefits do not vary much;

67. Riker "Political Science," 177.

3. the interaction of individual choices and actions result in a social equilibrium.[68]

The theologian (and the attentive social scientist) will note that these presuppositions are asserted at the outset of theorizing; they are not proven or derived out of empirical study of social action. And yet, these assumptions subtly outline a very precise theory of human nature and rationality, and a not-so-subtle economic ideology. In the presuppositions of rational choice theory, there is no place for the determination of ends; reason's sole purpose is to employ the means at hand to achieve whatever particular end is desired.

For Stark, the first premise of rational choice theory regarding the nature of rationality assumes that humans seek rewards and avoid costs. Thus, any "rational" choice will be guided by this preference, and his interpretation of religion emerges out of this perspective. He argues that, because some desired rewards are in limited supply, or remain beyond the capacity of some people to achieve, individuals often substitute a "compensator" for a desired reward. A compensator is an explanation or proposal for an alternative manner to obtain a desired reward, often through elaborate and lengthy methods. Religion serves to provide compensators in the absence or unavailability of certain rewards, principally the desire for immortality. Stark writes, "it usually is necessary to enter into a long-term exchange relationship with the divine and with divinely inspired institutions, in order to follow the instructions" on how to achieve the desire goal over the longer term; "churches rest upon these underlying exchange relationships."[69]

From this premise, Stark deduces axioms such as the idea that less powerful people will be more likely to accept compensators. He also suggests that, when a religious organization weakens its emphasis on supernaturalism and an afterlife, it inevitably weakens itself, due to a diminished ability to offer the promise of powerful compensators. This explains, he concludes, why liberal mainstream Christian churches are in decline. It is noteworthy that this analysis leads Stark to challenge rather than support the secularization thesis. Instead of expecting a general decline of interest in religion, spurred on by the spread of modernity and

68. For a brief summary of these basic assumptions, see: Iannaccone, "Framework for the Scientific Study of Religion," 26; Stark and Bainbridge, *Theory of Religion*.

69. Stark, "Bringing Theory Back In," 6–7.

scientific knowledge, he argues that secularization is a self-limiting process. Although some people might abandon their religious traditions, Stark suggests that their children will likely be religious. While major religious denominations may decline, new faiths and traditions will emerge that offer more credible and supernatural compensators[70] The general logic behind Stark's argumentation against secularization is that access to desired rewards will always be limited, and so therefore the need for compensators will always be required to pacify disappointed or frustrated desires.

Some of the language Stark employs to describe this approach to religion reveals the extent to which macroeconomic theoretical models inform the assumptions of rational choice theory. His explanatory concepts are often drawn from the vocabulary of economics. Religious communities are referred to as "firms." Those that "specialize" will flourish in the "religious economy." Those that fail to offer a compelling enough compensator will decline. He argues that, "Religious economies are like commercial economies in that they consist of a market of current and potential customers, a set of firms seeking to serve that market, and the religious 'product lines' offered by the various firms."[71] This view is employed to support his challenge to the secularization thesis: "to the degree that a religious economy is competitive and pluralistic, overall levels of religious participation will tend to be high." In other words, as the "monopoly" of mainline Christian churches declines, the emerging pluralistic and "free" religious market will result in increasing "religious" activity and exchange, as individual "religious investors" diversify what Lawrence Iannaccone calls their "religious portfolios."[72] It is suggested that, in a "free market," flexible institutions will prosper.

The first task for the theologian is dialogue with such a sociological approach is to question an overly immediate translation of these findings to the practicalities of pastoral ministry: church outreach and mission, planning of service times, and so forth. Even in an environment in which academic theology is suspicious of social science, pastors and lay people on the ground are frequently quick to employ any theory that appears to assist them to understand how their fellow Christians work, and how

70. Ibid., 18–19.
71. Ibid., 16–17.
72. Iannaccone, "Voodoo Economics?" 81.

to respond in kind. However, at the same time, the patterns of behavior observed by Stark and Iannaconne are nevertheless important for the church to have brought to its attention. The fact that Christians are as prone to be shaped by their social-economic climate as any other human beings is an important pastoral challenge for theologians and pastors to confront directly.

The deeper task for the theologian is to inquire into the assumptions and value commitments made in this theoretical model. Is this really how all human beings make their decisions? Even when they do, are they subsequently satisfied with the results? Such a critical engagement with rational choice theory does not necessarily require or involve any particularly *theological* method or insight. Is the contribution of the theologian to this debate, then, only to ask the social scientist to be a better social scientist?

Although there is something to be said for even that role, theology can offer more than this. Staying with the present illustration, let us revisit the third presupposition of rational choice theory regarding social equilibrium. The notion that existent social forms represent the stable outcome of different strategic actions has been challenged by the social scientist Theodor W. Adorno. But when he did so, he was often accused of being a theologian. This example is instructive. Adorno employs a concept of what he calls the social "totality." If the study of social action concerns itself only with the interactions between human beings without attending to their "objectified form," he argues that it acts as if "everything really depended on these interpersonal relationships," and not on larger social mechanisms. "What disappears from sociology is not only the decisive element whereby social activity is able to maintain itself at all, but also knowledge of how it maintains itself, with what sacrifices, threats and also with what potentialities for good."[73] For Adorno, the social whole cannot simply be reduced to the sum of its parts.

Adorno's speculative concept of "social totality" intends to suggest a dialectical theory of society, in order to hold open a notion of "society as a thing-in-itself."[74] As such, it serves to "give a name to what secretly holds the machinery together."[75] The concept provides a way to appreciate Marx's critique of ideology in sociological method, and it prevents

---

73. Adorno, *Introduction to Sociology*, 142.

74. Adorno, *Positivist Dispute*, 12.

75. Ibid., 68.

treating social structures and experiences as "natural" or *a priori*. Adorno argues that positivist empirical studies of social action fail to account for how objective social structures shape the subjective actions of human agents. To ignore this is to ignore the mediated nature of all knowledge and experience, and of the contradictions contained within human society. To Adorno, modern society, with its ongoing disparities in distribution of wealth, access to education and health care, is irrational:

> By calling this society irrational I mean that if the purpose of society as a whole is taken to be the preservation and the unfettering of the people of which it is composed, then the way in which this society continues to be arranged runs counter to its own purpose, its *raison d'être*, its *ratio*.[76]

Thus, while rational choice theory might observe how some individuals behave, Adorno's critical perspective insists that the seemingly "rational choices" that individuals make, in order to determine the manner and extent to which their subjectivity is shaped by the larger social whole. Adorno argues that failure to attend to the reality of the social totality results in an undialectical separation between *actuality* and *potentiality*. In *Negative Dialectics*, he refers to the example of freedom to explain what he means: "Emphatically conceived, the judgment that a man is free refers to the concept of freedom." But as the individual encounters barriers to its actions, "the concept of freedom lags behind itself as soon as we apply it empirically." Such a confrontation forces the concept to contradict itself, as the particular individual seeks to be free, but must also diminish what the concept of freedom implies practically "for utility's sake."[77]

Adorno's social theory wrestles with this dilemma. The contradiction between the concept of freedom and the particular experience of social unfreedom cannot simply be resolved in thought. Instead, the "potential for freedom calls for criticizing what an inevitable formalization has made of the potential." The tension that arises because of the concept's unrealized *potentiality* results in a criticism of its *actuality*. Without a dialectical concept of society, he argues, one cannot distinguish between a society's actuality and its potentiality. The *status quo* will be taken to be society's only possible form.

76. Adorno, *Introduction to Sociology*, 133.
77. Adorno, *Negative Dialectics*, 149–51.

Adorno's concept of social totality remained vague and unformulated, and was frequently dismissed by his critics as a theological concept that was not to be taken seriously; however, his approach represents a helpful place to begin to reconceive the debate between theology and sociology. It is an advance beyond the rejection of social theory by Milbank and Hauerwas, for it continues to acknowledge that the society in which Christians think and act exists prior to them, and thus has the capacity to shape them in often unrecognized ways. Yet Adorno's general concern also signals to theology that it need be suspicious of the inherent assumptions and value judgments made by social science, and thus need to simply ignore the very real issues brought to theology's attention by Milbank. Finally, the notion that existing society cannot be immediately reduced to some self-evident social facts or patterns coincides well, and can be strengthened and nurtured by, a theological concern for the reality beyond the self-evident present before it.

Christian theology brings its own concerns and commitments to the study of society, including attention to the grace of God, but also charity, reconciliation and redemption. These basic orientations or concerns can serve to heighten attention to the tension between actuality and potentiality, or redeemed and unredeemed in more properly theological terminology. Adorno himself frequently employed theological concepts to describe the distinction between the present reality of social life, and a hope that the world could be better than it is.

This critique of Milbank, as well as of rational choice theory, illustrates that theology benefits from an engagement with social science. As a discipline, theology requires assistance in understanding its own social location, and the social dynamics which impact on the life of the church and its members. But the interaction between theology and sociology is not one which only ought to humble theology. Theological assumptions may be called into question by the dialogue, but so, too, sociological presumptions. In the conversation between theology and social science, theology holds open attention to unrecognized reality, which is too frequently ignored by social science's focus on describing the immediately existing that presents itself. Theology introduces distinct concerns and questions about social experience that may otherwise remain ignored or unrecognized. Theology's concern to focus primarily on the acts of God in the world does not replace the usefulness of social analysis for the church, but theology can enhance social theory's scrutiny of presently existing reality. The two disciplines have different habits and disciplines, but there no need to define them as inherently at war. The fruitfulness of the dialogue will depend on how the other looks upon those it engages with. For this reason, Martin and Adorno represent much more promising guides for how to proceed with the conversation between theology and social science than either Milbank or Hauerwas.

9

Theology and Politics:
The Intellectual History of Liberalism

CHRISTOPHER INSOLE

Definitions and Histories of Liberalism

THEOLOGIANS, WHEN DISCUSSING "LIBERALISM" in the context of political philosophy, are apt to pull out of their hat whatever they have stuffed
into it before the show began: what sort of creature emerges—cuddly,
mingy, or verminous—reveals more about the temperament and prejudices of the theologian than anything else. The definition is already tailor
made to fit the evaluation. "Liberalism" is found to be—because in truth it
is defined to be—secular, individualistic, and morally corrupt, or ordered
to justice and human flourishing. Introducing an historical dimension to
the discussion can actually make things worse, in that we can feel more
learned, and so become more taken in by our prejudices. True, what we
now tailor is a whole intellectual history and narrative, but still this description can be shaped for us, or by us, in such a way that most of the
evaluative work has already been smuggled in.

Here, for example, are two rival intellectual histories of liberalism,
which feed parasitically off each other's crudity. On the one hand, there
is a Whiggish genealogy, which tells the following narrative about the

emergence of liberalism. Liberalism arrived not a moment too soon after the Reformation and the Wars of Religion: a wise, gracious, and soothing host, settling down the fractious religious delinquents of warring Europe, Catholic against Protestant. Before the liberal state: warfare, religious fanaticism, oppression, and intolerance (bad). With the liberal state: peace, freedom, and toleration (good). In the wake of William Cavanaugh's influential work,[1] many theologians now set against this a rival history of liberalism, which is much less flattering to its subject. The rise of the liberal state, according to this counter-narrative, is to be understood against the context of the dispute running through the middle ages concerning whether authority and power was held by the Church, or by temporal rulers. Luther's contribution is massively to centralize power in the prince, as opposed to the Pope. The absolutist prince of Lutheranism, opposed to the trans-national claim of the Roman Catholic Church, is secularized by thinkers such as Hobbes, and set on its way to becoming the bureaucratic state of late-capitalism. This totalizing state claims to save us from a category of "violent religion" (which category it largely invents), while actually demanding allegiance to the new religion of nationalism enforced by violence. In both cases we have a genealogy which is supposed to give us the key to the meaning of "liberalism." By uncovering *the* intellectual history of liberalism, we now know its hidden aspirations and deepest motivations, enabling us to come to judgment about it.[2]

In my view, neither of these narratives is helpful. They do serve though to illustrate the danger in starting with a single definition, or historical narrative, for as complex a phenomenon as liberalism. In reflecting more widely on the interface between "Theology and Politics," I would suggest that our thinking is immeasurably improved when theologians do not *begin* with metaphysically and theologically freighted definitions and narratives. Rather, we should begin with a set of *practices*. These practices, I suggest—whatever we think of them, and however far we think contemporary politics has fallen away from them—make up what we know of as "constitutional liberalism," where and when it exists: the restriction of the use of coercive public power to sustaining peace and

1. See Cavanaugh, "Fire Strong Enough" and *Theopolitical Imagination*, esp. ch.1. For a fuller response to Cavanaugh, see my "Discerning the Theopolitical."

2. Manent's *Intellectual History of Liberalism*, it should be said, does not indulge in unhelpful reductionism, but sets out admirably a range of thinkers and concerns that constitute the diverse liberal tradition.

justice (giving to each their due), rather than to enforcing ultimate truth or unity of belief; the protection of individuals within a framework of rights and liberties; the separation of powers (between the law-makers, law-enforcers and those who interpret the application of the law), and the mixed constitution (elements of rule of the one, the few and the many). Representation is taken to be the basis of authority, and the rule of law the manifestation of this authority. Such law is established by consent and is oriented to the welfare of the people governed by it. The law protects and enshrines certain rights, which cannot be violated or trumped. The law is understood to have a limited external scope, allowing subjects to pursue their own ends within a tolerant and pluralistic society, inasmuch as they do not put peace or justice at peril. In constitutional liberalism, the law has authority rather than the individual ruler, and the ruler is held accountable for their use of authority: so a further set of practices, such as freedom of speech and association, arise as an expression of the commitment to the accountability and transparency of power. The internal circumscription of the powers of the state, and the limited external scope of the law, means that the state allows and facilitates semi-autonomous public institutions, such as churches and universities, which institutions are protected within a framework of law, but where it is not within the purview of the law to determine, say, the truths of physics or of theology. Only where most or all of these practices are adhered to, more or less well, do we have constitutional liberalism.

If we begin with this fairly loose "family resemblance" concept of constitutional liberalism, we are in a position to illuminate the complexity of the subject. This must be better than having to balance our precarious pile of historical bricolage, just long enough to take our pristine snapshot, to put in the album with the sticker "liberalism" next to it. Thinking of liberalism in terms of this set of practices can help us to understand how some thinkers join us for some of the party, but leave—or storm out—before it really gets going: so, for example, Hobbes is often called a "liberal" thinker because he has something to say about rights and liberties, and about representation and consent. We each have a right to self-preservation, and because of the war against all in the state of nature, we can only secure this right by contracting amongst ourselves to create an absolute sovereign, capable of keeping the peace. The sovereign acts, but as we have created the sovereign from our act of consent, in the ultimate analysis, we are the authors of the sovereign's actions. For this reason, dissent from the sovereign is actually a form of self-contradiction. This is a notion of "representation" in the strongest possible sense. We are the *authors* of the absolute sovereign's actions.

By all means we can talk of Hobbes as a "liberal" thinker, and of Hobbesian liberalism. But we must be sure to be specific. Because we only have the one term "liberalism" where about eleven might suffice, we need to differentiate other strands and traditions of liberalism. Consider: Hobbes deplores the mixed constitution, the separation of powers, freedom of speech and association, and the notion that the law has authority over the ruler. Just as there must be no internal division of sovereignty, for Hobbes, there must also be no external limitation on the authority of the state: with there being no public space not under the control of authoritarian state structures. This immediately reveals the at best partial success of any theological engagement with politics—certainly at work in the Cavanaugh narrative outlined above—which is convinced that Hobbes, and Hobbes' absolute state, is the key to understanding "liberalism" as such.

So we see that some forms of liberalism do not endorse all the practices listed above, or prioritize the practices differently. We can do some of the work of clarification by talking specifically. Just to add the term "constitutional" to our liberalism might help to pick out liberalisms that are committed to constitutional practices. But even where there is agreement on the importance of a practice, it can be capable of a number of quite different metaphysical underpinnings and justifications. History reflects this conceptual complexity by embodying in different thinkers and movements quite opposed justifications for similar practices. The practices, we might say, are over-determined by theory: a number of normative frameworks can and have been offered for them.

The first task of theology in relation to politics, and to political philosophy, should, I would suggest, be this: to avoid reductionism. Theologians should resist the temptation, in themselves and others, to cut intellectual corners by a speedy appeal to the "foundations" of liberalism. As Wittgenstein said, "don't think, but look."[3] Look first of all at the complexity of what might be meant by "liberalism." And then, Wittgenstein again, "I'll teach you differences."[4] Theologians have a great deal to offer in separating out the complexity of normative strands in the various

3. Wittgenstein, *Philosophical Investigations*, §66.
4. Rhees, *Recollections of Wittgenstein*, 157.

geological strata of liberalism, just because so many of these differences have their ultimate grounding in theological convictions and disputes. It is ironic that it is often the very same theologians who pride themselves both on being post-foundationalist and properly attentive to *practices*, who should themselves appeal to the "foundations" of liberalism and neglect a range of concrete practices when thinking about politics. Interesting to reflect also on Wittgenstein's insight that "what it is we believe" is not fixed simply by "mental contents," but is expressed in the full weave of our behavior and practices. This might put a question mark against the not unfamiliar figure of a theologian who announces an opposition to "liberalism," alongside an active and positive engagement and protective instinct towards some or all of the practices listed above.

In case, for some, this begins to smell too hygienically Wittgensteinian—practices *rather than* metaphysics, with metaphysics as a sort of idle wheel in the mechanism—I should say that I do not mean to imply that these practices float free of theory. There should be no dualism in our understanding of practices and theory, as if a practice, such as the preservation of rights, is not already imbued with an anthropology and a metaphysics. This notion that we can have certain practices without any (at least implied) substantial theory or metaphysics is one that the liberal theorist John Rawls himself pedals. If theologians can be too quick to start with metaphysical foundations, secular political philosophers can often be observed nimbly steadying themselves on the branch that they are sawing off, denying that there are any such foundations while patently standing on them. The precise claim I want to make is this: theological and metaphysical premises do a *great deal of work* in framing, constituting and justifying the practices listed above, and the practices are always to some extent framed, constituted, and justified by theological, quasi-theological, or metaphysical assumptions and premises. The opposite of good theology is not no theology, but bad theology. That we begin our engagement by discerning practices does not mean that this is where we will stay, or where we will end up. But we must learn to disaggregate, and to discern diversity and nuance before we begin to adjudicate. Aphorisms such as "don't think but look," and "I'll teach you differences," point to the diversity of practices involved in liberalism, and to the range and diversity of theoretical and metaphysical underpinnings for these practices. It is to the speedy and reductive resort to monolithic foundations that I object, rather than a more nuanced, historically curious and theologically sensitive interest in foundations.

For the remainder of this chapter, I intend to take just one of the practices listed above as a lens through which to look at some wider considerations. Focusing on the notion of the mixed constitution will enable us to reflect first of all on the role of democracy. Secondly, it will point us—through a brief encounter with medieval ecclesiology—to the importance of doctrinal themes in the emergence of liberalism. Finally, I will look at the Kantian reconstruction and defense of liberal practices. The only practice that Kant rejects is the mixed constitution. Understanding why Kant does this will take us deeper into some of the very distinctive and theological origins of apparently secular underpinnings for liberal constitutionalism, which are widely understood as hostile to theological reasoning. In particular, it takes us to secular underpinnings such as we find in John Rawls, and Rawlsian reconstructions of the tradition. It is dismaying when the "theology and liberalism" debate just becomes the "theology and John Rawls' debate: as if liberalism was discovered in 1971 with the publication of his *Theory of Justice*. Liberalism was no more discovered in 1971 than sex was in 1963. At the same time, Rawlsian/Kantian liberalism is for many the dominant expression of this tradition. It demands our attention.

There will be distinct changes of gear between the sections of the chapter: from a consideration of democracy, to medieval ecclesiology and then a concluding section on Kant. My hope is that the progression exemplifies the virtues of the methodology of attention and disaggregation before adjudication, which I have been recommending. We discern first of all what the practice is, and its role in constitutional liberalism, and use this to explore two very different theological and metaphysical groundings for constitutional practices (first of all ecclesiology, and then Kantian reason).

The Mixed Constitution

The Role of Democracy

The specific arrangements of different mixed constitutions can be very complex, but it is clear enough what is being sought. A mixed constitution works between the need to come to political judgment, whilst not trusting any single mechanism for discerning the right course of action. The monarchical mechanism, of course, does not require a King or a Queen: a president of a republic also embodies the principle of "rule by one." In the UK the monarchical mechanism is represented symbolically by the sovereign, but exercised concretely through the Prime Minister's royal prerogative. Monarchy can deliver swift and effective action; but Prime Ministers, Kings and Presidents are only human, and can err. A small group of expert rulers—with, it is hoped, particular capacities or opportunities for political wisdom—incorporates a greater range of experience and perspectives than the monarchical principle, but can itself become beholden to particular interest groups or segments of society. In the UK the House of Lords plays this role: made up of life peers with expertise in a range of professions, Anglican Bishops, and hereditary members, who in theory are supposed to have the advantages of stability, independence and historical memory.

Democratic rule, where some part of the people decide directly or through representatives (such as the House of Commons), extends the process of discernment to a wide range of interest groups, and can disrupt the plans of a cozy elite. But it also extends it to those without the means—the time, expertise and experience—of discernment, and is vulnerable to the injustices and preoccupations of the mob. Supporters of the mixed constitution reject pure monarchy, pure aristocracy, and pure democracy, and insist that these three mechanisms act as checks and balances upon one another. This constitutional instinct is concerned to limit the absolutizing pretensions and powers of the state, and the same momentum that supports a mixed constitution will also seek legal protection and relative independence for strong public institutions below the level of the state. It is crucial to constitutionalism that there should be more levels of political reality than the individual and the state.

Concentrating on the mixed constitution has the one distinct advantage that it enables us, immediately and incontrovertibly, to put democracy in its place, and to harness as an ally of liberalism significant contemporary theological critiques of "liberalism" (so-called). One of the most deleterious conflations in political theology is the sense that constitutional liberalism and democracy are either the same thing, or that liberalism gets its normative value by virtue of *being the product of a democratic process*. In fact, democracy is one of the practices supported within the framework of constitutional liberalism; but it is not the framework itself,

179

and it is not the source of constitutional liberalism. As Oliver O'Donovan puts it, "rather than underpinning justice, democracy is a task of justice on the narrow front of political representation," so that "by providing a just settlement to thorny conflicts of representation, democracy adds a further layer to liberal government."[5]

This is not meant to imply that democracy is *the* practice that guarantees representation: all levels of the constitution are *representative*, as is our involvement in voluntary associations. All these mechanisms are intended to represent our true interests, as they meet questions of public power and coercive law. Being properly represented is not like some sort of interactive reality show, where you must "have your say" by phoning in your opinion or your vote. Edmund Burke told his Bristol electorate that it was his duty to "sacrifice his repose, his pleasures" and "his satisfactions, to theirs," and "in all cases, to prefer their interest to his own." The representative owes the represented "his unbiased option, his mature judgment, his enlightened conscience," but "he betrays" instead of serving them if he "sacrifices it to [their] opinion."[6]

Where democracy—as a form of collective autonomy—is seen as the source of normativity, the foundation rather than an implication, then it is more than likely to become a danger to other practices of constitutional liberalism. To put it simply: if democracy is the *source* of truth, rather than one of its protectors, some of the practices of liberalism are put on a very precarious footing: why bother to preserve freedom of speech and association, or certain rights and liberties, if the general will that bestows these things, has determined that they are to be taken away (in the interests of security say)?

Because democracy is one of the practices of liberalism, and owing to the expansion of both liberalism and democracy in roughly the same places at the same time, their conceptual distinguishability is not widely appreciated. The tradition of reflection about constitutional liberalism— running through Locke, Burke, de Tocqueville,[7] Mill, and Arnold—is a litany of caution about the role and impact of democracy. In 1923 Carl Schmitt goes as far as to identify the essence of democracy as the "assertion of an identity of governed and governing, sovereign and subject . . .

---

5. O'Donovan, *Ways of Judgment*, 174.

6. Burke, "Speech to the Electors of Bristol," 446–48.

7. See, for example, Manent, "Tocqueville,"

the quantitative (the numerical majority or unanimity) with the qualitative (the justice of the laws)."[8] Schmitt considered democracy to be fundamentally at odds with constitutional liberalism, which he interpreted as resting upon a transcendent conception of truth, alongside a sense that discussion and openness is the best way to approach this truth. Citing the "liberal Burke" as a paradigmatic example, Schmitt argues that "the belief in parliamentarianism . . . belongs to the intellectual world of liberalism . . . not to democracy," such that "discussion means an exchange of opinion that is governed by the purpose of persuading one's opponent through argument of the truth or justice of something, or allowing oneself to be persuaded of something as true or just."[9]

Schmitt's observations have some bite when one reflects that he was the leading jurist during the Weimar Republic, attempting during the early 1920s to preserve order against extreme anti-constitutional elements, such as fascism and communism. Schmitt discerned these movements harnessing democracy at the cost of constitutionalism, and became convinced that the incoherence of mixing liberal and democratic grounds for the political was one of the factors pulling the infant Republic apart. His *Crisis of Parliamentary Democracy*, written in 1923, he described later as a "warning and cry for help."[10] Schmitt wanted President von Hindenburg to use extraordinary powers to protect the whole constitution against an overactive democratic gland. In May 1933, in the interests of "order"—as he saw it—Schmitt threw his lot in with the National Socialists. This was because Schmitt was enough of a Hobbesian to think that the greatest political evil was disorder, with order of any sort better than chaos and civil war. Totalitarianism he understood as opposed to liberalism, but as on the same continuum as democracy: the expression of a democratic logic, whereby the general will constructs truth. The question of how the general will is construed (through the ballot box, or through the great man) being a secondary and more technical matter.

If there is a lesson from all this, it is that many critiques of "liberalism" from contemporary theologians are better understood as cultural critiques of democracy, which are in fact part of a liberal tradition as old

---

8. Schmitt, *Crisis of Parliamentary Democracy*.

9. Ibid., 6–8.

10. Ibid., xxxviii.

as liberalism itself.[11] The same anxieties that we find in Edmund Burke, de Tocqueville, and Matthew Arnold tend to surface in figures such as John Milbank and Stanley Hauerwas: the corrosive impact of a homogenizing, permissive, licentious, commercial, and individualistic society, without proper cultural formation, ecclesial involvement, historical memory, social integration, appropriate authority, or social and communal virtues. Only if we have already conflated democracy with liberalism do these critiques look like anything other than a defense of recognizably liberal practices and institutions.

Schmitt, Burke, and warnings about democracy: this might all sound—it might be—rather reactionary. Against this, it should be noted that being aware of the distinction between liberalism and democracy does not always lead to a *critique* of an overactive democratic dimension. Consonant with our methodological principle to look for differences and variety, there are in the liberal tradition a variety of construals of the value of democratic processes, even where the status of democracy as a means to an end, rather than an end in itself, is well understood. We can understand all this, but still think that there is not enough democracy about, or not the right sort of democracy, perhaps because it is insufficiently supported by the virtues and social structures that are necessary for its healthy flourishing. Thinkers more on the left of liberalism understand that equality is a necessary aspect of liberty and the protection of individuals, and understand democracy as a necessary expression and protection of this equality. An anxiety about too thin a theory of the state, which leaves individuals vulnerable to a morally neutral economic sphere, is precisely the concern of nineteenth-century liberals such as T. H. Green, J. S. Mill, and Hobhouse. And then there is the republican model of liberalism, harking back to the Greek city republics, which emphasizes the

---

11. It should be clear that some defenses of democracy in a wider sense are not directly targeted by such cultural critiques of democracy. So, for instance, when Stout defends "democracy" in *Democracy and Tradition* he is best construed as defending a set of practices and virtues that underpin constitutional liberalism, although as Little insightfully points out, Stout obscures this point by disavowing the term "liberal." Little correctly warns that by abandoning the term "liberalism," Stout risks surrendering "with one hand what he has gained with the other," as "rescuing the word 'liberal' is no trivial undertaking, since the idea of '*liberal* democracy,' properly understood, and as opposed to '*illiberal* democracy' is indispensable both to the contemporary worldwide discussion of democracy and, as a matter of fact, to much that Stout himself appears to favor about American Democracy" (288). See Little, "On Behalf of Rights."

importance of a virtuous public space, and which highly values democratic traditions (this is a strong tradition in North America, embodied
in de Tocqueville, and represented recently by Jeffrey Stout). Again, the
point is that when theologians worry about too small a conception of
the state, a lack of equality, or the atrocities of global markets, they are
not necessarily stepping outside of recognizably liberal traditions: or, at
least, they are expressing concerns first and frequently expressed by liberal thinkers.

Doctrine and the Mixed Constitution

Now for the first change of gear, to more historical concerns. In this section I will outline very briefly the way in which medieval ecclesiology is
one of the main conduits for the practice of the mixed constitution. I say
"one of the main conduits" because—again acknowledging differences—
there are others: for example, a republican tradition—coming through
Machiavelli, Harrington, and Montesquieu—derives an interest in constitutional checks and balances more directly from the classical sources,
Aristotle and Polybius. Here again we have case of the same practice being capable of different construals and justifications. My focus here will
be on the ecclesial and theological tradition, and the particular way it has
construed the practice.

But before that, we need to face a blunt question: who cares? That
is, who cares what the genealogy is? Is it simply of academic antiquarian
interest to uncover the medieval historical roots of a practice? Well, we
should care, for the following reason. Precisely if we want to be attentive
to the different textures and possibilities of liberal practices, it helps us to
recover some of the motivations and aspirations of the original practices,
in their original context. We might find that we have become coarsened
and deaf to the history of the present, replacing a rich polyphony with an
irritating jingle. As I will show, this is in fact what we find: that when the
church meets the liberal tradition, it misunderstands itself and that tradition if it meets it as an alien and secular innovation. Aspects of liberalism
are in fact ecclesial traditions, with strong doctrinal support.

This gives the lie to the "Whiggish" of the two narratives I set out at
the beginning. The liberal state is not simply a post-Reformation solution to delinquent warring "religions." It would be more true to say that

constitutional liberalism finds its roots in strands of medieval ecclesiology. Such debates arise from a profound reckoning with the question of the relationship between salvation and the use of power given that every individual must be, in Augustine's words a "question to themselves before God"[12]—that is to say, that even a pope, prince or sacred college of cardinals can err, for who is without some sin in this life? We find in medieval ecclesiology a sustained meditation on the need to come to political judgment, where some judgments approximate the good more than others, against the backdrop of our inability to make judgments, given imperfection and sin. Sin which is individual, communal and structural, pervasive but not uniform, and which cannot be eliminated from human nature by social formation, virtue, the best of intentions, or any process or mechanism of social engineering or historical progress.

Of particular importance is the conciliar movement of the fourteenth and fifteenth centuries, which sought to contain the monarchical power of the pope within a mixed constitution—embodying elements of the one, the few and the many—such that the whole church was perceived to be present most authoritatively in a representative council. The conciliarists made an appeal on three fronts: to the notion of the mixed constitution supported by Aristotle, to representative structures in Roman and canon law where the head is answerable to the collective body, and to the Mosaic polity of the Old Testament, which the conciliarist Jean Gerson characteristically describes as "the best government just as it was under Moses . . . mixed from three polities: regal in Moses, aristocratic in the seventy-two elders, and timocratic since the rectors were chosen under Moses from the people and from single tribes."[13] "Timocracy" means here the virtuous form of rule by the many in Aristotle, of which democracy is the corrupt version. Gerson's framing of a mixed constitution for the church is representative of the movement: "we can divide the ecclesiastical polity into papal, collegial, and synodal (that is, of the general council). Papal [rule] imitates regal, the collegial [rule] of the Lord Cardinals imitates aristocracy, general synodal [rule] imitates polity or timocracy; or rather it [ecclesiastical polity] is a perfect polity that results from all."[14]

---

12. Augustine *Confessions* X.33.50.

13. Gerson, *Oeuvres Completes*, in Blythe, *Ideal Government*, 251.

14. Gerson, in Blythe, *Ideal Government*, 250.

The causal link between these medieval conciliarists and the emergence of liberal constitutional principles in the sixteenth and seventeenth centuries has been demonstrated beyond question by historians (such as John Neville Figgis, Francis Oakley, Brian Tierney, and James Blythe):[15] the only possible debate is one concerning degrees of emphasis relative to other traditions. Such ecclesiastical constitutionalism enters the political blood stream through early defenses of Anglicanism, which conveniently construe the Church of England as being in continuity with the conciliar medieval Catholic Church. Marsilius of Padua, one of the most important fourteenth-century conciliarists, is translated into English within a year of the break with Rome, and given a preface that explicitly draws attention to the continuity and preservation of constitutional practices.[16] Richard Hooker's *Laws of Ecclesiastical Polity* is also steeped in such constitutionalism, with explicit parallels drawn between ecclesiastical and temporal governance.

15. The classic work here is Figgis' *Political Thought From Gerson to Grotius*. If there were problems with Figgis' approach, they would be the following: first of all, he did not trace the origins of conciliarism far back enough, and secondly, he did not explain how the conciliarist thought of the middle ages fed into "secular" constitutionalism. Since Figgis, much work has been done on both fronts. On the foundations of conciliar thinking Brian Tierney has done groundbreaking work, demonstrating that the roots of conciliar thinking lie in canonistic glosses of the twelfth and thirteenth centuries, and showing the influence of the movement into the early modern period: see his *Religion, Law and Constitutional Thought 1150–1650*, and *The Foundations of the Conciliar Theory*. James Blythe has built on Tierney's work, showing the importance of the notion of the mixed constitution—derived from Aristotle and Biblical/Mosaic models—to a wide range of scholastic thinkers: see his *Ideal Government and the Mixed Constitution*. For the influence of conciliar thinkers on later resistance theories see Oakley, "On the Road." Oakley is putting the flesh on a suggestion made initially by Harold Laski that "the road from Constance to 1688 is a direct one" in "Political Thought in the Later Middle Ages" (41). For useful overviews of the scholarship in this area Burns, *Cambridge History of Medieval Political Thought*, ch.17, and Skinner, *Foundations of Modern Political Thought*, ch.4.

16. The Act of Supremacy, consolidating the split with Rome and declaring Henry VIII to be governor of the Church of England, was passed in 1534. One year later in 1535, we find the first English translation of Marsilius of Padua's radically conciliar treatise *Defensor Pacis*, sporting the royal coat of arms, and produced "with the king''s most gracious privilege." The translator, William Marshall, tells us that in Marsilius'' treatise, written two hundred years ago, "thou shalt find . . . the image of these our times most perfectly and clearly expressed and set out." Of particular relevance, Marshall instructs us, is the balancing and curbing of powers whereby "the officers and rulers" and "the multitude or commons" are "each to other established," "both parties keeping themselves within their own right, as it were within a certain limit or bounds," staking claim only to that which "the laws will give them leave." Marsilius of Padua, *Defensor Pacis*, 139.

In seventeenth-century debates concerning the resistance, if any, that might legitimately be exerted against the power of a monarch, we find interlocutors on all sides of the question acknowledging—lamenting or celebrating in speeches and pamphlets—the medieval ecclesiological roots of constitutional restrictions on the sovereign's power. In continuity with the medieval tradition, the concern is with the abuse of power. This theologically informed suspicion of power, and the determination to call the state to account in the face of a higher truth and authority, is found powerfully in the eighteenth century in a figure such as Edmund Burke.[17] And it is no accident that a leading nineteenth-century liberal, Lord Acton, should root his constitutionalism in his deeply help Catholic convictions. Commenting that the Christian is "bound by his very creed to suspect evil,"[18] Acton explicitly celebrates the liberal resistance to absolutism and the constitutional protection of the individual. It is against a background of doctrinal commitments, explicitly informed by his interest in medieval ecclesiology, that Acton frames his famous maxim that "power tends to corrupt and absolute power corrupts absolutely."[19] In terms of the narrative put forward by Cavanaugh, we might say that rather than the liberal state weighing in on the side of the prince in the medieval conflict between the pope and the prince, it stands against both, in refusing to locate absolute power anywhere; power is mistrusted, dispersed and held accountable within constitutional frameworks enshrined in law.

Oliver O'Donovan and Joan Lockwood O'Donovan are contemporary theologians who have done a great deal to keep this memory alive. Crude characterizations of Oliver O'Donovan's political theology as a version of "Christendom" hardly do justice to his success in bringing alive a tradition that makes rulers answerable to Christ, and attempts to build in concrete structures by which this answerability is made actual. The lesson for the theologian interacting with political philosophy should be clear. The doctrinal themes at the heart of ecclesiology—creation, fall, redemption, eschatology—are formative influences on the emergence of the structural curbing of power, and the pluralizing of sources of discernment and loyalty.

17. See my "Two Conceptions of Liberalism," and "Natural Law and Practical Reason."
18. Lord Acton, "Studies of History," 28.
19. Lord Acton, "Acton-Creighton Correspondence," 364.

A sense of the importance of the mixed constitution is strong in the historical memory of constitutional liberalism. That said, the mixed constitution is also one of the practices of liberalism that can seem most imperiled. Lacking the glamour of "rights," and because of the inflation of democracy, it is perhaps one of the least understood and valued. One can see the mixed constitution at risk whenever there are appeals to the obvious rightness and urgency of spreading democracy in the Middle East (rather than say good governance, justice and strong institutions); or where it asserted that the judiciary or a non-elected upper house can be easily by-passed because they are not "democratically elected." Political parties and governments cannot always be trusted to protect these constitutional restrictions on their own power, and we find liberalism in danger when "essentially plebiscitarian legitimations"[20]—appeals to the "democratic mandate"—are used to interfere with public associations, or to abolish historical protections and liberties (permitting an extensive period of detention without charge, to take a recent example).

Kantian Liberalism

And now for the final change of gear, into a more philosophical register, which through Kant will give us a line into contemporary Rawlsian construals of liberalism. Kant endorses all of the liberal practices listed at the beginning of the paper. All except one, which he condemns: and that is the mixed constitution. Kant is particularly puzzled at, and sarcastic about, the enthusiasm that the British have for this notion.[21] Understanding why Kant thinks this way provides us with an illuminating springboard, from which we can test my suggestion that liberal practices (bar the mixed constitution in this case) can be capable of very different systematic groundings, where the job of the theologian is to discern and then adjudicate the crucial premises and assumptions. Although Kant has more technical objections to a mixed constitution, to an extent he simply considers the whole palaver to be unnecessary. A mixed constitution seems like a good idea if truth is what we are after, and where the truth is complex and hard to discern, such that we diffract our discernment through a number of consensus seeking channels.

20. Hirst, "Introduction," 5.
21. Kant, "On the Common Saying," 82–83, and *Political Writings,* 186–87.

But truth, for Kant, is just not that hard to discern: not once you have the right method. Kant, like many early modern philosophers is enchanted by the paradigm of geometry and mathematics. If only the truths of religion, politics and metaphysics were as transparent and universal as "2+2=4," we would have the key to knowledge and civil peace. So when thinking about political philosophy—the scope and justification of the state's coercive power in relation to the individual—Kant attempts to apply a geometrical method: building up from first principles, using universal laws of reason, which any competent reasoner could employ. Geometers do not arrive at the truths of geometry on the basis of a consensus. They do not need to chew over the properties of a triangle with other geometers in order to come to agreement. Because the structure of reason is universal and transparent, any competent reasoner would arrive at the same truths: there will be consensus, simply because of the universality of reason. Applying the same paradigm to politics- Kant is happy to appoint a monarch with undivided power, just as long as the monarch is a competent reasoner. The monarch represents us because our interests are—obviously—represented by universal reason.

So the way it goes for Kant is something like this. The formal properties of reason itself determine the moral law: where there is universality and necessity, we have a categorical imperative. The mark of the moral law is its universalizability: act only on the maxim that I can at the same time will as a universal law. Among categorical imperatives, Kant creates two sets of distinctions: duties to others and duties to ourselves, and perfect and imperfect duties. Perfect duties (such as telling the truth) are always binding, in contrast to imperfect duties (such as cultivating one's talents, playing the piano and so forth) that can be fulfilled in a finite number of optional ways. The philosophy of political right concerns only perfect duties to others that require external coercion: "right is . . . the totality of conditions under which the will of one person can be unified with the will of another under a universal law of freedom."[22] Further, "the theory of right" is the sum of those laws for which an external lawgiving is possible."[23] From here Kant derives the *a priori* founding principles of an ideal constitution: "*freedom* for all members of a society . . . the *dependence* of everyone upon a single common legislation . . . legal *equality*

22. Kant, *Political Writings*, 133.
23. Ibid., 132.

for everyone."[24] Such an arrangement is "the only constitution which can be derived from the idea of an original contract, upon which all rightful legislation of a people must be founded."[25]

It might seem that here at least, in Kant, we have a properly secular justification for liberal practices (bar the mixed constitution, but a version of that can be put back in without much difficulty, and indeed, Rawls does put it back). Here at least we consult the structure of reason itself, which is conceived as independent of any particular traditional or confessional commitments. Kant of course is the muse behind John Rawls' thought-experiment of the "veil of ignorance," whereby to discern the fundamental laws that ought to govern our life together as citizens we are encouraged to imagine ourselves prior to being embodied in a particular situation, with a particular conception of the good. Those principles that we can agree on, in this hypothetical pre-born state, without religious convictions and economic interests, are—for Rawls—the ones that should constitute the norms of our political life. What Rawls is doing is to throw us, in a Kantian way, onto the structure of *a priori* reason itself: independent of our particular beliefs, experience, traditions and historicity.

Here at least, it might seem, the theologian faces a proper secular enemy, rather than another strand of theology, with a particular configuration and emphasis of doctrinal themes. This accounts for the whole industry sparked off by Rawls'—some felt rather illiberal—discourtesy to religious believers, when he seemed to insist, in his earlier work at least, that distinctively religious reasons should not be brought into public discussions. So here we have it: a secular versus a theological grounding of liberal practices.

Even this, though, would be much too quick. Rawls' guide here is Kant. Kant is in a tradition of continental rationalism, mediated through Leibniz, Wolff and Baumgarten. When these thinkers talk about God, they have in view a divine mind in two halves: the divine intellect and the divine will. The divine intellect, in this tradition, just *is* the structure of reason as such (it is the storehouse of all possibilities and necessities, some of which are made actual by the divine will). Reason is identical with the divine intellect. Crucially, in this tradition, the divine will can in no way "trump" or override reason: although this is not an external

24. Ibid., 99.
25. Ibid.

constraint upon God, precisely because reason is identical with the divine intellect. The shape of reason, for this tradition, is the shape of universality as such: which is discerned through *a priori* rules such as the principle of contradiction, of sufficient reason (everything must have a sufficient reason) and of perfection (the most perfect being will do the most perfect thing).

So if we were to ask whether God—when framing political principles, for example—could be permitted to give a "distinctively religious reason," the answer would have to be "no, God could not give a distinctively religious reason," if by that we meant a reason that did not conform to the universal structure of intelligibility as such. The injunction against specifically religious reasons in the Kantian tradition—and nobody tell the Kantians this—arises from an intellectualist doctrine of God: a tradition that identifies God with the structure of reason itself, and subordinates the divine will to the divine intellect. It arises from a theological rationale, where the critique of this rationale will itself be theological, relating to the doctrine of God, creation, fall and eschatology. And there is much to criticize in this tradition, from a theological point of view. The identification of God with mind, and then mind with *a priori* reason, and reason with necessity, would be one starting point. Another would be the disloyalty to the earth, to our creatureliness—our imperfection and sin—that is demanded by the search for a disembodied and absolute perspective on reason and morality. Kantians can be extremely ingenious at denying the accuracy of such an accusation, and in my view they need to be, given Kant's emphatic clarity that our noumenal selves need to be presumed to share God's non-spatial and non-temporal eternity, if the Kantian moral project is to get under way.[26]

Again, we might face the "who cares?" question: even if this is the origin of a particular thought experiment, how does it illuminate, conceptually or practically, the current issue? Well, the surprising presence of theology even here cuts both ways: it opens up a challenge to the secular political philosopher, and then to the theologian. To secular political philosophers who want to continue an unreconstructed Rawlsian line of ruling out "religious reasons" as irrational, there is the lesson that theological traditions can be extremely rational, in a way that even they could not help recognize. Furthermore, it illuminates, I think, a structural feature of any

26. For a full treatment, see my *Kant and the Divine Mind*.

attempt to build up to truth from human consent. This is the way it goes. In the face of a skepticism about arriving at the absolute and transcendent truth, perhaps because of a pluralism about perspectives on such truth, we come up with the promising idea that truth is in fact the product of consent, rather than something independent of the process of consent. But then actual concrete human individuals and groups can arrive at some very uncomfortable decisions: idiotic, unjust or—in hindsight—obviously "of their time." Well then, we must expand our notion of "consent" to mean not just any old consent, but the consent of ideal reasoners: truth is not the product of any old practice, but of an *ideal* practice of discernment. But now a real question arises as to what work is being done by the description of the practice as "*ideal:*" any synonym such as "useful" or "coherent" is likely in the end to collapse into something that looks very like good old-fashioned truth, even if it is not called that. *Why* is something ideal, or useful, or coherent ultimately, except that having *true* beliefs is ideal, and can be very useful and coherent? In other words: the collapsing of truth into reason and will is viable if the subject is the ideal subject. That is, if the subject is God. Anti-realism—the notion that the mind constitutes reality—works for God, because the divine mind does indeed constitute reality. Many secular attempts at anti-realism struggle, I think, because they need the ideal human cognitive subject to become more and more Godlike, when their disbelief in God was precisely one of the founding motivations for the antirealism.[27]

Now that the managers have taken over the university, and theologians are called upon to justify their existence in terms of their non-subject specific "transferable skills," one of these skills at least is this: the ability to sniff out small gods. Theologians are well trained to find the gathering "god concept" around which a particular discourse or practice is oriented: the efficiency of the manager, for example, or the "autonomy" of the Kantian, now stripped of its theological rationalism. Often the gathering concept, rather like the Wizard of Oz, is largely unexamined at close quarters. When finally all the noise stops, and the concept appears, like the Wizard, it can often be exposed as an unimpressive and angry little squirt of a concept.

On the other hand, to put the challenge the other way round, I have sometimes felt that there can almost be a perversity amongst religious

27. For a full treatment of the realism/anti-realism debate see my *Realist Hope.*

believers in the "theology and public reason" debate. It is hard to resist the conclusion that some religious believers find it rather thrilling to be high and mightily offended by the "liberal injunction" against the use of distinctively religious reasons. Rawls in his later works,[28] and some of his followers such as Charles Larmore,[29] have done much to qualify and nuance his earlier more restrictive statements. According to these later developments, all that is actually asked is that believers of all stripes—atheists included—be prepared to attempt to find grounds of mutual reciprocity and intelligibility with their interlocutors, assuming good faith on the other's part and acknowledging the complexity of the burdens of judgment.[30] On this account, we are dealing less with a substantive restriction on metaphysical content or motivation, and much more with an ethic of virtuous communication:[31] with a call for respect, empathy, consideration, and self-interrogation.

Once all these nuances are in, I do think there is at least a question to be put to the determined-to-be-offended religious believer, the "political correctness gone mad" brigade: what sort of religion does one have if the religious reason being offered is so completely incapable of being virtuously communicated? Is not the creator's command intelligible to the creature? Is not the God revealed to us, for us? Or to put it in terms of the germ of truth in rationalist theology, is it not the case, as Aquinas puts it, that God is not just "good" but "goodness" itself, or we might say, not just "reasonable," but "reason" itself. This is part of the mystery of the divine nature tracked by the doctrine of divine simplicity: that is, the mysterious unity and identity in God—which marks out God from any creature—between reason and will, nature and existence. The intellectualism that characterizes continental rationalism involves identifying God primarily with one arc of the mystery only. By making the half-truth the whole truth, even the half is lost: which describes the fate and inadequacy of both "voluntaristic" and "intellectualist" reductions of the divine nature.

---

28. See Rawls, *Political Liberalism*, and "Idea of Public Reason Revisited."

29. Larmore, "Public Reason."

30. See my *Politics of Human Frailty*, ch. 2.

31. This emphasis on the Christian virtues required for effective communication is insightfully explored by Biggar, in "Can a Theological Argument Behave?"

Conclusion

To draw things together then. Just by reflecting on one practice, the mixed constitution, we have been able to illumine some of the diverse theological sources—conceptual and historical—of politics, and political philosophy. We hope thereby to turn the behemoth "liberalism" into a more finely grained and diverse concept, which commands attention and care from theologians. In "liberalism," the theologian should not find a theologically neutral and secular politics, but something which is itself a theological tradition of sorts. Not all theological traditions are equally worthy of support. But to judge the truth of something, I must hear properly what is being said. Accordingly, the academic theologian's task in relation to politics can only become distinctively and properly theological—with a proper readiness to make theological judgments about politics—after a process of attention, discernment, historical curiosity and philosophical rigor. I ventured earlier that the opposite of good theology was not no theology, but bad theology. If we are honest about our creaturely embeddedness in the history and culture into which we are thrown, perhaps we could also say that for most of us, the opposite of good liberalism is not no liberalism, but bad liberalism. And we had better make sure that we know the difference.

10

On Theology, the Humanities, and the University

GAVIN D'COSTA

Introduction

I APPROACH MY TASK located as a Roman Catholic theologian (without a *mandatum*) working in a secular university in the United Kingdom within a Faculty of Arts. In this paper I want to argue that there is an inherent drive within Catholic theology, wherever it operates, that requires four moves within the university, any university, but especially where that university claims to be a Catholic university. The moves would of course be negotiated very differently according to the nature of the university. In a secular university they might take place in a more ad hoc manner involving informal cell groups across the disciplines linking philosophy with physics or theology with politics, as well as developing large scale research projects drawing upon public funding to explore the interrelation between the disciplines that is presupposed within a Catholic world view. My concern to be tradition-specific is not sectarian or un-ecumenical, but stems from a respect for the different traditions within theological communities and their sometimes different foci of authorities. If one were a Kuperyian or a Lutheran or a Mennonite or a Jerry Falwell evangelical, the vision of what the university might be and of what its goals and presuppositions are is likely to be shaped by different assumptions, authoritative texts, and notions of control over such a project. This is not to say there is any single Catholic vision, but for the sake of my argument, I shall be drawing upon recent magisterial sources to guide my arguments. To be tradition-specific is also useful to limit the field of discussion given an already impossibly wide canvas.

What are the four moves which theology requires were it to be situated within a Catholic university? First, theology must recognize itself to be the queen of the sciences and not, as it is in most universities, just another discipline in the humanities. This involves an internal argument within the discipline, which has to shake off various coils before rebirth might happen. What are such coils? The first might be the liberal Protestant assimilation of theology to history, followed by the liberal Catholic equivalence that inevitably followed. The second might be the slow process of assimilation of theology to the various disciplines in the humanities so that theology in turn it becomes deconstructive, feminist, structuralist, and so on. This is not to say that these movements within the humanities are not interesting or important, but simply to say that theology is its own discipline and not cultural theory. The third would be to trace how this assimilation of theology to heathen gods and goddesses carries right through to the social sciences (in some brands of liberation theology that give hermeneutical priority to Marxism), and even the natural sciences (in some brands of eco-theology that configure God to gaia). In the last one hundred years theology has morphed into other disciplines (adopting their methods and presuppositions), which generates a serious challenge to the vocation of the "theological theologian," rather than the culturally assimilated theologian.[1]

This is not a rewinding the clock to a pre-modern period, for that is culturally impossible. Rather, I want to argue for an intellectual engagement to recover the disciplinary integrity of theology, whose object of concern, to put it in Aristotelian disciplinary terms, is God. I am not arguing that theology should be out of relation to the other disciplines, but rather than these disciplines have proper objects of study which are not formally God, but whose disciplinary operations are related to God's

---

1. See John Webster's helpful plotting of this task, where he advances a very similar argument about theology to my own—but not about theology's overall role in the university, precisely due to his distrust of reason and institutions presumably resulting from his Reformation presuppositions. See Webster, *Theological Theology*.

created world. Only once theology has gained its proper disciplinary rigor, as faith seeking understanding, as an explication of what has been given to us in the gospels, tradition, and magisterium, can theology speak with its own integrity, with its own voice. Rather than be assimilated to other disciplines, it needs to be able to borrow and learn from them, but also to challenge and question them—but that is to move to a later step in my argument. For now, the first task of theology is to recover its own vocation as being ecclesial.[2] For only when theology attends to God (and thus be a practice of the church—hence, ecclesial theology), can theology begin to help us relate to the unity of the intellectual disciplines and be queen of the sciences. But the first discipline that it must relate to, for it is already related to that discipline through its very practices, is philosophy.

Second, theology must work together with philosophy, as its traditional handmaiden, to be able to engage with the intellectual disciplines of the university. It must also work with philosophy because all conceptual thinking requires philosophical rigor for its purification—and theology is also always a type of conceptual thinking in its best ecclesial forms. This is an admittedly complex and contentious claim given the state of "philosophy" in the academy. There are two distinct claims here, both of which have been thoughtfully mapped out by Alasdair MacIntyre, and here I will repeat the outcome of some of his discussion without being able to repeat all his arguments.[3] The first claim is that philosophy has a genuine autonomy with its own rules and procedures that are best practiced by the philosopher. The history of philosophy shows that it takes on all sorts of shapes and forms. The history of Catholic philosophy, which is what I am particularly concerned about here, is a history of a discipline that starts with figures such as Gregory of Nazianzen and Augustine in the patristic period, followed by Anselm, Bonaventure, and Aquinas in the Middle Ages, and Newman, Rosmini, Maritain, Gilson, Edith Stein, and Elizabeth Anscombe in the modern period, to name a very small but important sample.[4] MacIntyre shows that in this long history, the genuine autonomy of philosophy is itself justified by theology, which recognizes that where reason is unclouded by unruly and disordered passion it has the genuine ability to move towards the truth of God. This was the point

2. See Congregation for the Doctrine of the Faith, *Instruction on the Ecclesial Vocation of the Theologian.*

3. MacIntyre, *God, Philosophy, Universities.*

4. John Paul II, *Fides et Ratio.*

of the teaching of Vatican I, *Dei Filius*, chapter 2.[5] The second claim is that an unencumbered philosophy (one that was not explicitly hostile to Christian theism—and thus belonging to any number of traditions: Platonist, Aristotelian, Analytical and so on), might be harnessed by theology to develop the project of apologetics, preaching, and teaching in the explication of the true faith, and thus in dogmatics. This was precisely the case when Aquinas adapted and developed the Aristotelian heritage that he discovered through the translations from the Greek and Arabic sources. Aquinas also realized that there were elements of Aristotle that were inimical to the Christian vision and these he challenged, but through rational argument and internal criticisms. The point is that both theology and philosophy are mutually dependent, although theology takes the lead in noting when philosophy has arrived at conclusions that are inimical to Christian faith. This process is a complex one and takes years of dispute to clarify what is at stake. Only through this positive relationship, where philosophy is both autonomous and dependent, can theology build a bridge whereby it might interact with the intellectual disciplines of the university.

Third, this theological-philosophical engagement with the disciplines must actually cover the entire curriculum, not just the humanities. This will require a complex process of conversations with intellectuals who require interdisciplinary skills that very few possess. It will also require that careful discernment whereby theology is allowed to call into question presuppositions or methods that are inimical to God, while fully respecting the autonomy of each discipline related to its precise subject matter. I will be outlining the very complex dynamics present in this operation in a single discipline below, but it is important to note this repeated dual claim: just as with philosophy, so every discipline, has a genuine autonomy which must spring from the subject matter that is addresses; while every discipline should be open to critically examining whether some of its presuppositions (naturalism, absolutist forms of functionalism, and so on) actually inhibit both its encounter with the subject of

5. MacIntyre, *God, Philosophy, Universities*, 151–52, including the important concluding statement after his exposition of *Dei Filus*: "Part of the gift of Christian faith is to enable us to identify accurately where the line between faith and reason is to be drawn, something that cannot be done from the standpoint of reason, but only from that of faith. Reason therefore needs Christian faith, if it is to do its own work well. Reason without Christian faith is always reason informed by some other faith, characteristically an unacknowledged faith, one that renders its adherents liable to error" (152–53).

its disciplinary specialism and the interrelation of that specialism with the other specialisms of the university. Such conversations and cultural generation will take many decades to establish. In what follows later, I will only comment on the humanities given the remit of our conference.

Fourth, through this process of interdisciplinary conversations over many generations the universities might be one legitimate body that is involved in the cultivation of "Christian culture"—a concept that is at the heart of such an enterprise. Underlying this concept of a Christian culture is something quite unique to theistic religions (and thus a unique form of Islamic and Jewish culture are also possibilities): a vision of creation as related and structured towards a single end—giving glory to God. This entails the assumption that underlying the different intellectual disciplines of the modern university there is a unity, a real relationship, rather than the fragmentary utilitarian relationships that tend to dominate within modern research universities, driven as they are by funding from governments, pharmaceutical companies, arms industries, and private businesses. The unity and intelligibility of the disciplines is formed precisely by its relationship to God, creator of all things that have intelligible form. In what follows I shall pick up some threads from all four moves, accepting this is a rather piecemeal stab at the question, but one that at least opens up some strategic questions.

Some Recent, Relevant Moves

There is a telos within Catholic theology that demands that it be part of a wider intellectual operation, that it be the engine to generate a Christian culture. Pope Benedict XVI's "controversial" Regensburg Address highlighted this nicely when he argued for the restoration of reason within theology, against voluntaristic and fideist models of theology (deriving from Duns Scotus in the Christian tradition; and in parallel from Ibn Hazm within Islam).[6] This restoration is required after what Benedict calls the "modern self-limitation of reason, classically expressed in Kant's 'Critiques,' but in the meantime further radicalized by the impact of the natural sciences."[7] This cultural development which characterized the

6. Here, MacIntyre fails to track the significance of Scotus' nominalism as fundamentally corrosive to Christian philosophy as does Benedict (see MacIntyre, *God, Philosophy, Universities*, 99–101).

7. Benedict XVI, "Meeting with the Representatives of Science."

European situation resulted in an intellectual ethos that had profound epistemological and ontological implications: an inability to think metaphysics. Let me cite Benedict in full: "First, only the kind of certainty resulting from the interplay of mathematical and empirical elements can be considered scientific. Anything that would claim to be science must be measured against this criterion. Hence the human sciences, such as history, psychology, sociology and philosophy, attempt to conform themselves to this canon of scientificity."[8] Benedict could have extended his reflections to the place of postmodern deconstructionism in the academy, for this tradition has also called into question modernity's restricted canon of "science" and has precipitated an intellectual reconfiguration in the human and social sciences. In this sense some strands of postmodernity are allies to theology in calling into question certain problematic aspects of modernity. However, postmodernity's reconfiguration (more often in principle rather than institutional practice) has been along the lines that further fragments the disciplines, in part by refusing metaphysics, and in part by conflating all disciplines into basic discourses of power (following Foucault, and of course, Nietzsche). This inevitably transforms most disciplines into cultural studies.

But even in this new disarray there are benefits: for students and researchers are asking what the nature of their discipline is? This genealogical sensitivity is important, not to dissolve all into power, but to recognize that there is a theological narration to be undertaken in showing why theology and the disciplines have been so increasingly functionally and financially configured in the modern university. Nevertheless, the way in which the disciplines may be re-envisaged is not the sole province of deconstructionists, but also part of the public debate in which theology has much to say—a point to which I will return shortly. But let us return to Pope Benedict's thread.

Benedict goes on: "A second point, which is important for our reflections, is that by its very nature this method [referring to what has been translated as 'scientificity'] excludes the question of God, making [God] appear an unscientific or pre-scientific question. Consequently, we are faced with a reduction of the radius of science and reason, one which needs to be questioned."[9] This constricting radius must be challenged by Catholic theology within the university. This also makes clear that the

8. Ibid.
9. Ibid.

questions cannot simply be limited to the humanities as the modes of privileged knowledge are today often generated from the social and natural sciences which then shape other disciplinary models of both practice and theory. If the university is concerned with an alleged search for truth, the models of truthful knowledge and their disciplinary practices are most significant. This is why Benedict finishes his lecture envisaging the conversational and dialogical role of theology within the university: "In this sense theology rightly belongs in the university and within the wide-ranging *dialogue* of sciences, not merely as a historical discipline and one of the human sciences, but precisely as theology, as inquiry into the rationality of faith."[10] In steering theology away from being assimilated into the humanities or natural and social sciences *per se*, Benedict restores and recovers the uniqueness of the discipline and in doing so, allows the space for theology's inter-disciplinary relationship to be properly explored.

We have to turn to Benedict's predecessor to flush out the Regensburg vision, for Pope John Paul II saw that theology must not only get on with its own thing, its own discipline, its own object of study—God—but with its handmaiden "philosophy," what Benedict has been calling "reason"; it needs to rethink culture.[11] Benedict is more of an Augustinian compared to John Paul II, although Tracey Rowland has done a good job of decreasing the distance between them regarding Thomism.[12] Both, however, are adamant on the importance of growing a Christian culture. Before attending to Pope John Paul II, a slight clarification is in order, for here a crucial question arises, and one which cannot be ignored for long: is the notion of a "Christian culture" too closely allied with what has been deemed "Christendom" by Stanley Hauerwas and relentlessly criticized? Are Benedict and John Paul II engaged in a deeply flawed project? The complexity of this question is well bought out in Hauerwas's book, *The State of the University*.[13] Hauerwas develops, elaborates, and thinks through a very intriguing claim: being Christian should make a difference to being in a university because being Christian shapes our knowledges of the world, the relation between these knowledges, and their final meaning and purpose. Hauerwas is burning John Henry Newman's torch but

10. Ibid. Emphasis mine.
11. See below where I attend to this task.
12. Rowland, *Culture and the Thomist*.
13. Hauerwas, *State of the University*.

typically with more fire and smoke. Hauerwas rightly notes that Christians start from a difficult position as they have generally been educated by the very institutions that they now seek to reform. Our Christian discipleship has been shaped by these distorted knowledges. We have become too assimilated. You can see that Hauerwas and I are in basic agreement in this respect, but I want to focus on three points that help develop and distinguish my own argument from his—and which throws further light on the notion of a "Christian culture."

First, Hauerwas suggests that universities as they exist in the United States are primarily a production of modernity where their goals are shaped by the accumulation of money. Their stated aims are often reducible to service to the state, powerful funding of elites, and the promotion of reason over tradition and practices; and in a postmodern mode, their own self-consumption. In this, he is following Alasdair MacIntyre's earlier analysis.[14] Hauerwas gives delightful textual depth to these claims. He shows that knowledges are shaped and perpetuated by the presuppositions of the institutions that generate knowledge. In modern day U.S.A., these presuppositions are often alien to Christian ones, for Christians, argues Hauerwas, believe that all knowledge is orientated to love, worship, and praise of the one true God. On this first point then there are two interesting questions that are not fully addressed. First, Hauerwas alludes to John Milbank's related and rather "precocious" position: that only theology can save the secular university, if the university is the university by virtue of its commitment to truth.[15] In Milbank's view theology alone can embody and serve this goal for it alone is the adequation of knowledge with the supremely infinite and actual real God. Thus the legitimacy of all disciplines depends on their at least implicit ordering towards theology, assuming that this means participation in God's self-knowledge. For Milbank, without theology, disciplines are "objectively and demonstrably null and void." Hauerwas backs off from this position by turning to Newman, but in so much as Hauerwas refuses Newman's privileged role for philosophy in the great synthesis between the disciplines, and instead wishes to argue that theology is intractably philosophical, it is difficult to see why Hauerwas actually rejects Milbank's position. He seems to give two reasons: first, theology is only a "queen" "if humility determines her

14. MacIntyre, *Three Rival Versions*.
15. Milbank, "Conflict of the Faculties," 39–58.

work"; and second, Milbank's would be a nostalgic reclaiming of the habits of Christendom and Constantinianism.[16] I'm not sure these reasons are convincing.

Humility is an important brake to pride and hubris, but pride and hubris are not traditional characteristics required by theology to operate. Neither are they required by Milbank's claims. If the Virgin Mary is seen as the archetype of a "queen," rather than worrying secular role models such as Boadicea, Queen Victoria, and the like, humility, obedience, and even audacity might characterize theology, the servant queen of the sciences. Newman actually uses Mary as the typographical figure of the faith of the unlearned and the great doctors of the church: "[Mary] is our pattern of Faith, both in the reception and in the study of Divine Truth. She does not think it enough to accept, she dwells upon it; not enough to possess, she uses it; not enough to assent, she develops it; not enough to submit to reason, she reasons upon it; not indeed reasoning first, and believing afterwards, with Zacharias, yet believing without reasoning, next from love and reverence, reasoning after believing. And thus she symbolizes to us, not only the faith of the unlearned, but of the doctors of the Church also."[17] Hauerwas needs to de-secularize his queen, such that the role of theology as queen of the sciences can be developed properly.

Second, Christendom and Constantinianism are heresies for Hauerwas, but I want to suggest there is quite a difference between a Catholic university and a Catholic state which runs universities—even though both must be concerned about the abuse of power. While the Catholic state is not really an issue in Europe or North America, the question of a Catholic university is. Hauerwas falsely and instinctively equates a Christian university with Constantinianism. I say instinctively because there is no further argument given for his derisive remarks. For example, he writes: "I am not trying to argue for something called the Christian university. Sam Wells has pointed out to me when 'Christian' is used as an adjective you can be confident that you are reproducing the habits of Constantinianism."[18] That may be so in some cases, but there is no argument for why this must always be the case, such as in "Christian churches against the war in Iraq," "Christian hospices," and so on. This move on

16. Ibid., 31.

17. Newman, "Sermon XV," 313.

18. Hauerwas, "State of the University," 7.

Hauerwas's part ironically drives him to conform to secular modernity's privatization of religion and thereby replicate his *bête noir*, liberal Protestantism. How so? By refusing to see that the logic of his argument must lead to the proposal for a Christian university; to instinctively mistrust institutions; to fail to recognize that the Christian university is rooted in the heart of the church and not extrinsic to the church—see below.

Only through such a move can the "secular," "modern," and "postmodern" institutions that shape our society be called into question in an institutionally embodied manner. The question of alternative knowledges affecting a wide range of disciplines is too important to be left to *ad hoc* individuals, notwithstanding their important contributions. Rather it requires structured and long-term institutional support and curriculum development if it is to be sustained. Oddly, Hauerwas draws on Catholics like MacIntyre and Newman who both strongly support entities like "Catholic universities," but Hauerwas never properly attends to this implication. Nor does Hauerwas attend to *Ex corde ecclesia* in which John Paul II set out a picture of a modern Catholic university, developing Newman's insights and taking seriously the troublesome particularities that arise in developing such radical options. Hauerwas's neglect is uncharacteristic, because the materiality of such institutions is about alternative practices that are required of Christians, and only thus is the university seen to arise out of the "heart of the church" (*ex corde ecclesia*). Hauerwas's ambivalent ecclesiology might explain this problem, but its repercussions are in danger of undermining rather than supporting and advancing his overall thesis.

The second feature of Hauerwas's argument is to highlight how alternative knowledges might look. He does this through imagining an alternative construal of the "field" using an essay by Yoder where the church engages ad hoc with anyone, but always in solidarity with everyone, especially the dispossessed and weak, to seek justice in proclaiming the crucified Lord. Hauerwas is suspicious of any theory of dialogue, a third language, to mediate between traditions. However, in avoiding tradition-specific universities, Hauerwas is in danger of weakening the possibility of this type of engagement. He might well retort that tradition-specific universities might not want such engagements, and while this is true, it is not the case with the type of Methodist Texan Christianity he defends, or the type of Catholicism I am advocating. Hauerwas is well aware of the wider implications of his argument. For example, he writes:

> ... if you believe as MacIntyre and I believe that usury is a practice that Christians must avoid, then how the knowledge called economics is understood may well be different from the understanding of those who do not share our views about usury. If you think that force can only be justified on just war grounds, then how you understand the relations between states may be very different from the assumptions of those that assume some form of a balance of power model is necessary for pursuing those research agendas called international relations. Or if you believe, as Christians do, that creation is a more fundamental notion than nature, that may well make a difference in the kind of distinction you think necessary between the study of botany and biology. Surely, for Christians who believe all that is created has purpose, the attempt to understand life mechanistically must be questioned.[19]

There are limits to Hauerwas's bonfire of the disciplines: pure mathematics will not be touched in the least, chemistry hardly at all, politics somewhat, and history, ethics, and metaphysics very much so. Hauerwas is drawing from Newman at this point, but Hauerwas avoids serious argument about what will and will not be changed and why some disciplines are apparently utterly immune from being part of this interdisciplinary conversation and related positively to the theistic canopy. Astronomy, physics, botany, and biology have all impacted upon religious claims. What might be at stake are the reductionist naturalistic presuppositions undergirding some sciences, obviously not the correct autonomy of the sciences as such. It would be unfair to press this point as Hauerwas is a theologian and not a natural scientist or social scientist, but this is simply to highlight an area that requires more development for Hauerwas's thesis to be even more wide-ranging and convincing than it already is.

To conclude these comments on Hauerwas, I want to suggest that the architectural structure that Hauerwas is groping towards is to be found in what I take to be the contemporary re-staging of Newman's vision of the university: John Paul II's splendid document: *On Catholic Universities* (1990); and its younger sibling published eight years later: *Faith and Reason* (1998), upon which Benedict's Regensburg lecture is grafted. This will help establish my orientation to the question of the relationship between theology, the university and the humanities and how the humanities might be re-visioned within a Catholic outlook.

19. Ibid., 53.

The "Catholic outlook" as I call it is theoretically best nourished within a Catholic university where it is assumed that the dogmatic truths of the faith are accepted and intellectual endeavor is undertaken from that starting point—in each and every discipline. This is the challenging and refreshing assumption that since all creation is God's creation, in principle, no form of authentic knowledge properly gained from any discipline will contradict the truth of Christianity in terms of dogma; but instead, that all disciplines will further illuminate those truths and deepen our understanding of them and their penetration within human culture. *On Catholic Universities* succinctly expresses the dialectical tension within this initially smug-sounding claim: "A Catholic University's privileged task is to unite existentially by intellectual effort two orders of reality that too frequently tend to be placed in opposition as though they were antithetical: the search for truth, and the certainty of already knowing the fount of truth." Clearly, while the truths of the disciplines are not revealed truth, their fount is. Put like this, the distinction between theology and the other disciplines is properly highlighted, but not in terms of affording theology special knowledge properly the preserve of lawyers, literary specialists, biologists and economists. Hence the dialogue between the disciplines takes place with a proper confidence of their respective integrities, autonomy in the sense outlined above, and legitimate fields: "While each academic discipline retains its own integrity and has its own methods, this dialogue demonstrates that methodological research within every branch of learning, when carried out in a truly scientific manner and in accord with moral norms, can never truly conflict with faith. For the things of the earth and the concerns of faith derive from the same God."[20]

Theology and Literature

To conclude this essay, let me turn to one department found in most Humanity Faculties today and tease out a little what I have been saying above when applied to English Literature. I should say that I've got half a degree in English, taught the subject in a Theology and Literature degree that once ran at Bristol and love reading novels and poetry. As you can see,

---

20. John Paul II, *Ex Ecclesiae Corde*, 17. I have attended further to this argument in *Theology in the Public*, 77–111.

I'm not really qualified for what follows, but I will try and illustrate some of the issues through use of those who are more qualified.

There are many sets of questions that might be discussed in an English department within the type of university I envisage. They might range from the perennial question regarding the canon of literature to be taught, the hermeneutics of reading that canon, and the question of the relation of literature to the Bible: how our reading one from the other is different, if at all and how literature might be the site of the deepening of revelation. Let me say a few words about literary approaches before focusing on a couple of very significant contributions to this debate.

In terms of hermeneutics and literary theory, one might ask three questions. Is the literary theory employed by a reader explicitly inimical to the Christian vision and such that it might actually distort the proper reading of a literary text? Are students aware that every approach to reading implicitly contains a world-view with all sorts of presuppositions of an ontological, aesthetic, and ethical nature? And finally, what sort of moral responsibility is there from teachers to bring this question to the fore?

Examples regarding the first question might be found in certain Marxist, naturalistic, mechanistic, psychoanalytic, feminist, deconstructive literary approaches where students are trained to analyze literature within a worldview whose presuppositions are deeply critical of orthodox Christian faith. Showing this to be the case is of course part of the project that would have to be carried out by literary critics who are also Christians or at least suitably sensitive to what is at stake. In practice there is of course no single "psychoanalytical" school, so one might find serious differences between Lacan, Kristeva, Irigaray, Fromm, and Freud when we look at their reading of literary classics. Some of these readings indeed lead to a deeper appreciation of aspects of Christian faith, as I have argued elsewhere in my analysis of Luce Irigaray.[21] It is also appropriate to put questions from our Christian perspective as I tried to with Irigaray, suggesting that some of her own concerns and goals are best arrived at through Catholic Christianity rather than the French feminist psychoanalytical tradition she has developed. There is an important place for the type of dialectical argument between these two "rival traditions," to use MacIntyre's phrase, where there is a recognition of profound differences in paradigmatic starting points, but the subsequent need to

21. See *Sexing the Trinity*, chapters 1–2.

genealogically narrate what MacIntyre calls the "opponents" history and to then explain, better than they, how the internal lacunae within that tradition might be better explained from a Thomist perspective.[22] This engagement with "rival" traditions of enquiry underlines the significance of the reading strategies adopted for every strategy comes out of a "tradition" and is thus embedded within a series of wider metaphysical and ontological concerns. The contention from within the Christian tradition is that Christianity is the truthful and thus the most comprehensive narration of all that there is—a contention made while this narration is yet to be done within the church; and while this narration has already been achieved in the resurrection of Christ.

Here I follow Hans-Georg Gadamer in agreeing with a basically humanistic orientation of reading texts: allowing that texts challenge our horizons of understanding, while our horizon also generates questions to the texts. [23] But I want to further develop upon Gadamer, in exploring the specific dynamics when our "horizon" is constituted by Catholic Christianity. Are there specific "Catholic" hermeneutical strategies? I think there must be. This would involve two complex set of tasks. First, it would require criticizing reading strategies that are closed to the transcendent or that employ reductive assumptions (Marxist, naturalist, and so on), without in any sense arguing that employing these strategies does not shed interesting light on literature. Second, one would be constructively developing and exploring multiple ways of reading literature as a Christian. The Catholic horizon must be one that constantly moves towards a richer and wider appreciation of all creation in its particularities. In this movement it must of necessity become vulnerable to challenge and questioning, but with a confidence that since God is creator of all, the entire creation and the study of that creation, both natural and social, is worthwhile both in its particularity as well as in relation to the whole. What might all this mean when reading literature?

One illustration of what I'm arguing for is presented in Nicholas Boyle's fine work *Sacred and Secular Scriptures.*[24] I've chosen Boyle because of his standing amongst secular intellectuals in scholarship on Goethe and for his rather daring claim that one might be a better reader

---

22. See MacIntyre, *Three Rival Versions,* and *Whose Justice?*

23. Gadamer, *Truth and Method.*

24. Boyle, *Sacred and Secular Scriptures.*

of the Western literary canon were one to be a Catholic Christian. Boyle of course, is coming out of a longer and variegated tradition of Christian humanism to be found in writers like Coleridge, Arnold, Ruskin, and T. S. Eliot.[25] I want to turn to Boyle's argument only to suggest that the issues he raises should be central to the debate within Literature departments within the humanities.

Boyle's argument is presented in three parts and this Catholic hermeneutics has as its central hero a Lithuanian Jew—Emmanuel Levinas. When Boyle uses the term "Catholic," it does not mean Roman in any narrow sense, but a drawing in from whatever wisdom is to be found in whichever quarter. In part one he looks at the question of the Bible as literature. In part two he outlines, on the basis of this discussion, a Catholic hermeneutical approach to literature in which literature is seen as an *preparatio* (my term) for the Bible as well as an explication of various biblical moments: "Secular scriptures in short are the way in, the prolegomena, to the sacred scriptures. They provide the commentary that makes the original text accessible, the atmosphere of application, elaboration, and response that the written law needs in order to breathe and live."[26] But the Bible belongs to a community of ritual practices in which there is conviction that the temporal mediates the divine, first in Israel, then in Christ, and then in constructed artifacts like buildings, literature and rituals which are lit by the light of revelation and themselves illuminate the manner in which that revelation is imbricated within the textures of culture. In part three he tests this approach with respect to works by Pascal, Goethe, Melville, Jane Austen, Rupert Brooke, and finally J. R. R. Tolkien.

Here I want to look a bit more closely at part I. Boyle traces the eighteenth-century German attempt to resolve the deist and historicist criticisms of the Bible. He traces how Herder and German Romanticism addressed this problem by arguing that the Bible is best understood as poetry, which saved "meaning," but failed to distinguish the difference between secular and sacred literature. Through this move, the anchor mooring the Bible to the church was removed. Schleiermacher on the other hand, refused the aesthetic turn and provided a historic hermeneutic. This placed authorial intention and historical study at the centre, and thus the academy, not the church as primary interpreter of Scripture. Hegel is

25. For background on this, and advancing a similar thesis, see Oser, *Return of Christian Humanism*.

26. Boyle, *Sacred and Secular Scriptures*, 142.

the half-hero in this section of Boyle's analysis in restoring the Bible to the church which Herder and Schleiermacher effectively cut off. Hegel was also able to transcend the reason-revelation split of the eighteenth century by recasting the entire debate so that the two are now intrinsic parts of an unfolding dialectic as well as foregrounding the political significance of Christianity. Even so, for Boyle, in this process Hegel problematically cuts off Christianity from its Jewish root, its biblical tradition.

In Boyle's narrative, Frei and Ricoeur enter the picture next. Hans Frei is seen as failing to transcend the Calvinist *sola scriptura* which implausibly steers around mediation, the community of church for Boyle. Paul Ricoeur is seen as the three-quarters-hero in this section for restoring the complexity of forms to Scripture in the complex task of interpretation, even if too tightly and formally. Ricoeur draws upon the earlier Romantic tradition in one strong sense which is all important for Boyle's argument: Ricoeur argues that revelation is given in the Bible and other great literature, precisely by its opening up a new world to us, its readers. Here Ricoeur is deeply dependent on Gadamer. According to Ricoeur, what makes biblical revelation specific is that in all its "different forms of discourse [it is] directed towards a single vanishing point, the Name of the Unnameable."[27] It is thus like the "Atlantis of being" that is revealed through its reading. In one sense Ricoeur is a little bit too low Protestant for Boyle for he also manages to side-step the ecclesial context of reading. For Boyle, Levinas supplements Ricoeur in bringing out both the ethical and the ritual aspects that forms a traditioned reading practice. This is highlighted in Levinas's tracing of two branches of Judaism that issued from the destruction of the Temple. One branch acts as if the temple is now no longer central and it is reading alone that counts. The other branch still recognizes the importance of temple Judaism, which Boyle argues is continued in Catholic Christianity, where there is presence beyond the text pointing to one who is signified: "the material and particular presence of God in the world, first in rituals and in a building and then in a man and subsequently in other rituals and other buildings and other people insofar as they are related to this man." Boyle, developing this, suggests the radiation of revelation within culture such that if the Bible is revelation, then all culture that has been generated through the

27. Ibid., 71.

impact of the Bible has been shaped by and gives shape to the unfolding of this revelation—sometimes in ways that bypass authorial intention.

Boyle then articulates and develops his Catholic reading strategy. His basic argument is that secular literature (in part following Ricoeur) shares in revelation formally: (a) in as much as "Literature is language free of instrumental purpose, and it seeks to tell the truth;" (b) in so much as any act of representation is an "event of forgiveness," because "works of literature are made out of language, out of the original symbolic exercise of my preoriginal responsibility for my neighbor, they have at their heart a principled universality which fits them to participate symbolically in that interaction of Law and loss and reconciliation which Christians call Atonement;" and (c) "Of course, a secular author cannot get it right all the time and the greatest always err by giving too much rather than too little."[28] What is important here is not whether Boyle's argument actually succeeds, but rather the importance of his attempt to develop a Christian hermeneutic of "secular" literature which also illuminates the way we should read our "sacred" literature. The rest of the book undertakes this task.

An aside on theology: Boyle argues that nineteenth-century French literature from Chateaubriand to Victor Hugo was "drenched in the Bible" whereas the rationalist scholastic theologians of that time plundered the Bible as proof text. He suggests that literature of this period is going to be more helpful and illuminating in reading the Bible than are the theological tracts—and vice versa. While this fails to do full justice to minor non-scholastic currents in nineteenth-century France, Boyle's point is well taken: theology can learn richly from secular reading traditions. And, in terms of our overall concern, secular literature might best be read from a religious perspective. It is a sort of win-win situation.

Boyle's book at least raises important questions showing a two-way interaction between literature that is not formally revelation and the Bible, which is. It also shows that reading the two genres (sacred and secular) together is deeply illuminative and is actually required for a proper appreciation of western literature. It would be intriguing to apply Boyle's approach to non-western, non-European literature shaped by other scriptural traditions, but that takes me too far from my primary concern. Boyle's book is also important in raising the challenge that a Catholic

28. Ibid., 125 and 133.

approach does better service to the task of reading literature than many of the literary theories employed at present.

I would be intrigued to know if George Steiner would find Boyle's book a building upon Steiner's own thesis in *Real Presences* (as Boyle himself claims).[29] Steiner, from a very different angle that might be characterized as "non-institutionalized Jewish and Christian biblical would-be believer," argues that great literature (and music and art) presupposes a transcendental "real presence" for its embodiment. Steiner throws down a challenge that also informs Boyle's thesis: "[T]he act of reading in the fullest sense, of the act of reception and internalization of significant forms within us, is a metaphysical and, in the last analysis, a theological one. The ascription of beauty to truth and to meaning is either a rhetorical flourish, or it is a piece of theology."[30] I cite Steiner precisely because what I think is missing from his remarkable book is actually provided by Boyle's book: the underpinning of the authority of revelation, and the church that mediates it, to ground this interpretative community. Boyle would acknowledge that these are not premises that can be argued for from some neutral starting point, but which, once held, can actually be defended. Steiner fails to offer this level of rationality to defend his own position, although that may be due to his profound recognition of the failure of modernity's traditioned reason to justify anything other than itself. Boyle is I think analogous to MacIntyre who still believes in dialectics, while Steiner is like John Milbank, who employs rhetorical persuasion in the belief that dialectics is futile. Whether this analogy is correct or not, I hope to have at least opened one type of conversation that is required about the act of reading literature in a Literature department. There are many other sorts of conversation, not least about the actual canon to be honored, with an intriguing illustration to be found in Lucy Beckett's *In The Light of Christ: Writings in the Western Tradition* (which is reading literature in the way Boyle does without Boyle's attention to the manner of reading it).[31]

Looking at one discipline and two contributions to that discipline in terms of my overall argument about theology, the university and the humanities is less that a tip of the iceberg, and more like feeling the waters

29. Steiner, *Real Presences*. Referred to most appreciatively in Boyle, *Sacred and Secular Scriptures*. 6, 67, 89, 143.

30. Steiner, *Real Presence*, 215–16; cited by Boyle, *Sacred and Secular Scriptures*, 6.

31. Beckett, *In the Light of Christ*. This question of the canon typically bypasses the question of hermeneutics, as is the case in Bloom's classic, *Closing of the American Mind*.

cooling around our toes before the iceberg appears. It would be helpful to systematically work through the humanities and ask the same questions.[32] There is a huge task ahead if the institutional form of this kind of dialogue of the disciplines is to take place. It has been my primary contention that structurally such a dialogue might more easily take place within a Catholic university. It has also been my contention that ecclesial theology requires such a setting for its own telos to be fulfilled. In history of course, Catholic universities have not always been beacons of such projects but have sometimes doused the light with a vengeance.[33] But in principle, they at least should be committed to establishing a curriculum of studies that displays the truth that God created the world, and created it good, and that all forms of intellectual sciences, not least humanities, are interrelated to one another because together they illuminate God's wonderful and fallen creation. Together and on their own, they serve to illuminate the glory of God (indirectly) as well as the grandeur of God's creation (directly). This project is impossible without the restoration of theology as the queen of the sciences.

32. In historical studies, there would be no better start to the debate than Augustine's *City of God* and Christopher Dawson's historiographical concept of "Catholic culture." Marsden provides an interesting (although obviously slightly dated bibliography) in his excellent work *Outrageous Idea of Christian Scholarship*.

33. Such is the verdict of Burtchaell, *Dying of the Light*.

Epilogue

Initium Sapientiae Timor Alterius and the Constituents of the University

CHRISTOPHER CRAIG BRITTAIN

THE ESSAYS THAT MAKE up this collection come to the question of the relationship between theology, the humanities, and the university at a time when the traditional boundaries and concerns of this debate have shifted profoundly. Perhaps the dramatic nature of the present challenges facing the university is what accounts for the absence of any reference by this book's contributors to a once celebrated theological reflection on the purpose of higher education: John Henry Newman's *The Idea of the University*. This is noteworthy, given that, at least in the popular imagination, the values and cultural status surrounding the institution of the university remain, to a large degree, not unlike those expressed by Newman just over one hundred and fifty years ago:

> If then a practical end must be assigned to a University course, I say it is that of training good members of society. Its art is the art of social life, and its end is fitness for the world . . . It does not promise a generation of Aristotles or Newtons, of Napoleons or Washingtons, of Raphaels or Shakespeares, though such miracles it has before now contained within its precincts. Nor is it content on the other hand with forming the critic or the experimentalist, the economist or the engineer, although such too it includes within its scope. But a university training is the great ordinary means to a

great but ordinary end; it aims at raising the intellectual tone of society, at cultivating the public mind, at purifying the national taste,
at supplying true principles to popular enthusiasm and fixed aims
to popular aspiration, at giving enlargement and sobriety to the
ideas of the age, at facilitating the exercise of political power, and
refining the intercourse of private life. It is the education which
gives a [person] a clear, conscious view of their own opinions and
judgments, a truth in developing them, an eloquence in expressing
them, and a force in urging them.[1]

There is much in Newman's *The Idea of the University* that will not
resonate with the contemporary reader; for example, his assumption that
the concept of "Right Reason," when consistently exercised, "leads the
mind to the Catholic Faith." Given the state of the university today, rent
by ideological critique, the demands for practical relevancy, and powerful markets interests, there appears to be little that would lead one to be
drawn to Newman's unified theory of first principles, or even his notion
of a purified "national taste." As Bill Readings has argued in *The University in Ruins*, "the notion of culture as the legitimating idea of the modern
University has reached the end of its usefulness" as "the University is becoming a transnational bureaucratic corporation."[2]

Some enthusiasm, nevertheless, does remain in contemporary debates for elements of Newman's vision in the above quotation: the practical
goal of cultivating a public mind, and on training good members of society—albeit understood differently from Newman's original intention. But
even this understanding of the university has recently come under attack.
To highlight how the essays in this volume represent significant resources
for carrying forward the wider debate over the future of the university,
my closing remarks will revisit two recent treatments of knowledge and
citizenship in modern democratic societies: Jeffrey Stout's *Democracy
and Tradition* and Rowan Williams' *Lost Icons*. After briefly revisiting the
contemporary tensions with which universities struggle, the discussion
highlights a significant gap in Stout's defense of the legitimacy of religious
discourse in the public sphere. It shows that his argument admits that
many religious adherents will find it difficult to find a home in public
institutions like the university, but that it does little to analyze why this
is so, nor does it propose ways to respond to such tensions. This suggests

1. Newman, *Idea of the University*, 134.
2. Readings, *University in Ruins*, 3–5.

that his position requires a fuller treatment of subjectivity, which, I argue, is present in the work of Rowan Williams. Bringing the work of these two thinkers into a conversation with each other serves to illuminate further how each of the essays in this volume offer substantial contributions to a deeper understanding of both the challenges and potential that exists for a vigorous role for theology in the contemporary university.

Prior to turning to Stout and Williams, I will first recall some of the challenges and tensions that the contributors to this book have articulated so powerfully.

The Crisis Facing Theology and the Humanities in the Modern University

After theology was displaced from its throne as "Queen of the Sciences," a position it enjoyed during the Middle Ages, it was conceived of as being a threat to scholarly objectivity and excellence. As the modern university took shape in the nineteenth century, theology lost its former role as the unifying source of knowledge and morality, and this function was relocated as being more properly the role of the humanities. The increasing prominence of natural science and technical knowledge in the Academy frequently led to concerns over the fragmentation of education into disparate disciplines with little capacity to shape the character of the citizen. In the United States, for example, as denominational colleges were gradually replaced by the modern university, the concept of character formation continued to be emphasized by university and government officials.[3] Although the notion of open scientific inquiry was sometimes considered to be a moral guide in and of itself, more frequently the humanities were regarded as the sphere in which virtue and character could be nurtured. As such, the human sciences were thought to offer resources to guide the wise and judicious deployment of technological knowledge and skill. Although theology was no longer considered to be the source of a unifying divine wisdom, the humanities were thought to offer the alternative of a common culture and canonical reference point around which to focus the moral task of the university. Julie Rueben's study of this process signals that this vision was largely eroded in the early decades of the twentieth century: "In this transition from the classical college to the modern

3. Rueben, *Making of the Modern University*, 61–87.

university, the older ideal of the unity of truth was largely gutted . . . Unity has given way to fragmentation; diverse and specialized programs were loosely held together under a single administrative structure."[4]

This fragmentation of knowledge within the Academy, along with heightened societal suspicion of the cultural and class hegemony of the traditional beneficiaries of the classical university education, has thus shifted the ground under the debate over theology's place in the modern university. If it is indeed true that, as Bill Readings describes it, "the grand narrative of the University, centered on the production of a liberal, reasoning, subject, is no longer readily available to us," then prior conceptions of theology in the Academy will be challenged. For much of the nineteenth and twentieth century, Christian theologians lamented the decline of status, even legitimacy, of theology as a respected academic discipline in the university. What is striking at the beginning of the twenty-first century is how often theologians are now joined in such protests by colleagues from all the other disciplines of the human sciences. In a certain sense, the humanities are experiencing the fate suffered previously by theology as an academic discipline.

Defending the Traditional "Liberal Arts" Education

Martha Nussbaum has recently offered a vigorous defense of the traditional vision for the humanities and their place in a "Liberal Arts" education." In her view, the danger confronting higher education in the contemporary context is that, faced with increasingly global economic competition, with the requisite concerns for technological innovation and profit, universities are increasingly reducing education to the acquisition of instrumental skill. The result is a "forgetting of soul." She argues that such over-emphasis on science and technology threatens to result in the complete marginalization of the humanities. But the humanities, she continues, are the source of some of the more vital characteristics required for a healthy democracy: "the ability to think critically; the ability to transcend local loyalties and to approach world problems as a 'citizen of the world'; and, finally, the ability to imagine sympathetically the predicament of another person."[5]

4. Ibid., 267.
5. Nussbaum, *Not For Profit*, 6–7.

Nussbaum's position resonates to some degree with a number of the chapters in this volume. In the essays by John Webster, David Jasper, Simon Oliver, Laurence Hemming, and Gavin D'Costa, a strong case is made for the fact that theology is of central importance for *knowledge* as such, the absence of which thus has profound implications both the intellectual and social roles of the university.

Although Jeffrey Stout would likely disagree with a number of the points developed by each of these authors, his recent book *Democracy and Tradition* outlines a perspective that would not only welcome such arguments into the contemporary Academy, but would consider such vigorous challenges to the norms of secular reasoning to be crucial for the university's health, as well as that of liberal democracy. His position is also one which resonates with Martha Nussbaum's vision for the humanities. For these reasons, it is instructive to turn briefly to an analysis of one aspect of this important book.

Stout on Resident Aliens and the Alienated Theologian

In *Democracy and Tradition*, Stout explores the exercise of public reasoning in modern democratic societies. He argues against the assumption on the part of many liberal political theories that debates within the public sphere must assume a neutral perspective with regards to any conceptions of the good, so that all public deliberations over policy and ethical issues must be undertaken on the basis of a commonly understood notion of rationality without reference to privately held religious perspectives or traditions. He describes theorists like Jürgen Habermas, Richard Rorty, as well as John Dewey and Charles Peirce, as advocating a "Jeffersonian compromise" with religion: a view that insists that, "we should limit conversation to premises held in common, thereby excluding the [public] expression of religious premises."[6] Stout's intriguing position is that democracy does not in fact require such a rigid notion of value-neutral or tradition-free public reasoning. He suggests that such a policing of public discussion over policy undermines the stability and health of democratic societies, for it discourages religious adherents from articulating their motivations and opinions clearly in the public sphere, thereby hindering transparency and clarity of communication between citizens.

---

6. Stout, *Democracy and Tradition*, 86.

Over the course of Stout's book, two character types serve as the heroes of his narrative. First, Stout calls for the sincere and patient "secular" non-religious person to embody a hospitable openness to listen to the claims of people of faith. The second sort of individual applauded by the book is the religious adherent who willingly engages in public reasoning in the public sphere. What is of particular interest for the present discussion is how these two character-types are bordered by two more problematic antagonists: the "resident alien" and the "alienated theologian."

The Resident Alien

One of Stout's concerns in *Democracy and Tradition* is his observation that some religious adherents and theologians describe liberal democracy as being inherently anti-religious. In his examination of the work of Stanley Hauerwas, for example, Stout notes that Hauerwas understands democratic liberalism to represent a threat to Christian virtue and practice. Hauerwas argues that all theoretical and moral standpoints are conditioned. There exists no universal or neutral standpoint from which all particular or biased perspectives can be judged. Thus, he argues that the notion of a value-neutral "secular" public sphere is in fact misleading, serving only to mask specific value-laden interests (capitalism, consumerism, nationalism, etc.) that lie behind the discourse legitimated by liberal political theory.

Stout is sympathetic up to a point with Hauerwas's position, agreeing that all discursive positions are contextually conditioned by particular interests. What he is concerned with, and what he intends to challenge, is the tendency in Hauerwas's position towards sectarianism. Stout becomes alarmed when people of religious faith like Hauerwas describe themselves as "resident aliens" in a hostile secular society. He reads such a reaction as resembling a strategy not unlike a defensive "circling of the wagons" in which religious communities effectively withdraw from public debate, thereby impoverishing the dynamism and health of democratic exchanges between the different communities that make up civil society. Furthermore, Stout warns that, "Theologies designed to articulate, defend, and reinforce resentment of the secular are symptoms of the disease they are meant to cure. They are the ideological expression of the enclave society."[7]

7. Ibid., 115.

The Alienated Theologian

In addition to his concern with the self-described "resident alien," Stout also refers to what, following Van A. Harvey, he calls the "alienated theologian." He notes that "thinkers committed to exercising the vocation of theology in a democratic context often experience a tension between the virtue of open-minded charity in listening to others and their calling as expounders of the commitments of their ecclesial community."[8] Stout observes that, once theologians enter sincerely into dialogue with others, "they have felt the force of reasons at odds with their confession of faith."[9] This reference to the "alienated theologian" in Stout's book is brief, but significant. For although he notes the ongoing struggle of some theologians to maintain the beliefs of their tradition in the midst of participation in public reasoning, he does not dwell very long with this problem. This is a significant gap in his argument, given his particular emphasis that, "democracy will suffer greatly if orthodox Christians are unable to find a way to maintain their own convictions." [10]

The Christian in Public

Stout's argument is much more interested in, for lack of a better term, the "confidently public theologian," who serves a crucial role for the viability of the book's entire argument. But the displacement of the "alienated theologian" in favor of the public theologian occurs too quickly. On the one hand, Stout argues that adherents of religious traditions should feel welcome to enter debates in the public sphere and voice the particular concerns and perspectives of their tradition. And yet, at the same time, he also claims that, "There are in fact many situations in which the introduction of religious premises into a political argument seems a sign of bad taste or imprudence on the part of the speaker." What is required, he continues, is "prudence and tact."[11] In opposition to Rorty, Stout does not consider religion a "conversation-stopper," but, it seems, religion

8. Ibid.

9. See Harvey, "Alienated Theologian." For an analysis of the tension between academic theology and scientific knowledge which argues for an inevitable clash between the two, see Wiebe, *Irony of Theology*.

10. Stout, *Democracy and Tradition*, 116.

11. Ibid., 86.

can, when invoked improperly, make conversation rather awkward, even vulgar.

Without greater clarity on this issue, Stout's engaging call for a renewed hospitality in the public sphere for religious discourse remains abstract and undeveloped. He neither explores the complexities experienced by the theologian in the academy, nor how the inhospitality of the university leads some to regard themselves as "resident aliens." As Van Harvey writes, "many American intellectuals regard theology . . . as something akin to astrology . . . They believe it to be divisive as well as obscurantist and therefore a threat to the common presuppositions on which civic discourse in a democracy must necessarily rest."[12]

Theology in the University

The essays in this collection develop a greater appreciation of the tensions that Stout alludes to but does not explore in detail, and nuance his discussion of the relationship between theology and knowledge in general. Although Stout's argument establishes some basic groundwork for theorizing the place of faith and theology in the university, there remain significant unresolved tensions among the very religious subjectivities that he describes. The fact that many feel themselves alien or alienated requires further analysis, for, in the end, Stout's pragmatic concept of knowledge makes little room for theological forms of reasoning.

On this latter point, the contributors to this book have much to offer. Hemming's deep probing of the complex relationship between secular and theological forms of reasoning calls into question the arrogance of modern subjectivity. Oliver's caution against conceiving of human knowledge as its own measure similarly challenges the strict rules governing the debate that Stout imagines in the public sphere. Webster's contribution suggests that, however hospitable the public sphere may be, it will be vital for theology to maintain a clear sense of the proper object of its inquiry. Moreover, D'Costa's defense of the concept of a "Christian university" cannot be simply classified as invoking a call to become a "resident alien," and thus his essay offers further nuance and complexity to this basic tension described by Stout.

12. Harvey, "On the intellectual marginality of American theology," 172.

When David McIlroy defends the value of mutual exchange between differing disciplines like law and theology as a way of establishing dialectical harmony and cross fertilization, he begins to explore the texture of the public interaction between theology and "secular" non-religious discourses in a more intimate manner than does Stout in his book. Joachim Schaper's essay represents a counter-example to that of Hauerwas, as he defends not only the appropriateness, but even necessity, of interdisciplinary dialogue with secular academic disciplines for the study of the Christian Bible. In Christopher Insole's contribution, Stout might find his closest ally, if only perhaps due to Insole's clarification that "the opposite of good liberalism is not no liberalism, but bad liberalism." Like Stout, Insole offers an important response to accusations that political liberalism is inherently anti-theological.

These are substantial reflections to add to the conversation, for what Stout's study lacks is an analysis of the difficulty which the religious subject experiences when confronted by the tension of living in such a contested environment. One might add that, in our increasingly multi-cultural society, this tension is experienced not only by members of religious communities, but by most subjects in contemporary democracies. It is such a concern for the subject that other contributors to this book focus on. Jasper's call for a "theological humanism" is one which emphasizes subjective reflexivity, spurred on by the double love command to maintain a balance between the particular and the universal. My own essay encourages a similar form of reflexivity in theology through the use of disciplines such as sociology, while McIlroy presents a similar perspective on the interaction between theology and legal theory, and Schaper defends the importance of history for biblical studies. Kroeker offers a distinctive approach the question of the place of human beings in the Stoutian public sphere by arguing that embodied liturgical practices shape abstract concepts.

When viewed from the perspectives and concerns developed in the chapters of this book, it becomes apparent that, while Stout argues forcefully for the merits of including many voices and discourses in public debate, what receives less attention is the question of normativity and the legitimation of knowledge claims in such debates. This is likely due to Stout's reluctance to establish a rigid normative understanding of rationality in the Kantian sense. Yet leaving the resolution of such questions to pragmatic resolution leaves a number of significant issues unresolved.

To highlight once again the problem of the religious subject in Stout's argument, it is instructive to return to Stout's criticism of models of inter-subjective discourse that are based on "social contract" theory.[13] What is needed, he urges, is not a social contract, but social cooperation. The process of exchanging reasons in dialogue is all that is seems to be required. Dialogue partners will "hold one another responsible and implicitly impute to others the authority to keep normative track of one another's attitudes." He continues, "Why not count anyone as a 'reasonable person' who participates *responsibly* in the process of discursive exchange?"

Rather than a normative understanding of communicative procedural rationality, then, Stout advocates for intersubjective dialogue that is done "responsibly" and in "good taste," meaning that it is undertaken in a manner that listens to the other and is careful to articulate reasons for any claims made. Over the course of entering into public debate, what Stout calls the "kinematics of presupposition" will result in some knowledge claims receiving a favorable public hearing, and others unfavorable. He writes,

> If one cannot expect [theological] premises to be accepted or interpreted in a uniform way, it will not necessarily advance one's rhetorical purposes to assert them. And if theological premises therefore receive little discursive attention for this perfectly understandable reason, why would anyone have just cause for resentment of the resulting type of secular discourse? When people want to exchange reasons with others who differ from them theologically, this type of discourse is likely to increase drastically in significance. Resentment of this fact is indistinguishable from resentment of religious diversity.[14]

Does not a blunt reading of this statement imply, in effect, that those who feel like "resident aliens" are merely resentful of difference? Can the problem be so easily dismissed? Those religious adherents who continue to participate in discursive debate are to be applauded for successfully negotiating the complexities of modern discursive action. What might be expected, however, is that the more typical religious adherent in Stout's public sphere will remain the "alienated theologian," one who struggles to find a relevant way to articulate the particularity of their religious

13. Stout, *Democracy and Tradition*, 82.
14. Ibid., 99.

tradition in public acts of reasoning.[15] Stout's book gives little attention to understanding the resentment that many people of faith experience in the public sphere.

This absence is puzzling, given Stout's sensitivity and generosity when he upholds and defends the value of conversation and discussion. He writes, "Conversation is a good name for what is needed at those points where people employing different final vocabularies reach a momentary impasse."[16] What is at issue, however, is the instance when the impasse that emerges between differing "vocabularies" is far from *momentary*. Might it not be that numerous religious adherents have in fact attempted to articulate the particularities of their traditions in the public realm, and have failed to "justify" their claims in a manner that convinces others? What is the "alienated theologian" to do when she has entered into the exchange of "final vocabularies," and has left feeling wounded? What is clear is that Stout's position requires of the religious adherent—and all other citizens in democratic societies—two things: a virtue of openness and hospitality towards others, and willingness to separate personal beliefs and practices from the norms of the public sphere. When the debate is over, it is expected that the religious adherent will temporarily accept the verdict as representing the wisdom of the wider society—or, at least, hope that ongoing debate offers the future possibility that new arguments might change people's minds.

What Stout argues for is a procedural understanding of democracy as an open exchange of reasons. Essentially, it is an idealized procedure without clearly articulated norms.[17] Whatever happens after the exchange is left to the context and to those involved in the interaction. Is it not the case, however, that it is what happens *after the exchange* that is rather cru-

---

15. It is noteworthy that Stout appears to discuss theological discourse in isolation from the ritual practices in which theology finds its customary home. This is not difficult to understand, given his principle concern is with the interaction between people of differing faith traditions, yet, such a separation of religious discourse from religious practice is frequently criticized by theologians and scholars of religion. Hauerwas is one example of a Christian theologian who might argue along these lines, and Kroeker's essay in the volume raises related concerns.

16. Ibid., 90.

17. In this regard, Stout's position is actually not unlike that of Habermas' principal of universalization, in that it is intended as a procedural principal of practical argumentation that intends to resolved an issue through the force of the better argument. See Habermas, *Theory of Communicative Action*.

cial to the matter at hand? It is the *result* of a discursive exchange which will lead participants to celebrate, become alienated, or begin to describe themselves as "resident aliens." Will the participants of both sides of the debate remain committed to the procedural discursive presuppositions that Stout's democratic piety defends? The result of such exchanges might lead some to abandon democratic forms of communicative action and adopt more instrumental forms of social interaction. The fact of losing a debate does not, of course, mean that the disappointed participants will accept the verdict of the majority. Stout certainly acknowledges this, but his confidence in the ability of the general population to serve as "competent judges" of moral truths in contemporary debates is not developed sufficiently to address this problem; nor does his analysis explore the dynamics of subjectivity that impact on the intersubjective model he defends.

The Lost Soul

It is for this reason that Stout's inclusive political vision requires a more sophisticated analysis of subjectivity. In his book *Lost Icons*, Rowan Williams explores the struggles of the individual subject in contemporary society. In the face of the complexities brought on by the erosion of social consensus, Williams argues that the recognition "that the choices of the individual will cannot demand instant and unconditional fulfillment," implies "the necessity of spending time in the management of conflicts of interest or desire."[18] Williams notes that being able to negotiate difference "entails an assumption that differences can be *thought*, not just thrown against each other." His book focuses on the difficult process of learning and growth that the subject experiences in the encounter of difference and conflict. The implication he draws from this is the necessity of recognizing "that the self itself is learned or evolved, not a given, fixed system of needs and desires."[19] As such, Williams explores the importance for the subject to bear complexity and tension, and to mourn loss. His concern is that this necessity of bearing loss and complexity is in stark contrast with the idealized individual of Western society, which upholds self-contained and controlled models of the self. It also represents a very different

18. Williams, *Lost Icons*, 5.
19. Ibid., 6.

understanding of subjectivity from the one idealized by the liberal theory of the university: an autonomous individual made free and independent by the information that it acquires.

As part of this reflection on the challenges confronting the individual subject in contemporary culture, Williams explores the nature of education. He draws a parallel between the idealized self-contained individual and the notion that there is a single and fairly easily measurable standard of success in education. In contrast to this, Williams argues that education is "something that has to do with expressing and fostering a *corporate* responsibility." He continues, "since we currently don't seem to know, as a society, what we want to 'induct' children into or what we consider to be the foundation of moral legitimacy . . . it isn't surprising that we take refuge in treating education as the process of purchasing blocks of training material." Such a trend, in his opinion, impoverishes the ability of education to help students learn how to think about, and bear, complexity and difference. He continues, "for that requires both a fluency in the traditions, even the mythology, of the society you're in, *and* a confidence sufficient to test and challenge its inconsistencies or deceptions."[20]

This position connects Williams to Stout's concerns, as his argument illuminates the importance of encountering diverse ideas and traditions, even those which one might consider "mythology." What Williams' book adds to Stout's argument is an attention to the demands such an educational environment has on the individual subject. Williams names the dominant contemporary subjectivity a "Lost Soul." He argues that modern popular culture is reactive and prone to panic. It is "embarrassed by the inevitability of learning in and through time," because of its emphasis on short-term goals, its denial of diversity and difference, its defensiveness of ego in the face of endless complexity.[21] Such a situation represents, he continues, a loss of the self. For the demands of contemporary existence involve being involved in "narratives that are constantly being revised, re-edited."[22] The self must continue to grow and develop—to mourn and accept change—as new experiences and encounters result in growth and change.

20. Ibid., 35–36.
21. Ibid., 142.
22. Ibid., 144.

That this is difficult for an individual to bear is the focus of Williams' analysis: "negotiating with what is not myself spells frustration to a self that is simply looking for identity or self-presence." To be "a conscious subject is to be involved in thinking through what it is to experience check or limit."[23] Yet, for Williams, it is precisely the challenge of self-questioning that is the proper task of religious faith. He writes,

> Authentic religious . . . practice begins in the attempt to attend to the moment of self-questioning—to refuse to cover over, evade, or explain the pain and shock of whatever brings the self into question, to hold on to the difficulty before the almost inevitable descent into pathos and personal drama begins. 'The soul' is what happens in the process of such attention: 'it is a movement that begins whenever [one] experiences the psychological pain of contradiction.[24]

This description of the tension-filled status of the individual in contemporary society offers an analysis of subjectivity that connects with some of the general themes that Stout develops in his argument for inclusivity in democratic societies. It also resonates with Nussbaum's concern for the "forgetting of soul" in the contemporary university. Williams argues in a fashion similar to Stout for hospitality towards difference, and upholds the value of communication and debate. Yet Williams is more realistic about the difficulty and challenge that this ideal presents to the individual. Following through on such a proposal will amount to an experience that Williams calls "planned frustration."[25] In such processes, human beings—and not merely those who bear the title "theologian"—will indeed become alienated from themselves. One will inevitability encounter the fragmented and partial nature of one's own understanding and capacity. Contingency, rather than certainty, will be the norm. In this regard, the core of Williams' position also travels deeper into the challenges facing the modern university than does Nussbaum's, for "lost souls" are no less prominent, or problematic, in the humanities than they are in the natural sciences. The dynamics with which he is concerned are in, this sense, truly "multi-disciplinary."

23. Ibid., 146.
24. Ibid., 149.
25. Ibid, 150.

The Idea of a University?

Given this perspective, Williams argues that, "a good educational institution would be one in which conversation flourishe[s]."[26] It is here that the themes of Stout's democratic vision and Williams' examination of subjectivity converge with Newman's description of the ideal university. Such a linkage is not, of course, at the level of first principles or universal knowledge. Stout's pragmatic approach to knowledge and discourse, along with Williams' emphasis on contingency resist such an impulse. Rather, the convergence emerges along the line of Newman's concern for the training of good members of society, and cultivating the public mind. The Academy represents one of the primary places where public interaction by diverse members of society on issues of common concern take place. It is where one encounters "the other" of Williams' concern, and it is one of the venues in which religious communities explore the concerns of their tradition, and are engaged with by people from other traditions.

In a university that is—like the wider public sphere—fragmented by competing truth claims, agendas, and traditions, the criterion for education shifts from an exclusive emphasis on unifying truth, to the question of obligation. Both Stout and Williams argue for the importance, if not necessity, of fostering dialogue and communication between differences. That this is so difficult to achieve for the human individual is only one of the challenges confronting this vision. The university is in ruins, just as the autonomous subject is often alienated and reduced to a "lost soul." What Stout and Williams suggest to us, however, is that an expanded hospitality towards religious discourses represents an important and necessary advance for democratic societies, and for the development of new understandings of community. Should the university see fit to take up the lead in pursuing this goal, and in developing subjectivities able to embody this vision, it might well discover the core of its ongoing vital role in contemporary society.

Each of the essays collected in this volume seeks to nurture such a patience and sensitivity on the part of the subject towards knowledge of the otherness of reality. They approach theology as involving an attentiveness to that which lies beyond any form of knowledge which immediately presents itself in contemporary Western culture. Each essay embodies a different way to seek after a reality which cannot be reduced to the

26. Ibid., 89.

pressures and fluctuating trends presently sweeping the Academy. Thus, while the contributors of this book do not share a single vision of how one should interpret or embody the motto *Initium Sapientiae Timor Domini*, what they do communicate is a collective commitment to a closely related position: *Initium Sapientiae Timor Alterius*. For each author explores from differing angles the reality that the fear of the "other" is the beginning of wisdom (where, of course, "fear" is taken to imply *respect*, as opposed to being frightened of the stranger). Such a pursuit, as some of the book's contributors have sought to emphasize, is not the exclusive realm of theology, but few can question the vigorous focus with which contemporary theologians like those assembled in this volume seek to attend to a reality than remains elusive (and thus "other") to what immediately presents itself, and, indeed, is the "Other" beyond all particular "others." Such patient and attentive discipline to this task, nurtured and inspired by an ancient and rich tradition, may be theology's best argument for a legitimate and significant role in the contemporary university.

Bibliography

Acton, Lord. "Acton-Creighton Correspondence." In *Essays on Freedom and Power*, 357–374. Boston: Beacon, 1948.

———. "Studies of History." In *Essays on Freedom and Power*, 2–29. Boston: Beacon, 1948.

Adorno, Theodor W. *Introduction to Sociology*. Translated by Edmund Jephcott. Edited by Christoph Gödde. Stanford: Stanford University Press, 2000.

———. *Negative Dialectics*. Translated by E. B. Ashton. New York: Continuum, 1995.

———. *The Positivist Dispute in German Sociology*. Translated by Glyn Adey and David Frisby. London: Heinemann, 1976.

Allard, G.-H. "La technique de la 'reductio' chez Bonaventure." In *S. Bonaventura 1274–1974*, vol. 2. Rome: Collegio S. Bonaventura, 1974.

Anderson, J. N. D. *Law, Liberty & Justice*. London: Stevens, 1978.

Anselm. *Basic Writings*. Translated by S. N. Deane. 2nd ed. Chicago: Open Court, 1962.

Aristotle. *Metaphysics I–IX*. Translated by Hugh Tredennick. Cambridge, MA: Harvard University Press, 1996.

Aristotle. *The Nicomachean Ethics*. Translated by J. A. K. Thomson. Harmondsworth: Penguin, 1976.

Aquinas, Thomas. *Commentary on Aristotle's Metaphysics*. Translated by John P. Rowan. Notre Dame, IN: Dumb Ox, 1995.

———. *Summa Theologiae*. Translated by the Fathers of the English Dominican Province. Londo: Sheed & Ward, 1920.

Augustine. *The City of God against the Pagans*. Translated by R. W. Dyson. Cambridge: Cambridge University Press, 1998.

———. *Confessions*. Translated by Gillian Clark. Cambridge: Cambridge University Press, 1993.

———. *De Doctrina Christiana [On Christian Doctrine]*. Translated by R. P. H. Green. Oxford: Clarendon, 1995.

———. *The Literal Meaning of Genesis*. Translated by Edmund Hill. Hyde Park, NY: New City, 2002.

Balthasar, Hans Urs von. *Henri de Lubac: Sein organisches Lebenswerk*. Einsiedeln: Johannes, 1976.

Barclay, O. "The nature of Christian morality." In *Law, Morality and the Bible*, edited by B. N. Kaye and G. J. Wenham, 125–50. Leicester, UK: InterVarsity, 1978.

Barth, Karl. *Church Dogmatics* IV/3. Edinburgh: T. & T. Clark, 1961.

Bibliography

Barton J. *The Nature of Biblical Criticism*. Louisville: Westminster John Knox, 2007.

Beckett, Lucy. *In the Light of Christ: Writings in the Western Tradition*. San Francisco: Ignatius, 2006.

Benedict XVI. "Meeting with the Representatives of Science: The Lecture of the Holy Father." September 12, 2006. Online: http://www.vatican.va/holy_father/benedict_xvi/speeches/2006/september/documents/hf_ben-xvi_spe_20060912_university-regensburg_en.html.

Berman, H. J. *The Interaction of Law and Religion*. London: SCM, 1974.

Bérubé, C. *De la philosophie à la sagesse chez Saint Bonaventure et Roger Bacon*. Rome: Instituto Storico dei Cappuccini, 1976.

Biggar, Nigel. *Behaving in Public: Christian Ethics outside the Church*. Grand Rapids: Eerdmans, 2011.

Bloom, Alan. *The Closing of the American Mind*. New York: Simon & Schuster, 1987.

Blythe, James. *Ideal Government and the Mixed Constitution*. Princeton: Princeton University Press, 1992.

Bonaventure. *On the Reduction of the Arts to Theology*. Edited by Z. Hayes. Saint Bonaventure, NY: Franciscan Institute, Saint Bonaventure University, 1996.

Bonhoeffer, Dietrich. *Creation and Fall; Temptation: Two Biblical Studies*. New York: Macmillan, 1959.

Boulnois, Olivier. *Être et Représentation: Une genealogie de la métaphysique moderne à l'époque de Duns Scot*. Paris: Presses Universitaires de France, 1999.

Boyle, Nicholas. *Sacred and Secular Scriptures: A Catholic Approach to Literature*. London: Darton Longman & Todd, 2005.

Brittain, Christopher Craig. *The Weight of Objectivity: Critical Social Theory and Theology*. Saarbrücken: Lampert, 2010.

Burke, Edmund. *The Works of the Right Honourable Edmund Burke*. 6 vols. London: Henry G. Bohn, 1854–56.

Burns, J. H. *The Cambridge History of Medieval Political Thought c.350–1450*. Cambridge: Cambridge University Press, 1988.

Burnside, Jonathan. "Criminal Justice." In *The Jubilee Manifesto*, edited by Michael Schluter and John Ashcroft, 234–54. Nottingham: InterVarsity, 2005.

———. *The Signs of Sin: Seriousness of Offence in Biblical Law*. Sheffield, UK: Sheffield Academic, 2003.

Burnside Jonathan P., and Nicola Baker, editors. *Relational Justice: Repairing the Breach*. Winchester, UK: Waterside, 1994.

Burtchaell, James Tunstead. *The Dying of the Light. The Disengagement of Colleges and Universities from their Christian Churches*. Grand Rapids: Eerdmans, 1998.

Cavanaugh, William T. "'A Fire Strong Enough to Consume the House': The Wars of Religion and the Rise of the State." *Modern Theology* 11:4 (1995) 397–420.

———. *Theopolitical Imagination: Discovering the Liturgy as a Political Act in an Age of Global Consumerism*. London: T. & T. Clark, 2002.

———. *Torture and Eucharist: Theology, Politics, and the Body of Christ*. Oxford: Blackwell, 1998.

Chesterton, G. K. *Orthodoxy*. London: Hodder & Stoughton, 1996.

Clark, William. *Academic Charisma and the Origins of the Research University*. Chicago: University of Chicago Press, 2008.

Clark, Timothy. *Martin Heidegger*. London: Routledge, 2002.

Coakley, Sarah. "Introduction: Re-thinking Dionysius the Areopagite." *Modern Theology* 24:4 (2008) 531–40.

Colwell, John E. *Living the Christian Story: The Distinctiveness of Christian Ethics.* Edinburgh: T. & T. Clark, 2001.

Connolly, William. *The Augustinian Imperative: A Reflection on the Politics of Morality.* Thousand Oaks, CA: Sage, 1993.

Congregation for the Doctrine of the Faith. *Instruction on the Ecclesial Vocation of the Theologian.* 1990. Online: http://www.vatican.va/roman_curia/congregations/cfaith/documents/rc_con_cfaith_doc_19900524_theologian-vocation_en.html

D'Costa, Gavin. *Sexing the Trinity.* London: SCM, 2000.

———. *Theology in the Public Square: Church, University, and Nation.* Oxford: Blackwell, 2005.

Cullen, Christopher. *Bonaventure.* Oxford: Oxford University Press, 2006.

Nicholas of Cusa. "*De Possest.*" In *A Concise Introduction to the Philosophy of Nicholas of Cusa*, 3rd ed., translated and edited by Jasper Hopkins. Minneapolis: Arthur J. Banning, 1986.

———. "*De Sapientia.*" In *Nicholas of Cusa on Wisdom and Knowledge*, translated by Jasper Hopkins. Minneapolis: Arthur J. Banning, 1996.

———. "*De Docta Ignorantia.*" In *Selected Spiritual Writings*, translated by H. Lawrence Bond. New York: Paulist, 1997.

Daiches, David. *God and the Poets.* Oxford: Clarendon, 1984.

Danto, Arthur C. *The Abuse of Beauty: Aesthetics and the Concept of Art.* Chicago: Open Court, 2003.

Davies, Oliver. *The Creativity of God: Word, Eucharist, Reason.* Cambridge: Cambridge University Press, 2004.

De Man, Paul. *The Resistance to Theory.* Manchester: Manchester University Press, 1986.

Derrida, Jacques. "Force of Law: The 'Mystical Foundation of Authority.'" *Cardozo Law Review* 11 (1990) 919–1045.

Dodaro, Robert. "Augustine's Secular City." In *Augustine and His Critics*, edited by Robert Dodaro and George Lawless, 231–259. London: Routledge, 2000.

Dooyeweerd, Herman. *Encyclopedia of the Science of Law, Volume 1: Introduction.* Lampeter: Edwin Mellen, 2003.

———. "Kuyper's wetenschapsleer." *Philosophia Reformata* 4 (1939) 193–232.

———. *A New Critique of Theoretical Thought.* Cardiff: Edwin Mellen, 1997.

———. "De staatkundige tegenstelling tussschen Christelijk-Historische en Anti-revolutionaire partij." III (c.1923–24) 5. Mimeographed article, Dooyeweerd Archive, VU, Amsterdam.

———. *In The Twilight of Western Thought.* Nutley, NJ: Craig, 1975.

Dostoevsky, Fyodor. *The Brothers Karamazov.* Translated by R. Pevear and L. Volokhonsky. New York: Vintage, 1990.

———. *Crime and Punishment.* Translated by David Magarshack. Harmondsworth, UK: Penguin, 1966.

Edwards, James C. *The Plain Sense of Things: The Fate of Religion in an Age of Normal Nihilism.* University Park: Pennsylvania State University Press, 1997.

Ellul, Jacques. *The Theological Foundation of Law.* Translated by Marguerite Wieser. London: SCM, 1961.

Evans, G. R. *Old Arts and New Theology. The Beginnings of Theology as an Academic Discipline.* Oxford: Clarendon, 1980.

Figgis, John Neville. *Political Thought From Gerson to Grotius, 1414–1625*. New York: Harper, 1960.

Finnis, John. *Aquinas: Moral, Political, and Legal Theory*. Oxford: Oxford University Press, 1999.

Ford, David. *Christian Wisdom: Desiring God and Learning in Love*. Cambridge: Cambridge University Press, 2007.

———. *Shaping Theology: Engagements in a Religious and Secular World*. Oxford: Blackwell, 2007.

Foucault, Michel. *Discipline and Punish: The Birth of the Prison*. Translated by Alan Sheridan. New York: Vintage, 1977.

Fraassen, Bas van. *The Empirical Stance*. New Haven, CT: Yale University Press, 2002.

Funkenstein, Amos. *Theology and the Scientific Imagination*. Princeton: Princeton University Press, 1986.

Gilby, Thomas. *Between Community and Society: A Philosophy and Theology of the State*. London: Longman Green, 1952.

———. *Principality and Polity*. London: Longman Green, 1958,

Gadamer, Hans-Georg. *Truth and Method*. 3rd ed. Translation revised by Joel Weinsheimer and Donald G. Marshall. London: Continuum, 2004.

Gellner, Ernest. *Relativism and the Social Sciences*. Cambridge: Cambridge University Press, 1985.

Gilson, Étienne. *The Unity of Philosophical Experience*. San Francisco: Ignatius, 1999.

Griffiths, Paul. *Lying: An Augustinian Theology of Duplicity*. Grand Rapids: Brazos, 2004.

Gross, Alan. *The Rhetoric of Science*. Cambridge: Harvard University Press, 1990.

Gunton, Colin. *Father, Son and Holy Spirit: Essays Toward a Fully Trinitarian Theology*. Edinburgh: T. & T. Clark, 2003.

Habermas, Jürgen. *A Theory of Communicative Action*. 2 volumes. Translated by Thomas McCarthy. Boston: Beacon, 1987.

Hadot, Isletraut. *Arts libéraux et philosophie dans la pensée antique*. Paris: Études augustiniennes, 1948.

Harrison, Carol. *Augustine. Christian Truth and Fractured Humanity*. Oxford: Oxford University Press, 2000.

Harvey, Van A. "The Alienated Theologian." *McCormick Quarterly* 23:4 (1970) 234–66.

———. "On the Intellectual Marginality of American Theology." In *Religion and Twentieth-Century American Intellectual Life*, edited by Michael J. Lacey, 172–92. Cambridge: Cambridge University Press, 1989.

Hauerwas, Stanley. *After Christendom? How the Church Is to Behave If Freedom, Justice, and a Christian Nation Are Bad Ideas*. Nashville: Abingdon, 1991

———. *The State of the University: Academic Knowledges and the Knowledge of God*. Oxford: Blackwell, 2007.

———. *With the Grain of the Universe: The Church's Witness and Natural Theology*. Grand Rapids: Brazos, 2001.

Hays, Richard B. "Reading the Bible with Eyes of Faith: The Practice of Theological Exegesis." *Journal of Theological Interpretation* 1 (2007) 5–21.

Hebden Taylor, E. L. *The Christian Philosophy of Law, Politics and the State*. Nutley: NJ, Craig, 1966.

Hegel, G. W. F. *Glauben und Wissen*. Hamburg, Felix Meiner, 1962.

———. *Hegels theologische Jugendschriften*. Edited by H. Nohl. Tübingen: Mohr/Siebeck, 1907.

———. *Phänomenologie des Geistes*. Hamburg: Felix Meiner, 1988.

Heidegger, Martin. *Being and Time*. Translated by John Macquarrie and Edward Robinson. Oxford: Blackwell, 1962.

———. *Die Grundbegriffe der Metaphysik: Welt, Endlichkeit, Einsamkeit*. Edited by Friedrich-Wilhelm von Herrmann. In *Gesamtausgabe*, 102 vols., A29/30. Frankfurt: Klostermann, 1983

———. *Hegels Phänomenologie des Geistes*. Edited by Ingtraud Görland. Frankfurt: Klostermann, 1988.

———. "Letter on Humanism." In *Pathmarks*, translated by Frank A. Capuzzi, edited by William McNeil, 239–76. Cambridge: Cambridge University Press, 1998.

Helmer, C. "Schleiermachers exegetische Theologie: Urteilsbildung und Korrespondenz in der neutestamentlichen Wissenschaft." In *Schleiermachers Dialektik: Die Liebe zum Wissen in Philosophie und Theologie*, edited by C. Helmer, C. Kranich, and B. Rehme-Iffert, 55–77. Tübingen: Mohr/Siebeck, 2003.

Helmer, C. "Schleiermacher's Exegetical Theology and the New Testament." In *The Cambridge Companion to Schleiermacher*, edited by J. Mariña, 229–48. Cambridge: Cambridge University Press.

Hemming, Laurence Paul. *Postmodernity's Transcending: Devaluing God*. Notre Dame, IN: Notre Dame University Press, 2005.

Henderson, R. D. *Illuminating Law: The Construction of Herman Dooyeweerd's Philosophy 1918–1928*. Amsterdam: Free University of Amsterdam, 1994.

Hirst, Paul Q., editor. *Pluralist Theory of the State: Selected Writings of G. D. H.Cole*. Translated by J. N. Figgis and H. J. Laski. London: Routledge, 2005.

Holmes, Steve. "Can Punishment Bring Peace? Penal Substitution Revisited." *Scottish Journal of Theology* 58 (2005) 104–23.

Hoff, Johannes. "The Rise and Fall of the Kantian Paradigm of Modern Theology." In *The Grandeur of Reason*, edited by Conor Cunningham and Peter Candler, 167–96. London: SCM, 2010.

Hopkins, Jasper. "Nicholas of Cusa (1401–1464): First Modern Philosopher." In *Renaissance and Early Modern Philosophy (Midwest Studies in Philosophy, vol. XXVI)*, edited by Peter A. French and Howard K. Wettstein, 13–29. Oxford: Blackwell, 2002.

Howard, T. A. *Protestant Theology and the Making of the Modern German University*. Oxford: Oxford University Press, 2006.

Howard, Thomas A. *Religion and the Rise of Historicism: W. M. L. de Wette, Jacob Burckhardt, and the Theological Origins of Nineteenth-Century Historical Consciousness*. Cambridge: Cambridge University Press, 2000.

Hugh of Saint Victor. *The Didascalicon*. Edited by J. Taylor. New York: Columbia University Press, 1991.

Iannaccone, Laurence R. "Framework for the Scientific Study of Religion." In *Rational Choice Theory and Religion*, edited by Lawrence A. Young, 25–44. New York: Routledge, 1997.

———. "Voodoo Economics? Reviewing the Rational Choice Approach to Religion." *Journal for the Scientific Study of Religion* 34:1 (1995) 76–89.

Ignatieff, Michael. *The Lesser Evil: Political Ethics in an Age of Terror*. Edinburgh: Edinburgh University Press, 2004.

Insole, Christopher. "Discerning the Theopolitical: a Response to Cavanaugh's Reimagining of Political Space." *Political Theology* 7:3 (2006) 323–35.

———. "Kant and the Divine Mind: Transcendental Idealism and Freedom." Forthcoming.

————. "Natural Law and Practical Reason." In *The Cambridge Companion to Edmund Burke*, edited by David Dwan and Christopher Insole. Cambridge: Cambridge University Press, forthcoming.

————. *The Politics of Human Frailty: A Theological Defence of Political Liberalism*. Notre Dame, IN: University of Notre Dame Press, 006.

————. *The Realist Hope: A Critique of Anti-Realist Approaches in Contemporary Philosophical Theology*. Farnborough: Ashgate, 2006.

————. "Two Conceptions of Liberalism: Theology, Creation and Politics in the Thought of Immanuel Kant and Edmund Burke." *Journal of Religious Ethics* 36:3 (2008) 447–40.

Jackson Bernard S. *Studies in the Semiotics of Biblical Law*. Sheffield, UK: Sheffield Academic, 2000.

John Paul II. *Ex Ecclesiae Corde. On Catholic Universities*. August 15, 1990. Online: http://www.vatican.va/holy_father/john_paul_ii/apost_constitutions/documents/hf_jp-ii_apc_15081990_ex-corde-ecclesiae_en.html.

————. *Fides et Ratio. On the Relationship between Faith and Reason*. September 15, 1998. Online: http://www.vatican.va/holy_father/john_paul_ii/encyclicals/documents/hf_jp-ii_enc_15101998_fides-et-ratio_en.html.

Kierkegaard, Søren. *Philosophical Fragments*. Edited and translated by Howard V. Hong and Edna H. Hong. Princeton: Princeton University Press, 1985.

Lagerlund, Henrik, editor. *Rethinking the History of Skepticism: The Missing Medieval Background*. Leiden: Brill, 2010.

Jordan, Mark. *The Alleged Aristotelianism of St. Thomas Aquinas*. The Étienne Gilson Series 15. Toronto: Pontifical Institute of Mediæval Studies, 1990.

————. *Rewritten Theology: Aquinas After His Readers*. Oxford: Blackwell, 2006.

Jowett, Benjamin. "On the Interpretation of Scripture." In *Essays and Reviews*, 7th ed., edited by Fredrick Temple, 330–433. London: Longman, Green, Longman, and Roberts, 1860.

Kant, Immanuel. *The Critique of Practical Reason*. Translated by Thomas Kingsmill Abbott. Whitefish, MT: Kessinger, n.d.

————. *Critique of Pure Reason*. Translated by Norman Kemp Smith. London: Macmillan, 1993.

————. "Perpetual Peace: A Philosophical Sketch. 1795." In *Political Writings*, edited by H. S. Reiss, 93–130. Cambridge: Cambridge University Press, 1991.

————. *Political Writings*. Edited by H. S. Reiss. Cambridge: Cambridge University Press, 1991.

Karger, Elizabeth. "Ockham's Misunderstood Theory of Intuitive and Abstractive Cognition." In *The Cambridge Companion to Ockham*, edited by Paul Vincent Spade, 204–26. Cambridge: Cambridge University Press, 2000.

————. "Ockham and Wodeham on Divine Deception as a Skeptical Hypothesis." *Vivarium* 42 (2004) 225–36.

Kimmerle, H. "Hermeneutical Theory or Ontological Hermeneutics." *Journal for Theology and the Church* 4 (1968) 107–21.

Kitchen, K. *On the Reliability of the Old Testament*. Grand Rapids: Eerdmans, 2003.

Klemm, David E., and William Schweiker. *Religion and the Human Future: An Essay on Theological Humanism*. Oxford: Blackwell, 2008.

Kroeker, P. Travis, and Bruce Ward. *Remembering the End: Dostoevsky as Prophet to Modernity*. Boulder, CO: Westview, 2001.

Kuyper, Abraham. *Principles of Sacred Theology*. Grand Rapids: Eerdmans, 1954.

Larmore, Charles. "Public Reason." In *The Cambridge Companion to John Rawls*, edited by Samuel Freeman, 368–93. Cambridge: Cambridge University Press, 2003.

Laski, Harold. "Political Thought in the Later Middle Ages." In *The Cambridge Medieval History*, edited by John B. Bury, 8:620–45. Cambridge: Cambridge University Press, 1936.

Lindbeck, George A. *The Nature of Doctrine: Religion and Theology in a Postliberal Age*. Philadelphia: Westminster, 1984

Little, David. "On Behalf of Rights: A Critique of Democracy and Tradition." *Journal of Religious Ethics* 34:2 (2006) 287–310.

Lockwood O'Donovan, Joan. *Theology of Law and Authority in the English Reformation*. Atlanta: Scholars, 1991.

Lovin, Robin W. *Christian Faith and Public Choices: The Social Ethics of Barth, Brunner and Bonhoeffer*. Philadelphia: Fortress, 1984.

Lubac, Henri de. *Catholicism: Christ and the Common Destiny of Man*. Translated by L. C. Sheppard. 1938. London: Burns, Oates & Washbourne, 1950.

———. *The Mystery of the Supernatural*. Translated by Rosemary Sheed. 1965. Reprint, Montreal: Palm, 1967.

———. "Sur la philosophie chrétienne." *Nouvelle Revue Théologique* 63 (1936) 225–53.

MacIntyre, Alasdair. *After Virtue: A Study of Moral Theory*. 2nd ed. Notre Dame, IN: University of Notre Dame Press, 1984.

———. *God, Philosophy, Universities: A Selective History of the Catholic Philosophical Tradition*. Lanham: Rowman & Littlefield, 2009.

———. *Three Rival Versions of Moral Enquiry: Encyclopaedia, Genealogy, and Tradition*. London: Duckworth, 1990.

———. *Whose Justice? Which Rationality?* London: Duckworth, 1988.

Manent, Pierre. *An Intellectual History of Liberalism*. Translated by Rebecca Balinski. Princeton: Princeton University Press, 1996.

Marion, Jean-Luc. *Being Given: Toward a Phenomenology of Givenness*. Translated by Jeffrey L. Kosky. Stanford: Stanford University Press, 2002.

———. "The Possible and Revelation." In *The Visible and the Revealed*, translated by Christina M. Gschwandtner et al., 1–17. New York: Fordham University Press, 2008.

———. "The Saturated Phenomenon." In *The Visible and the Revealed*, translated by Christina M. Gschwandtner et al., 18–65. New York: Fordham University Press, 2008.

Maritain, Jacques. *Primauté du Spirituel*. Paris: Librairie Plon, 1927.

Marsden, George. *The Outrageous Idea of Christian Scholarship*. New York: Oxford University Press, 1997.

Marshall, Christopher. *Beyond Retribution: A New Testament Vision for Justice, Crime and Punishment*. Grand Rapids: Eerdmans, 2001.

Marlet, Michael. *Grundlinien der kalvinistischen "Philosophie der Gesetzidee" als christlicher Transzendentalphilosphie*. Munich: Karl Zink, 1954.

Marrou, H.-I. *Saint Augustin et la fin de la culture antique*. Paris: Boccard, 1938.

Martin, David. *Reflections on Sociology and Theology*. Oxford: Oxford University Press, 1997.

McGinn, Bernard. "Three Forms of Negativity in Christian Mysticism." In *Knowing the Unknowable: Science and the Religions on God and the Universe*, edited by John W. Bowker. London: I. B. Taurus, 2008.

McIlroy, David H. *A Biblical View of Law and Justice.* Carlisle, UK: Paternoster, 2004.

———. "Idols and Grace: Re-envisioning Political Liberalism as Political Limitism." *Political Theology* 11 (2010) 205–25.

———. "The Role of Government in Classical Christian political thought." In *God and Government*, edited by N. Spencer and J. Chaplin. London: SPCK, 2009.

———. "Towards a Relational and Trinitarian Theology of Atonement." *Evangelical Quarterly* 80 (2008) 13–32.

———. "A Trinitarian Reading of Aquinas's Treatise on Law." *Angelicum* 84 (2007) 277–92.

———. *A Trinitarian Theology of Law: In Conversation with Jürgen Moltmann, Oliver O'Donovan and Thomas Aquinas.* Milton Keynes, UK: Paternoster, 2009.

———. "What's at Stake in Natural Law?" *New Blackfriars* 89 (2008) 508–21.

Milbank, John. *Being Reconciled: Ontology and Pardon.* London: Routledge, 2003.

———. "The Conflict of the Faculties: Theology and the Economy of the Sciences." In *Faithfulness and Fortitude: In Conversation with the Theological Ethics of Stanley Hauerwas*, edited by Mark Thiessen Nation and Samuel Wells, 39–57. Edinburgh: T. & T. Clark, 2000.

———. "The Second Difference: For a Trinitarianism Without Reserve." *Modern Theology* 2/3 (1986) 213–34.

———. *The Suspended Middle: Henri de Lubac and the Debate Concerning the Supernatural.* London: SCM, 2005.

———. *Theology and Social Theory: Beyond Secular Reason.* Oxford: Blackwell, 1990.

Milton, John. *Paradise Lost.* Edited by Stephen Orgel and Jonathan Goldberg. Oxford: Oxford University Press, 2004.

Moberly, R. W. L. "Biblical Criticism and Religious Belief." *Journal of Theological Interpretation* 2 (2008) 71–100.

———. "'Interpret the Bible Like Any Other Book'? Requiem for an Axiom." *Journal of Theological Interpretation* 4 (2010) 91–110.

———. "What is Theological Interpretation of Scripture?" *Journal of Theological Interpretation* 3 (2009) 161–78.

Moltmann, Jurgen. *The Coming of God: Christian Eschatology.* Translated by Margaret Kohl. London: SCM, 1996.

———. *A Theology of Hope: On the Ground and the Implications of a Christian Eschatology.* 5th ed. Translated by James W. Leitch. London: SCM, 1967.

Murdoch, Iris. *The Fire and the Sun: Why Plato Banished the Artists.* Oxford: Oxford University Press, 1977.

Murrmann-Kahl, M. *Die entzauberte Heilsgeschichte: Der Historismus erobert die Theologie 1880–1920.* Gütersloh: Gütersloher Verlagshaus Gerd Mohn, 1992.

Newlands, George. *Generosity and the Christian Future.* London: SPCK, 1997.

Newman, John Henry. *The Idea of the University.* Notre Dame, IN: University of Notre Dame Press, 1982.

———. "Sermon XV: The Theory of Development." In *Fifteen Sermons Preached Before the University of Oxford*, 312–51. Oxford: Oxford University Press, 2006.

Nietzsche, Friedrich. *On the Genealogy of Morals.* Translated by W. Kaufman and R. J. Hollingdale. New York: Vintage, 1967.

Nussbaum, Martha. "Narrative Emotions: Beckett's Genealogy of Love." In *Why Narrative? Readings in Narrative Theology*, edited by Stanley Hauerwas and L. Gregory Jones, 216–48. Grand Rapids: Eerdmans, 1989.

——. *Not For Profit: Why Democracy Needs the University*. Princeton: Princeton University Press, 2010.

Nygren, Anders. *Agape and Eros*. London: SPCK, 1953.

Oakley, Francis. "On the Road from Constance to 1688: the Political Thought of John Major and George Buchanan." *Journal of British Studies*, 2 (1962) 1–31.

William of Ockham. *Quodlibetal Questions* (Quodlibeta Septem). Vol. 5. Translated by Alfred J. Freddoso and Francis E. Kelley. New Haven: Yale University Press, 1991.

——. *Philosophical Writings*. Edited and translated by Philotheus Boehner. Edinburgh: Hacket, 1957.

O'Donovan, Oliver. *The Desire of the Nations: Rediscovering the Roots of Political Theology*. Cambridge: Cambridge University Press, 1996.

——. *Resurrection and Moral Order: An Outline for Evangelical Ethics*. 2nd ed. Leicester: Apollos, 1994.

——. *The Problem of Self-Love in St. Augustine*. New York: Yale University Press, 1980.

——. *The Ways of Judgment*. Grand Rapids: Eerdmans, 2005.

Oliver, Simon. *Philosophy, God and Motion*. London: Routledge, 2005.

Olthuis, James H. "Dooyeweerd on Religion and Faith." In *The Legacy of Herman Dooyeweerd: Reflections on Critical Philosophy in the Christian Tradition*, edited by C. T. McIntire, 21–40. Lanham, MD: University of America Press, 1985.

Oser, Lee. *The Return of Christian Humanism: Chesterton, Eliot, Tolkien, and the Romance of History*. Missouri: University of Missouri Press, 2007.

Pascal, Blaise. *Pensées*. Edited by L. Brunschwicg. Paris: Hachette, 1897.

Paffenroth Kim, and Kevin L. Hughes, editors. *Augustine and Liberal Education*. Lanham: Rowman & Littlefield, 2008.

Panaccio, Claude, and David Piché. "Ockham's Reliabilism and the Intuition of Non-Existents." In *Rethinking the History of Skepticism: The Missing Medieval Background*, edited by Henrik Lagerlund, 97–118. Leiden: Brill, 2010.

Pannenberg, Wolfhart. *Wissenschaftstheorie und Theologie*. Frankfurt am Main: Suhrkamp, 1987.

Peace, Richard. *Dostoevsky: An Examination of the Major Novels*. Cambridge: Cambridge University Press, 1971.

Pedersen, O. *The First Universities. Studium generale and the Origins of University Education in Europe*. Cambridge: Cambridge University Press, 1997.

Phillips, D. Z. *Religion and the Hermeneutics of Contemplation*. Cambridge: Cambridge University Press, 2001.

Plato. *Republic*. Translated by Desmond Lee. Harmondsworth, UK: Penguin, 2007.

Pollmann, Karla, and Mark Vessey, editors. *Augustine and the Disciplines: From Cassiciacum to Confessions*. Oxford: Oxford University Press, 2005.

Popkin, Richard. *The History of Scepticism from Savonarola to Bayle*. Oxford: Oxford University Press, 2003.

Pratchett, Terry. *Hogfather*. London: Victor Gollancz, 1996.

——. *Reaper Man*. London: Victor Gollancz, 1991.

——. *Thief of Time*. New York: Doubleday, 2001.

Rawls, John. "The Idea of Public Reason Revisited." In *Collected Papers*, edited by Samuel Freeman, 573–615. Cambridge: Harvard University Press, 1999.

——. *Political Liberalism*. New York: Colombia University Press, 1993.

——. *A Theory of Justice*. Cambridge: Harvard University Press, 1971.

Rea, Michael. "Introduction." In *Analytic Theology: New Essays in Philosophy of Religion*, edited by Oliver Crisp and Michael Rea, 1–30. Oxford: Oxford University Press, 2009.

Readings, Bill. *The University in Ruins*. Cambridge: Harvard University Press, 1996.

Reno, R. R. "Theology's Continental Captivity." *First Things* (April 2006). Online: http://www.firstthings.com/article/2007/01/theology8217s-continental-captivity---18.

Reuben, Julie A. *The Making of the Modern University: Intellectual Transformation and the Marginalization of Morality*. Chicago: University of Chicago Press, 1996.

Rhees, Rush, editor. *Recollections of Wittgenstein*. Oxford: Oxford University Press, 1984.

Ricoeur, Paul. *Oneself as Another*. Translated by Kathleen Blaney. Chicago: University of Chicago Press, 1992.

Riker, William H. "Political Science and Rational Choice." In *Perspectives on Positive Political Economy*, edited by James E. Alt and Kenneth A Shepsle, 163–81. Cambridge: Cambridge University Press, 1990.

Ridder-Symoens, H. de, editor. *A History of the University in Europe 1: Universities in the Middle Ages*. Cambridge: Cambridge University Press, 1992.

Rist, John. *Augustine: Ancient Thought Baptized*. Cambridge: Cambridge University Press, 1994.

Rorty, Richard. *Philosophy and the Mirror of Nature*. Princeton: Princeton University Press, 1979.

Rowland, Tracey. *Culture and the Thomist Tradition: After Vatican II*. London: Routledge, 2003.

Sagovsky, Nicholas. *Christian Tradition and the Practice of Justice*. London: SPCK, 2008.

Schleiermacher, F. D. E. *Brief Outline of Theology as a Field of Study: Translation of the 1811 and 1830 Editions, with Essays and Notes, by Terrence N. Tice*. Schleiermacher Studies and Translations 1. Lewiston, NY: Edwin Mellen, 1990.

———. *Hermeneutik und Kritik: Mit einem Anhang sprachphilosophischer Texte Schleiermachers*. 4th ed. Edited by M. Frank. Frankfurt am Main: Suhrkamp, 1990.

———. *Universitätsschriften; Herakleitos; Kurze Darstellung des theologischen Studiums* KGA, 1. Abt., Bd. 6. Edited by D. Schmid. Berlin: de Gruyter, 1998.

Schmitt, Carl. *The Crisis of Parliamentary Democracy*. Translated by Ellen Kennedy. Cambridge: MIT Press, 1996.

———. *Political Theology. Four Chapters on the Concept of Sovereignty*. Translated by George Schwab. Cambridge: MIT Press, 1985.

Simons, Herbert W. "Introduction: The Rhetoric of Inquiry as an Intellectual Movement." In *The Rhetorical Turn*, edited by Herbert W. Simons, 1–31. Chicago: University of Chicago Press, 1990.

Skinner, Quentin. *Foundations of Modern Political Thought*. Vol. 2, *The Age of Revolution*. Cambridge: Cambridge University Press, 1972.

Sokal, Alan, and Jean Bricmont. *Intellectual Impostures*. London: Profile, 1998.

Southern, R. W. *Scholastic Humanism and the Unification of Europe*. 2 vols. Oxford: Blackwell, 1995.

Spier, J. M. *An Introduction to Christian Philosophy*. Translated by D. H. Freeman. Philadelphia: P. & R., 1954.

Stark, Rodney. "Bringing Theory Back In." In *Rational Choice Theory and Religion: Summary and Assessment*, edited by Lawrence A. Young, 3–23. London: Routledge, 1997

Stark, Rodney, and William Sims Bainbridge. *A Theory of Religion*. New York: Peter Lang, 1987.

Steiner, George. *The Death of Tragedy*. London: Faber & Faber, 1963.

———. *Real Presences*. Chicago: Chicago University Press, 1991.

Stout, Jeffrey. *Democracy and Tradition*. Princeton: Princeton University Press, 2004.

Strauss, D. F. M. "Justice, Legal Validity and the Force of Law with Special Reference to Derrida, Dooyeweerd and Habermas." *South African Journal of Philosophy* 28 (2009) 65–87.

Strickland, Wayne G., Walter C. Kaiser, Douglas J. Moo, Willem A. Van Gemeren, and Stanley N. Gundry. *Five Views on Law and Gospel*. Grand Rapids: Zondervan, 1996.

Stump, Eleonore. "The Mechanisms of Cognition." In *The Cambridge Companion to Ockham*, edited by Paul Vincent Spade, 168–203. Cambridge: Cambridge University Press, 2000.

Schweiker, William. *Theological Ethics and Global Dynamics in the Time of Many Worlds*. Oxford: Blackwell, 2004.

Tierney, Brian. *The Foundations of the Conciliar Theory*. New enlarged edition. Leiden: Brill, 1998.

———. *Religion, Law and Constitutional Thought 1150–1650*. Cambridge: Cambridge University Press, 1982.

Tournai, Stephen of. *Die Summa des Stephanus Tornacensis uber das Decretum Gratiani*. Edited by J. F. von Schulte. Geisen, 1891.

Troeltsch, E. "Über historische und dogmatische Methode in der Theologie." In *Gesammelte Schriften*, II:729–53. Tübingen: Mohr/Siebeck, 1922.

Webster, John. *Theological Theology*. Oxford: Clarendon, 1998.

Wesley, John. *Sermons on Several Occasions*. London: Epworth, 1975.

Wiebe, Donald. *The Irony of Theology and the Nature of Religious Faith*. Montreal: McGill-Queen's University Press, 1991.

Williams, Rowan. *Grace and Necessity: Reflections on Art and Love*. London: Continuum, 2005.

———. *Lost Icons: Reflections on Cultural Bereavement*. Harrisburg: Morehouse, 2000.

Williams, Stephen N. *The Shadow of the Antichrist: Nietzsche's Critique of Christianity*. Grand Rapids: Baker, 2006.

Witte, John. *God's Joust, God's Justice: Law and Religion in the Western Tradition*. Grand Rapids: Eerdmans, 2006.

———. *Law and Protestantism: The Legal Teachings of the Lutheran Reformation*. Cambridge: Cambridge University Press, 2002.

Wittgenstein, Ludwig. *Bemerkungen über die Grundlagen der Mathematik*. Frankfurt: Suhrkamp, 1984.

———. *Philosophical Investigations*. Translated by G. E. M. Anscombe. Oxford: Blackwell, 1953.

Wolters, Albert M. "The Intellectual Milieu of Herman Dooyeweerd." In *The Legacy of Herman Dooyeweerd: Reflections on Critical Philosophy in the Christian Tradition*, edited by C. T. McIntyre, 1–18. Lanham: University Press of America, 1985.

Index

Index